# The School Principal

Over the past two decades, efforts to improve schools have significantly modified role expectations for principals. Today, school-level administrators are expected to be both visionary leaders and competent managers. Based on the conviction that administration is an amalgam of leadership and management, *The School Principal* emphasizes the need for practitioners to apply conceptual skills to make "what to do" decisions, to apply technical skills to make "how to do" decisions, and to apply relational skills to engage in democratic decision making.

Kowalski frames the book with a discussion of the nature of schools, the roles of principals, and their need to improve schools. The book then provides a balanced treatment of leadership and management, covering issues of personal behavior, instructional leadership, relationship building issues, finances, facilities, personnel management, pupil services, and maintaining safe schools. The text closes with discussion of the vital aspects of practice for contemporary principals, addressing problem solving, collaborative change strategies, and personal commitment to being a principal.

Special Features:

- Vignettes introduce the subject matter in the context of common challenges faced by practitioners.
- Knowledge-Based Questions and Skill-Based Activities prompt readers to engage with and reflect on the chapter content.
- *The School Principal* aligns with the Educational Leadership Consortium Council (ELCC) Standards.

Treating principals as concurrently visionary leaders and competent managers, this excellent text addresses the needs of aspiring and practicing principals, providing the tools to build effective and efficient schools.

**Theodore J. Kowalski** is the Kuntz Family Chair and Professor in Educational Administration, University of Dayton.

# The School Principal

## Visionary Leadership and Competent Management

*Theodore J. Kowalski*

Routledge
Taylor & Francis Group

NEW YORK AND LONDON

First published 2010
by Routledge
270 Madison Avenue, New York, New York 10016

Simultaneously published in the UK
by Routledge
2 Park Square, Milton Park, Abingdon, Oxon OX14 4RN

*Routledge is an imprint of the Taylor & Francis Group, an informa business*

© 2010 Taylor & Francis

Typeset in Bembo and Helvetica Neue by Prepress Projects Ltd, Perth, UK
Printed and bound in the United States of America on acid-free paper by
Edwards Brothers, Inc.

*Library of Congress Cataloging in Publication Data*
Kowalski, Theodore J.
The school principal : visionary leadership and competent management /
Theodore J. Kowalski.
p. cm.
Includes bibliographical references and index.
1. School principals—United States. 2. School management and organization—
United States. 3. Educational leadership—United States. I. Title.
LB2831.92.K69 2010
371.2'011—dc22
2009053638

ISBN 13: 978-0-415-80622-0 (hbk)
ISBN 13: 978-0-415-80623-7 (pbk)
ISBN 13: 978-0-203-85739-7 (ebk)

# Contents

# Detailed Contents

# Figures

# Tables

# Interface of ELCC Standards and Book Chapters

| Standard | Element | Book content |
|---|---|---|
| Standard 1.0: Candidates who complete the program are educational leaders who have the knowledge and ability to promote the success of all students by facilitating the development, articulation, implementation, and stewardship of a school or district vision of learning supported by the school community. | 1.1 Develop a vision<br>1.2 Articulate a vision<br>1.3 Implement a vision<br>1.4 Steward a vision<br>1.5 Promote community involvement in the vision | Chapters 1, 2, and 3<br>Chapters 2 and 3<br>Chapters 2 and 3<br>Chapters 2 and 3<br>Chapters 2 and 3 |
| Standard 2.0: Candidates who complete the program are educational leaders who have the knowledge and ability to promote the success of all students by promoting a positive school culture, providing an effective instructional program, applying best practice to student learning, and designing comprehensive professional growth plans for staff. | 2.1 Promote positive school culture<br>2.2 Provide effective instructional program<br>2.3 Apply best practice to student learning<br>2.4 Design comprehensive professional growth plan | Chapters 3, 4, and 10<br><br>Chapters 1, 4, and 5<br><br>Chapters 1, 4, 5, and 12<br><br>Chapters 4 and 8 |
| Standard 3.0: Candidates who complete the program are educational leaders who have the knowledge and ability to promote the success of all students by managing the organization, operations, and resources in a way that promotes a safe, efficient, and effective learning environment. | 3.1 Manage the organization<br>3.2 Manage operations<br><br>3.3 Manage resources | Chapters 2, 6, 7, 8, 9, and 10<br>Chapters 2 , 6, 7, 9, and 10<br>Chapters 2, 6, 7, and 8 |
| Standard 4.0: Candidates who complete the program are educational leaders who have the knowledge and ability to promote the success of all students by collaborating with families and other community members, responding to diverse community interests and needs, and mobilizing community resources. | 4.1 Collaborate with families and other community members<br>4.2 Respond to community interests and needs<br>4.3 Mobilize community resources | Chapters 3, 6, and 12<br><br><br>Chapters 1, 3, and 12<br><br><br>Chapters 1 and 12 |

| Standard | Element | Book content |
|---|---|---|
| Standard 5.0: Candidates who complete the program are educational leaders who have the knowledge and ability to promote the success of all students by acting with integrity, fairly, and in an ethical manner. | 5.1 Act with integrity | Chapters 1, 8, 9, and 13 |
| | 5.2 Act fairly | Chapters 1, 8, 9, 10, and 13 |
| | 5.3 Act ethically | Chapters 1, 8, 9, and 13 |
| Standard 6.0: Candidates who complete the program are educational leaders who have the knowledge and ability to promote the success of all students by understanding, responding to, and influencing the larger political, social, economic, legal, and cultural context. | 6.1 Understand the larger context | Chapters 1, 10, 11, and 13 |
| | 6.2 Respond to the larger context | Chapters 1, 10, 11, and 13 |
| | 6.3 Influence the larger context | Chapters 1, 10, and 13 |

# Preface

In the context of a reform-minded, information-based society, perceptions of the ideal school principal have changed considerably. During the first half of the previous century, for example, considerable emphasis was placed on running efficient and orderly schools. Today, however, the literature focuses heavily on school effectiveness. Specifically, most contemporary books and articles address topics such as transformational leadership, school restructuring, and learning communities. Though the importance of these issues is indisputable, standing alone they do not capture the realities of current practice.

This book, intended to meet the needs of aspiring and practicing principals, is nested in the conviction that outstanding principals continuously seek to have effective and efficient schools. They are concurrently visionary leaders and competent managers. Asked to describe the difference between these two essential administrative roles, the noted scholar Warren Bennis (1984) answered that managers ask "how and when," whereas leaders ask "what and why?" That is, principals as leaders focus on determining what needs to be done to improve schools; and they educate stakeholders and enlist their collaboration in and support for change initiatives. Principals as managers decide how to utilize human and material resources at the right times to ensure safe and efficient school environments.

The belief that outstanding principals both lead and manage is supported by evidence relating to countless efforts to improve low-performing schools. Those that are relatively well managed usually do not improve academically without visionary leaders; those that have visionary leaders do not usually improve unless they are well managed. Therefore, this book focuses on both the leadership and management roles assumed by contemporary principals. Theory is melded with tacit knowledge to provide knowledge and dispositions relevant to the challenges identified by successful principals.

The book has been divided into four sections. The first part examines the nature of schools and the roles of principals; the intent is to provide you with a basic understanding of the institution, the position, ongoing strategies to improve schools, and the essential role principals must play in implementing these strategies. The second part is devoted to leadership. The topic is examined from various perspectives including personal behavior, instructional leadership, and relationship building. Part III looks at managerial responsibilities—issues such as finances, facilities, personnel management, pupil services, and maintaining a safe and orderly school. The final section of the book covers three vital aspects of practice: problem solving, collaborative change strategies, and your personnel commitment to being a principal.

Each chapter has five features providing structural uniformity in the book. Collectively, they are intended to bridge theory and practice. These features are:

- *Vignettes preceding chapter content.* Though fictitious, the vignettes portray problems of practice commonly experienced by principals; and thus, they demonstrate the relevance of the content that follows.
- *Knowledge and skill objectives.* The last paragraph in each chapter introduction includes objectives regarding what you should know or be able to do after reading a chapter's content.
- *Reflections.* Each chapter ends with a summary section that prompts you to consider what you have read. The purpose is to encourage you to interface new knowledge with present knowledge and experiences.
- *Knowledge-based questions.* At the end of each chapter you will find questions that are intended to determine if you have acquired knowledge about key concepts.
- *Skill-based activities.* The skill-based activities suggested after the knowledge-based questions are intended to determine if you can apply the knowledge you have acquired.

These features and the overall content in this book are aligned with the Educational Leadership Consortium Council (ELCC) Standards. These criteria are used widely to evaluate both preparation programs and applicants for state licensing. An appendix in the front of the book interfaces chapter content with the standards.

I am indebted to several persons who helped me prepare this book. Elizabeth Pearn, my assistant, helped with technical aspects, such as editing and formatting. My doctoral assistant, Brother Michael Amakyi, CSSC, assisted with literature reviews and offered a myriad of constructive suggestions. My Routledge editors, Lane Akers and Heather Jarrow, provided encouragement, support, and creative ideas. Lastly, I thank the myriad graduate students and principals who taught me many things during my career.

Theodore J. Kowalski
University of Dayton

PART I

# Schools and Principals

## CHAPTER 1

# Complex Nature of Schools

*For decades, the Cross Creek School District has had the reputation of being one of the state's worst school systems. So, after James Eagan became state superintendent, he decided to visit the district to see firsthand if that standing was warranted. Accompanied by the district superintendent, he walked through each of the district's five school buildings, talked to the principals and several teachers at each site, and met with the school board president briefly after finishing the tour. When Dr. Eagan returned to the state capital, he told his deputy, "Without a doubt, this school system has the most deplorable facilities I have ever seen." He then detailed conditions that contributed to his evaluation.*

- *None of the three elementary schools had either a media center (library) or a computer lab. In fact, most elementary school classrooms did not have a single computer.*
- *Though all three elementary schools had small kitchens, two of them did not have cafeterias—students ate their lunches in either classrooms or hallways.*
- *The middle school, originally constructed as a high school in 1925, had very small classrooms, some with wooden floors. There was one small computer lab located in what had been a storage room. The building was generally dirty and a musty odor was pervasive.*
- *The high school, the district's newest facility, had been constructed 38 years ago. Since then, the building had not been renovated. Like the other schools, it provided little more than a basic shelter; most classrooms and the media center were small, the two science labs had outdated equipment, and access to computers was limited.*

*After sharing his perceptions, Dr. Eagan asked his deputy to conduct additional research on the district. Specifically, he wanted student data such as test scores, attendance figures, and graduation rates; he also requested fiscal data, such as tax rates, employee salaries, and per pupil expenditures. As expected, both sets of figures were low when compared with state averages. Approximately 40 percent of the students who enrolled at Cross Creek High School did not graduate; of those who did, only 13 percent continued their formal education and only 9 percent enrolled in 4-year colleges. The district ranked in the bottom 5 percent on the mandated state achievement tests. Fiscal data were equally depressing. Among 292 districts in the state, Cross Creek ranked last in the general fund tax rate (for operating expenses), 254th in the student transportation tax rate, last in the debt service tax rate (the district had no outstanding debt for school construction), 290th in average employee salaries, and 289th in per pupil expenditures.*

*Convinced that conditions in Cross Creek were inadequate, Dr. Eagan, with the unanimous support of the state board of education, wrote a letter to Cross Creek's superintendent and board president. He warned that, unless the school board took action to improve the district's facilities, he would recommend that the state board of education assume responsibility for operating the district—an option that rarely had been deployed in the state's history.*

*After receiving the letter, the Cross Creek superintendent met with the school board and the district's administrative staff. Though several principals urged the board members to reconsider their stance toward construction projects, their comments fell on deaf ears. Convinced that their political stance accurately reflected the will of most stakeholders, the board held a public meeting to discuss Dr. Eagan's threat. Two days later, the following letter, co-signed by the school board president and superintendent, was sent to the state superintendent.*

*Mr. Eagan,*

*The school board held a public forum 3 days ago to discuss your letter. A large number of residents attended. With few exceptions, the residents of this school district said they do not believe they can afford to fund major school construction projects. All five school board members agree. Most residents in this district attended the local schools, and they believe a good education is not measured by walls and bricks. They disagree with your assessments of our buildings and challenge your authority to eliminate local control. Economically, this is a poor community. Most residents are barely able to pay their property taxes. If you and the state board of education believe new schools are a priority, then fund the projects entirely with state funds. We have no objection to this solution. Otherwise, we believe that while our schools are old, our staff and community spirit ensure that students are receiving an adequate education.*

## INTRODUCTION

In an information-based and reform-minded society, adjectives such as "adequate," "efficient," "effective," and "good" (and their antonyms) have been used freely and carelessly to label schools. Because these adjectives have not been defined consistently, their connotations are imprecise. As demonstrated in the vignette about the Cross Creek school district, local stakeholders may see their schools as being adequate even though they are in a deplorable condition and lack basic features found in modern schools.

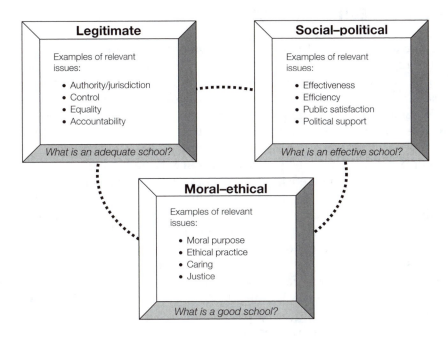

*Figure 1.1* Interacting Frames of Elementary and Secondary Schools.

This initial chapter looks at schools from three critical perspectives (see Figure 1.1). The first, a legal point of view or legitimate frame, addresses both the issue of local control and the extent to which schools are adequate institutions providing students equal opportunities. The second, a social–political point of view, addresses the extent to which schools are viewed as efficient and effective institutions. And the third, a moral–ethical point of view, addresses the extent to which schools are viewed as good and caring institutions. Each frame, but particularly the legitimate one, is complicated by the increased involvement of federal and state authorities in elementary and secondary education.

In order to comprehend the challenges faced by contemporary principals, you need to understand the complexity of the institutions in which they practice. Thus, after reading this chapter, you should be able to do the following:

* Identify the federal, state, and local government responsibility for public education
* Explain the relationships among laws, district policies, and school rules
* Identify society's interests in having efficient and effective schools
* Explain the importance of schools as moral institutions
* Express an understanding of the persistent tensions between societal and individual rights
* Differentiate the characteristics of adequate, efficient, effective, and good schools

## SCHOOLS: THE LEGITIMATE FRAME

Legitimate refers to what is legal; legitimate authority, therefore, pertains to power granted through a legal system (e.g., constitutions, laws, legal precedents). In the case of public elementary and secondary education, legitimate authority is dispersed, with federal, state, and local agencies being involved, albeit to different degrees. Governmental control of public schools focuses most intently on three values: liberty, adequacy, and equality. Liberty relates to individual freedom; in the case of education, it refers to citizen authority over schools (King, Swanson, & Sweetland, 2003). Adequacy is a relative concept in that it is continuously being redefined in a dynamic society; as an example, adequacy was redefined substantially after America transitioned from a manufacturing society to an information-based society (Schlechty, 1990). Fundamentally, this value deals with minimum acceptable levels, such as a minimum number of attendance days, a minimum length for a school day, and a minimum number of credits for high school graduation (Kowalski, 2006). Equality is defined as reasonably equal educational opportunities (King et al., 2003); often defined in terms of just and equitable distribution of resources, equality in a given state is measured by variations in revenue and spending among local districts (Crampton & Whitney, 1996). A school failing to provide reasonably equal opportunities for students (compared with those offered by other schools in the same state or district) may also be inadequate.

The concurrent pursuit of liberty, adequacy, and equality spawns legal conflict as demonstrated by lawsuits challenging state funding laws for public schools. For example, when local districts have had total or substantial leeway to raise revenues from the local property tax (i.e., considerable liberty), wealthy school systems have typically had much higher per-pupil expenditures than have poor school districts.[1] From a legal perspective, this condition can be problematic because opportunities afforded to students in wealthy districts are likely to exceed those afforded to students in poor districts. Moreover, the extent to which all districts in a state provide adequate educational opportunities is likely to vary. When a state's system of public elementary and secondary education is deemed by the courts to be inadequate or unequal, judges have commonly mandated state legislatures to fix the problem. At the same time, however, the courts have commonly found that some degree of inequity is acceptable in order to preserve liberty (King et al., 2003). Consequently, the legitimate frame of schools is basically characterized by two difficult assignments: balancing liberty, adequacy, and equality within a state and balancing federal, state, and local authority.

### Federal Authority

The U.S. Constitution does not mention education; thus, under provisions of the Tenth Amendment (powers not delegated to the federal government by the Constitution, nor prohibited by it to the states, are reserved to the states or to the people) education is deemed a state's right. Though public education remains a state responsibility, the federal government's role in this service has expanded, especially during the last half of the twentieth century. Justification for increased involvement has been based on the legal interpretation that the federal government may intervene if issues being addressed in or by schools are germane to the U.S. Constitution (including amendments) and federal laws.

Incrementally, the federal role in public elementary and secondary schools has become broader and more overt (Robelen, 2005). Support and opposition for federal interventions, however, have been inconstant, with political positions usually determined by the specific issue being addressed. Generally, dispositions toward federal involvement reflect the overall philosophical division in society (Radin & Hawley, 1988). Today, all three branches of the federal government intervene in public schools.

## Legislative Branch

The federal government can influence education by passing legislation deemed to serve a national interest by virtue of improving the effectiveness of public schools (LaMorte, 1996). Historically, Congressional involvement has produced four overriding themes: (a) constitutional rights of citizens, (b) national security, (c) domestic problems, and (d) concerns for a healthy economy (Kowalski, 2003). Since 1957, for example, the U.S. Congress has enacted several major laws that profoundly influenced curriculum, instruction, and governance. Four examples are identified in Table 1.1.

*Table 1.1* Examples of the Federal Government Exerting Legitimate Authority through Legislation

| *Legislation* | *Purpose* |
| --- | --- |
| National Defense Education Act of 1958 (NDEA) | Passed less than a year after the Soviet Union successfully launched the first space satellite, Sputnik, the law was intended to improve education in areas deemed essential to the nation's military defense. The primary subjects emphasized were mathematics, sciences, and foreign languages (Sufrin, 1963) |
| Elementary and Secondary Education Act of 1965 (ESEA) | Passed shortly after the Civil Rights Act of 1964, the law was intended to address equity issues and the needs of students from low-income families. Schools with the highest portion of poor children benefited most from the legislation. Funds were distributed to state agencies rather than directly to school districts (Ellis, 1983). Title I is arguably the most widely recognized aspect of this law |
| Education for All Handicapped Children Act of 1975 | Often called the civil rights act for special needs students, the law challenged traditional instructional practices and promoted the concepts of academic and social mainstreaming (now known as inclusion). The guiding principle was a free and appropriate public education (Singer, 1985). The law is now codified as the Individuals with Disabilities Education Act (IDEA) |
| No Child Left Behind Act of 2001 (NCLB) | This law is actually the current reauthorization of ESEA. It requires specific diagnostic and prescriptive activities intended to improve the effectiveness of public schools (Kowalski, Lasley, & Mahoney, 2008). Several notable requirements include student testing, data-based decision making, and choice for students in failing schools (Protheroe, Shellard, & Turner, 2003) |

### Judicial Branch

Federal courts may become involved in public education when pertinent federal law displaces inconsistent state law (Valente, 1987). Most notably, interventions have been based on applying the strict scrutiny standard to interpret the Fourteenth Amendment of the U.S. Constitution—an amendment intended to protect citizens and their individual rights from "various forms of arbitrary or capricious state action" (LaMorte, 1996, p. 5). In addition to establishing jurisdiction by litigation involving a federal constitutional question or federal statute, federal courts also may do so when litigants reside in more than one state (Reutter, 1985). Issues such as parental rights, student rights, the rights and authority of school officials (school boards, administrators, teachers, and other employees), and the rights of racial and ethnic minorities or other protected groups (e.g., racial discrimination, gender or age discrimination) have been addressed by federal courts (Kowalski, 2006). *Brown* v. *Board of Education* (1954), a U.S. Supreme Court decision that invalidated the long-standing concept of "separate but equal," is the quintessential example of the federal courts initiating and sustaining a major change in public elementary and secondary education.

### Administrative Branch

In 1979, the creation of a separate U.S. Department of Education (USDOE) expanded the role of the administrative branch of the federal government in public education (Campbell, Cunningham, Nystrand, & Usdan, 1990). Major responsibilities of the USDOE include (a) developing rules and regulations deemed necessary to enforce federal laws, (b) funding, sponsoring, and conducting research, (c) dispensing federal aid, and (d) managing federal grants. Since its inception, this agency has been politically controversial; opponents argue it erodes states' rights and proponents argue it is necessary to preserve federal interests.

## State Authority

In many ways, the growth of state power over public education paralleled the growth of federal power; however, state control has become more extensive and influential than the other two levels of government. The sweeping power of state government includes creating or abolishing school districts, setting funding formulas, and establishing a state-mandated curriculum (Sergiovanni, Kelleher, McCarthy, & Fowler, 2009). Since 1970, myriad lawsuits challenging the adequacy and equality of state systems of education have resulted in more centralized governance for public schools, primarily because of court mandates to rectify inadequate or unequal conditions.

### Legislative Branch

Provisions for public education are contained in state constitutions and in statutes promulgated by state legislatures. A state legislature has almost unlimited or plenary powers to determine basic education policy questions; however, this body may not enact laws violating either the federal constitution and statutes or the state's constitution (Alexander & Alexander, 2009). States also have established state boards of education, agencies that may have constitutional authority to set public education policy. In some states (e.g., Nebraska and Vermont), state boards have authority over state departments of education—agencies in the administrative branch of state government. Thus, the degree to which state boards function as a legislative body, an administrative body, or both is inconstant across the states (Kowalski, 2003).

### Judicial Branch

State courts have jurisdiction over disputes involving education that pertain to state constitutions and statutes. Historically, judges in these courts were reluctant to interfere with the authority of legislative and executive branches of state government to shape education policy (Alexander & Alexander, 2009). This tradition, however, has waned in some states, resulting in a proclivity toward judicial activism (Rebell, 1999), a process of broadly interpreting law that is criticized as setting new policy. Moreover, in a litigious society, the courts have become a common arbiter for disputes involving schools and school employees.

### Administrative Branch

State control over public schools was formalized by the appointment of state superintendents and the establishment of state departments of education (Butts & Cremin, 1953). In some states (e.g., Indiana and Oklahoma) the state superintendent is both the chief executive of the state department of education and, ex officio, the chair of the state board of education. Prior to 1930, state departments of education assumed an inspectoral role—one in which officials determined if local school districts were complying with state laws. Subsequently, they became more proactive in providing services to improve schools (Knezevich, 1984). Today, these agencies also play a pivotal role in administering federal programs, provide technical assistance to schools, and generate policy proposals for both legislatures and state boards.

## Local Authority

The concept of local control of public education is nested in liberty. In all but one state (Hawaii), much of the authority to govern public schools is relegated to local school boards—agencies that are legal extensions of state government (Kowalski, 2006). Until the middle of the last century, democratic localism was prevalent in America. In this political environment, citizens often influenced policy directly by expressing their political and philosophical views at school board meetings. This form of direct participation was rooted in two convictions: public education is both a public and private interest (Levin, 1987) and stakeholder influence in a democracy is a fundamental right (Levin, 1999; Skocpol, 1993).

After 1950, the evolution toward larger governmental agencies and the development of "professional" public administrators resulted in the rise of representative democracy (Levin, 1999). Public school districts certainly were affected by this trend. School consolidation and rapid population growth combined to produce fewer but bigger districts in which many citizens felt it was no longer productive to pursue their individual rights by confronting school officials directly. At the same time, state officials became concerned that unfettered local control would produce inadequate and unequal educational opportunities for some students. In a representative democracy, school board members, functioning as trustees, and superintendents, functioning as impartial professionals, are expected to carry out state policy and forge additional policy without political bias (Kowalski, 2006).

From their inception, local districts have been concurrently political entities (subdivisions of the state that serve to balance centralization and decentralization), legal entities (quasi-municipal corporations), geographic entities (defined by specific boundaries), social institutions (engaged in symbiotic relationships with their communities), and educational entities (agencies with specific responsibilities for transmitting knowledge and skills) (Knezevich, 1984). Though the specific scope of responsibility and authority granted to local boards varies slightly among the states, they generally have the following duties:

- Establish schools
- Erect school buildings
- Employ a superintendent
- Establish policy and rules necessary to govern the schools
- Raise and expend public funds (Campbell et al., 1990)

The normative role of local school boards has been challenged by several evolving political, social, and professional issues. For example, both the federal and state governments have assumed greater authority for public education; educators have demanded greater autonomy permitting them to function as true professionals; various stakeholders are demanding a more direct role in determining taxation and school-improvement initiatives.

## Policy, Rules, and Regulations

Collectively from a legal perspective, districts and schools operate under an intricate mix of laws, policies, and rules (or regulations). Thus, in order to understand schools, you need to know three relationships: (a) between laws and district policy, (b) between district policy and school rules, and (c) between legal constraints and principal decisions.

### District Policy

Policy approved by school boards sets both expectations and constraints for the operation of schools. Establishing public policy at the school district level is "the dynamic and value-laden process through which a political system handles a public problem" (Fowler, 2000, p. 9). The process focuses largely on setting parameters for determining what services are to be provided, to whom they are to be provided, and the manner in which they should be provided.

A school board's powers to create and enforce policy are granted by the state legislature, and all board policy decisions must conform to the limitations of relevant constitutional provisions, statutes, federal and state regulations, and common law (Imber & Van

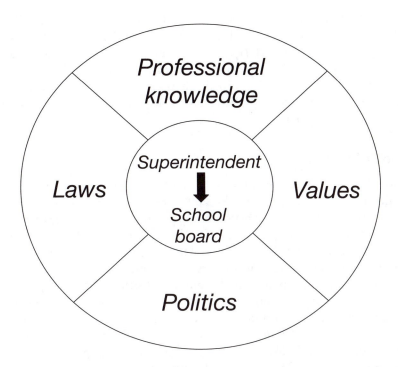

*Figure 1.2*  Factors Influencing School District Policy.

Geel, 1993). Formal policy decisions made by school boards produce policy statements that are placed in the district policy manual. Appropriately developed, they provide administrators and others with "a guide for discretionary action, a statement of purpose rather than a prescription for action" (Clemmer, 1991, p. 20). Ideally, district policies are recommended by the superintendent and they are grounded in defensible professional knowledge. They should focus on what is best for students, employees, and all other stakeholders. In reality, however, professional recommendations are often tempered or trumped by three other factors—laws, politics, and values (see Figure 1.2.)

Policy is often based on law (statutes or legal decisions) and is authoritative (Anderson, 1990). Thus, policy may restate federal or state laws, especially when school district personnel are held accountable for enforcing them. Laws pertaining to civil rights, the rights of disabled individuals, zero tolerance (e.g., pertaining to weapons in schools), and child abuse are examples (Kowalski, 2006).

In making policy decisions, board members may opt to use their own criteria. For example, they ignore the superintendent's recommendation and evidence provided to support it in favor of acting politically (e.g., bowing to public opinion, pressure group interventions, or the judgment of influential others). Ideally, board members are expected to be trustees, persons acting objectively to serve the interests of the entire community. As communities have become more diverse, many board members actually behave as political delegates acting on the basis of their own interests or those of supportive pressure groups. This behavior is especially common in larger districts, where boards are often factional, reflecting major economic, ethnic, social, political, and philosophical divisions (Björk & Keedy, 2001).

Values, such as liberty, equality, adequacy, and efficiency, also affect policy decisions (Stout, Tallerico, & Scribner, 1994). These values are basically enduring beliefs about what is desirable (Razik & Swanson, 2001). Though they are widely accepted, stakeholders do not agree about their relative importance. For example, persons favoring equality over liberty prefer more centralized governance and greater federal and state control over public education. Those favoring liberty prefer decentralization and a limited role for federal and state government.

## Rules and Regulations

Distinctions between district policy and school rules and regulations are often ambiguous, both legally and definitively (Kowalski, 2006). From a legal perspective, "regulation" is often used to describe non-constitutional and non-statutory rules promulgated by public departments, agencies, or bureaus (Imber & Van Geel, 1993). Whereas policy is legislative in nature (i.e., developed by school boards), rules and regulations are executive in nature (i.e., developed by administrators). Most often, rules and regulations provide direction for implementing policy. As an example, a district policy may give principals the discretion of suspending a student for a certain act; a rule may stipulate how the principal will use that discretion (e.g., an automatic 2-day suspension). Student handbooks contain most or all of a school's rules and regulations. Commonly, superintendents recommend approval of student handbooks prior to each school year. By approving the handbooks, school boards officially endorse school rules and regulations.

## Legal Constraints and Principal Decisions

Whereas laws and policy limit principal decisions, rules determine the extent to which principals restrict their own decisions and those made by other persons in the school. Sergiovanni (2009) posits that three pervasive factors affect administrative decision making:

- *Demands* stem from laws, policy, rules, and formal and informal position requirements (e.g., job descriptions). As an example, laws require principals to report incidents of child abuse.
- *Constraints* are an amalgam of community and school values, beliefs, and resources (both human and material). As an example, a principal may be constrained from adopting block scheduling because the community does not support the concept or because the school's physical environment is inadequate.
- *Choices* are the identifiable alternatives considered in relation to making a decision. As an example, a principal may identify reductions of custodial staff, student activities, or staff travel as alternatives for dealing with an impending budget reduction.

In developing rules, principals should weigh these factors with the following outcome in mind: increase choices in order to limit demands and constraints.

When laws, policy, and rules restrict choices, principals and teachers have fewer opportunities to exercise professional discretion. Thus, when forging rules and regulations, principals should consider the extent to which they are limiting choices.

The following typology developed by Clemmer (1991) identifies types of regulations based on discretion provided for decision makers:

- *Mandatory regulations* identify an issue requiring administrative action and do not allow decision-maker discretion. They are intended to ensure absolute consistency; the emphasis is on following a prescribed action, not on encouraging professional judgment. Zero-tolerance policies and regulations fall into this category. As an example, a principal may develop the following regulation: *Students caught smoking in a school building shall be suspended for 3 days.*
- *Directory regulations* identify an issue requiring administrative action and allow a limited level of decision-maker discretion. They are intended to promote consistency but acknowledge that contextual variables and professional judgment may need to be considered. As an example, a principal may develop the following regulation: *Students caught smoking in a school building normally will be suspended for 3 days; however, extenuating circumstances may merit a lesser or more severe punishment that must be approved by the superintendent.*
- *Discretionary regulations* identify an issue requiring administrative action and give the decision maker considerable discretion. The intent is to place considerable emphasis on contextual variables and the professional judgment of the decision maker. As an example, a principal may develop the following regulation: *Students caught smoking in a school building should be disciplined as deemed appropriate by the school principal.*
- *Proscriptive regulations* identify an issue requiring administrative action and give the decision maker complete discretion to handle the matter. The intent is to allow administrators to base their decision completely on contextual variables and professional judgment. As an example, a principal may develop the following regulation: *Board policy prohibits smoking in all areas of all school buildings; principals are expected to take necessary enforcement action.*

Some rules (e.g., those pertaining to weapons in a school) need to be mandatory, but generally, principals should try to provide professional staff the leeway to make decisions that affect students.

## SCHOOLS: THE SOCIAL–POLITICAL FRAME

Whereas the legitimate frame of schooling primarily is concerned with the values of adequacy and equality, the socio-political frame is primarily concerned with efficiency and effectiveness. From a social perspective, public schools are owned by citizens. As such, district residents are analogous to stockholders in a private corporation. There is, however, an important distinction between stockholders and stakeholders. In the private sector economy, decisions are based entirely or primarily on individual interests; for example, the type of refrigerator you purchase is not subject to public approval. Thus, stockholders usually act solely on the basis of personal interests (e.g., the amount of profit they will receive as a result of a decision). In the public sector economy, however, government officials (e.g., school boards and administrators) are expected to act on behalf of collective stakeholder (or society) interests.

Prior to 1950, the population of a typical school district was quite small and, therefore, stakeholders could directly pursue their individual interests by collectively deciding a course of action.[2] But, as noted previously, population growth contributed to the demise of democratic localism and rise of representative democracy (Levin, 1999). Under representative democracy, government officials, both elected and appointed, made decisions on behalf of stakeholders. As noted earlier, school board members ideally were to behave as trustees—that is, government officials who acted rationally and objectively to serve the interests of the entire community (Kowalski, 2006). In reality, however, two conditions politicized representative democracy:

- Society supports two broad goals for public education: serving society and serving individuals (Bauman, 1996). Local policy development occurs at a point where these two interests most directly collide. When threatened or angered by school officials who claimed to be acting in their best interests, citizens often resorted to political confrontation (e.g., seeking to replace incumbent board members or to oust the superintendent) in an effort to advance their interests or protect their rights (Levin, 1987).
- Scarce resources prevented school district officials from satisfying all stakeholder needs and wants; therefore, choices had to be made from among conflicting interests (Hanson, 2003). Commonly, groups with dissimilar and often competing interests sought to influence decisions made by school boards and administrators by forming coalitions (Wirt & Kirst, 2005).

## Schools as Efficient Institutions

Efficiency pertains to the relationships between inputs and outputs. In systems theory, schools are visualized as transformational institutions (Hoy & Miskel, 2005). That is, society provides inputs, such as students, financial support, staff, and facilities; educators and support staff deploy these inputs in an effort to transform students in a manner that complies with a school's designated mission; and, eventually, students return to society and the quantity and quality of their social contributions are outputs (see Figure 1.3). A school's efficiency level is based on the ratio of inputs to outputs; if inputs are high and outputs low, for example, a school would be considered inefficient.

Elevating efficiency can be done in two ways: increasing outputs while holding inputs constant or holding outputs constant while decreasing inputs (King et al., 2003). The following two tactics demonstrate how each option has been pursued:

- *Unfunded mandates.* State legislatures and state boards of education have often promulgated unfunded mandates. These requirements are enacted without provision for additional funding for local districts. As an example, some states have required students failing to meet state benchmarks on achievement tests to attend summer school; but the schools responsible for providing the additional service are given no additional summer-school funding. Unfunded mandates attempt to increase outputs without making a commitment to additional inputs.
- *Revenue freezes.* Freezing school district revenues is another efficiency-driven strategy. Concurrently freezing local tax levies and per-pupil state aid is nested in

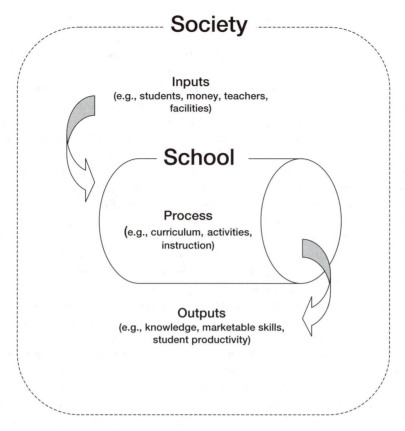

*Figure 1.3*  A School from a Systems Theory Perspective.

the assumption that school districts can at least hold outputs constant if inputs are reduced. Revenue freezes are de facto input decreases if the inflation rate is greater than zero and the district's enrollment is not declining.[3] Thus, revenue freezes typically exemplify an attempt to decrease inputs while holding outputs constant.

## Schools as Effective Institutions

Defining an effective school, especially at the national or state level, has proven to be an exceedingly difficult task, in large measure because stakeholders hold different values and expectations. Thus, disagreements over the social purposes of schooling can be traced as far back as the formative years of public education in this country (Spring, 1991). Equally notable, the distribution of political power has been dynamic. Groups holding competing values and interests have not dominated political policymaking arenas, as evidenced by abrupt and consequential policy shifts (Cuban, 1988). Thus, two political groups may disagree vehemently over the definition of an effective school, and a school that was defined as being effective 25 years ago may not be defined as such today. Even so, scholars in education increasingly recognize that a highly effective school is one in which impediments to learning are mitigated by purposeful interventions allowing all students to complete the curriculum as intended (Taylor, 2002). The extent to which this is accomplished is most often assessed by student achievement test scores.

Since the late 1970s, considerable effort has been made to determine the characteristics that make a school effective. One of the earlier studies on this topic was reported by Edmonds (1979). He identified several pervasive characteristics in institutions thought to be effective; they included features such as teacher job satisfaction, principal leadership and support, a culture conducive to learning, high student expectations, emphasis on basic skills, and parent volunteers. Another often cited study on effective school characteristics was conducted several years later by Purkey and Smith (1983). Their research affirmed several of Edmonds's findings (e.g., teacher job satisfaction, principal leadership, a positive school culture) and added several others, most notably (a) teacher collegiality, (b) teacher involvement in decision making, (c) instructional experimentation, (d) staff development, (e) sufficient time on task, (f) limited electives in the curriculum, (g) clear instructional goals, (h) an ordered and disciplined environment, and (i) school autonomy (i.e., freedom to experiment and make curricular and instructional adjustments). Several subsequent journal articles (e.g., Coyle & Witcher, 1992; Downer, 1991) essentially affirmed the validity of these characteristics.

In the mid-1990s, research by Zigarelli (1996) sought to determine again the validity of the previously identified characteristics. Using student achievement test scores to measure school effectiveness, he concluded that a significant association existed for five variables (high expectations for student performance, sufficient learning time, teacher satisfaction and collegiality, principal leadership and authority, and parental volunteerism) but did not exist for four other variables (teacher empowerment, continuing teacher education, principal management of the school, and warm relations between principals and teachers). Even more recently, Taylor (2002) posited that effective schools are characterized by eight conditions: (a) a clearly stated and focused mission, (b) a safe and orderly climate, (c) high expectations for students, teachers, and administrators, (d) opportunities to learn, (e) sufficient time on task, (f) instructional leadership being provided by all professional staff, (g) frequent assessments and evaluations of student progress, and (h) positive home–school relations.

In summary, determining the parameters of an effective school is complex because stakeholders disagree about the primary purposes of public education. Even when persons agree that student achievement should be the gold standard for determining effectiveness, studies on this topic have not produced entirely consistent findings. Nonetheless, the characteristics summarized by Taylor (2002) are now widely accepted in the profession as being the most relevant.

## SCHOOLS: THE MORAL–ETHICAL FRAME

Schools also are cast as moral institutions. In this vein, Noblit and Dempsey (1996) contend that schools are social institutions expressing societal values more than they are institutions achieving society's goals. Stakeholders across a state and even in many local districts, however, do not emphasize the same values. As examples, some see schooling largely as a technical enterprise transmitting knowledge and others see schooling largely as a moral enterprise promoting and reinforcing social values. Consequently, persons aligned with the former perception demand excellence and those aligned with the latter perception demand equity (Noblit & Dempsey, 1996).

From a moral–ethical perspective, schools can be described along a continuum from "bad" to "good." Though it is clear that good schools have moral purpose, this feature has not been interpreted consistently. Most notably, many persons construe moral purpose to mean teaching morality. Wardekker (2001) contends that teaching selected moral principles is arguably inappropriate in public schools serving a diverse democratic society. He envisions a moral school to be an institution that prepares students to handle plurality by participating in cultural activities in a critical way. Citizenship, respect for others, relationship building, community service, and helping every student to reach his or her potential are other examples of goals that have been linked to moral purpose. According to Cuban (1988), schools have moral purpose when educators in them are dedicated to molding virtuous and thoughtful persons.

Good schools also are places where you observe educators engaging in ethical practice. Leaders in these schools, both administrators and teachers, are aware of the moral dimensions of schooling and behave accordingly to teach and reinforce relevant values (Fuhrman, 2004). Ethical behavior for principals is especially critical in relation to dilemmas that require a choice between opposing alternatives, each of which has merit. When deciding what punishment should be administered to a student who has violated an important rule, for example, a principal often must decide between doing what is best for the school (e.g., suspending the student) and what is best for the student (e.g., finding an alternative punishment that allows the student to remain in school). Choosing between a good alternative (e.g., meeting your responsibility) and a bad alternative (e.g., neglecting your responsibility) actually is an easier and clearer decision.

One of the most recognized models for ethical practice in school administration was developed by Starratt (1991). It has three components:

- The *ethic of critique* pays particular attention to power relationships. It addresses the question: Whose interests are served by a decision?
- The *ethic of caring* focuses on human relationships such as cooperation, shared commitment, and friendship. It requires those who care for students or employees to encounter them "in their authentic individuality" (p. 195).
- The *ethic of justice* focuses on democratic participation and equal access to programs and resources. It demands attention to both the rights of individuals and the common good (societal rights).

In schools lacking moral purpose, decisions are made politically; that is, those in authority are swayed by self-interests or the interests of individuals and groups possessing substantial power. As a result, a politically driven principal is not inclined to protect persons who have limited power. The extent to which a school's professional staff members abide by ethical and moral standards plays an important part in determining what the institution is and what it will become (Beck & Murphy, 1996; Greenfield, 1995). Acknowledging that a universal definition of a good school may not be feasible, Cuban (1998) asserted that such schools satisfy stakeholders, set and reach achievable goals, and instill in students values, attitudes, and behaviors appropriate for living in a democratic society.

## REFLECTIONS

In order to understand what principals are expected to do and the actual challenges they face, you need to understand the complexity of their work environments. Today's schools vary considerably in size, location, resources, problems, and expectations; and contextual variability partially explains why principal roles and behavior are not homogeneous.

As you think about schools from a legal perspective, you should be acquainted with the concept of local control and the reasons why the state and federal levels of government have exercised authority to temper this concept. Legal requirements for schools to be adequate and to provide reasonably equal educational opportunities are fundamental issues in the legal domain that have been largely responsible for greater federal and state involvement.

As you think about schools from social and political perspectives, you should know the difference between societal and individual rights and the reasons why tensions between these entitlements have become progressively more intense. In addition, you should be able to define an effective school and identify characteristics validated through research. Stakeholders commonly demand that school officials take action to make public institutions more efficient and more effective. Responding to this requirement is complicated by two conditions. First, as districts and schools have become more diverse, stakeholders have often disagreed over the most important purposes of schooling; second, stakeholders have been inclined to assess school effectiveness almost entirely on the basis of student standardized test scores.

As you think about schools from moral and ethical perspectives, you should be able to articulate why moral purpose is important in a diverse democratic society. Moreover, you should be able to explain the critical nexus between ethical practice and moral schooling.

## Knowledge-Based Questions

1    Why are states responsible for public education?
2    What purposes are served by district policy and school rules?
3    What is the difference between an adequate school and an effective school?
4    What is the difference between an effective school and a good school?
5    When is a school efficient?
6    Why is it important for principals to be guided by ethical standards when attempting to resolve moral dilemmas?
7    What is the difference between visualizing a school as a technical institution and visualizing a school as a moral institution?
8    Why does conflict often exist between individual rights and societal rights?

## Skill-Based Activities

1    The vignette at the beginning of the chapter raises questions about legal authority for public schools. Take a position favoring or opposing the stance taken by the district superintendent and school board. Provide a rationale to defend your position.
2    Identify the three characteristics of an effective school you deem to be most important and provide a rationale for selecting each of them.
3    Explain why unfettered liberty would be likely to lead to inequities among districts and schools in a state.
4    Develop a defense for the position that schools can be both effective and efficient.
5    Identify at least two issues that you believe should be addressed by rules in each of the four categories discussed in this chapter (mandatory, directive, discretionary, and proscriptive).

## CHAPTER 2

# Principal Roles and Responsibilities

*June 3 was memorable for Judy Carrigan. The spring semester at Cantwell Middle School, a relatively new facility located in a serene rural setting, had ended the preceding day. Judy had arrived at the school around 9:30 a.m. that day with the intention of saying farewell to colleagues, packing her books, and returning to her apartment before noon. But after accomplishing her first two objectives, she remained in her classroom staring out the window and thinking about her next career challenge.*

*When Judy began teaching, she had not considered becoming an administrator. While she was completing a master's degree in social studies education, however, one of her professors, Dr. Arlene Myers, urged her to do so. She told Judy, "You have leadership potential and many schools need creative and collaborative principals." Judy followed the advice, completed courses to obtain a principal's license, and within a year found a new job.*

*Judy's memories of June 3 were vivid because she had convinced herself that day that she would be a successful assistant principal at Valley Middle School. Even before starting the position, Judy recognized that Valley and Cantwell were dissimilar middle schools. Valley was located in a large industrial city; it was nearly three times as large in enrollment; five times as many students came from low-income families qualifying them for free and reduced-price lunches; and three times as many students had failed to reach state benchmarks on standardized achievement tests. A dramatic difference in institutional climates, however, was a factor Judy had not foreseen. At Cantwell, the faculty and staff were cohesive and maintained a close and positive relationship with the principal. At Valley, employees were divided into cliques and most of them disliked and distrusted the principal. Most important, however, Judy's perceptions of her job responsibilities proved to be inaccurate. On June 3, she fantasized about being a change agent working closely with teachers and parents to build a vibrant learning community. Now 4 months later, she found herself supervising custodians, being responsible for controlling the cafeteria, and having contact with teachers and parents largely as a result of student discipline problems.*

*As one of two assistant principals, Judy had become increasingly disenchanted with her position. The principal, Max Davis, had purposefully not assigned her to work in the areas of curriculum and instruction—an assignment she had requested. He believed that, as a young and inexperienced administrator, she needed to learn how to manage a middle school. Judy also was disappointed because most teachers treated her and the other two administrators as adversaries. Persistent conflict between the school board and employee unions contributed to a climate of distrust in which the demarcation between teachers and administrators was distinct and unyielding.*

*As the end of the first semester neared, Judy often thought back to June 3 and asked herself why her perceptions then were so wrong. She no longer thought about being a successful assistant principal; her thought now vacillated between trying to survive and escaping from Valley Middle School.*

## INTRODUCTION

Educators transitioning from teaching to administration typically experience anxiety, and their ability to deal with their concerns depends largely on their knowledge of themselves and of the complexities of administration. Judy Carrigan found out quickly that her initial perceptions of being an assistant principal at Valley Middle School were incorrect—a discovery contributing to job dissatisfaction. Feeling disappointed and alone, she may make decisions that she later will regret. Her willingness and ability to analyze her situation accurately are critically important to her future.

Though generalizing about administrative roles can be precarious, most of us are inclined to do so. In reality, the conditions in any specific assignment are determined largely by three variables:

- *Individual differences.* Persons entering administration possess dissimilar attributes, such as needs, aspirations, knowledge, dispositions, skills, and experience. Thus, two individuals confronted with the same challenges may react to them very differently.
- *Role differences.* Not all administrative positions, including those with identical titles, have the same demands and expectations. This is most readily apparent in the variations found in principal and assistant principal job descriptions. But even when two principals have identical job descriptions, what is really expected of them may not be the same.
- *Institutional differences.* Schools are complex and unique institutions. Each one has a climate distinguishing it to some degree from others—similar to the way that personalities reveal individual differences. Moreover, as described in the previous chapter, communities served by a school can differ demographically, economically, politically, and philosophically.

The primary purpose of this chapter is to examine school administration by comparing past and present roles. Particular attention is given to contrasting public expectations with reality; that is, ideal and real roles are described and compared. After reading this chapter, you should be able to demonstrate the ability to do the following:

- Correctly differentiate among three key terms: management, leadership, and administration
- Distinguish between ideal and real roles
- Distinguish between formal and informal roles
- Identify traditional role expectations for principals
- Explain why some principals did not meet traditional role expectations
- Identify contemporary role expectations for principals
- Explain why some principals do not meet contemporary role expectations

## ROLE CONCEPTUALIZATIONS

Roles are basically functions integral to a position, and role conceptualizations are interpretations of those functions. In the past, principals were primarily conceptualized as managers, persons responsible for protecting resources, enforcing policy, and supervising employees. Today, however, many authors purposefully call principals leaders. In order to understand the functions assigned to and carried out by principals, you must be able to distinguish among three possible roles: *management*, *leadership*, and *administration*. You also need to know why persons disagree over the nature and importance of these functions. Research suggests that the extent to which you correctly understand these issues is likely to influence your behavior when you become an assistant principal or principal. Specifically, highly effective administrators usually have a more accurate and comprehensive understanding of their position and the various functions that it includes (Crow & Glascock, 1995).

### Principal as Manager

For much of the twentieth century, the principalship was viewed primarily as a managerial position, and understandably principals were commonly referred to as school managers. Until a few decades ago, this designation was viewed positively or at least neutrally. In fact, history reveals that superintendents and principals in the early to mid-1900s purposely emulated managerial behavior prevalent in private corporations in an effort to brand themselves as managers (Kowalski, 2006). Today, however, being labeled a manager is not especially advantageous or desirable, primarily because the role often has been associated with authoritarian and narcissistic behavior.

Properly defined, management focuses most directly on controlling resources and personnel, arguably essential assignments in any organization including schools. Specifically, managers allocate and protect resources and they monitor and evaluate employees. Consequently, persons performing this role are expected to make decisions about *how* things should be done. In the context of schools, management generally pertains to controlling resources and personnel to ensure that education and social goals are achieved (Hanson, 2003).

In order to understand why value judgments of management have changed, you need to know the difference between ideal and real roles. The former are prescriptive in nature and identify what principals are expected to do; the latter provide descriptions of what principals actually do. Over time, descriptive research, in both private and public organizations, produced a negative picture of managers. They were often depicted as autocratic, authoritative, impersonal, and task-oriented individuals who showed little interest in or empathy for the personal welfare of their subordinates (Schneider, 1994). This recurring characterization in the literature blurred distinctions between ideal and real managerial roles. That is, persons often evaluated the intentions of management based on actual managerial behavior (Yukl, 2005). When examined from an ideal role perspective, the need for management in schools is undisputable. For example, core managerial responsibilities—such as organizing, supervising, and evaluating (Kotter, 1990)—remain essential in all types of organizations.

## Principal as Leader

A study conducted over a 3-year period in California sought to identify how graduate students preparing to be principals defined leadership. The responses produced more than fifty separate definitions (Glasman & Glasman, 1997). This finding is not surprising in light of the fact that the term *leadership* has been added to the technical vocabulary of disciplines and professions without being defined precisely and uniformly (Yukl, 2005). Thus, hundreds of definitions are found in the literature. As a role conceptualization, however, leadership is often characterized by functions that distinguish it from management.

The concept of leadership almost always has positive connotations; as examples, leaders are commonly characterized as courageous, insightful, caring, and collaborative (Yukl, 2005). Functionally, however, leadership focuses most directly on organizational development (improvement). Leaders are expected to initiate new structures or operational changes when such alterations are in the best interests of the employing organization. In the case of education, principals functioning as leaders make decisions about *what* needs to be done to improve schools. For example, they work with others to build a vision for the future; they communicate and explain the vision to all stakeholders; they motivate and inspire stakeholders to work toward achieving the vision (Kotter, 1990). Culture building (a concept discussed more deeply later in the book) also is considered a primary leadership function, because lasting and meaningful change rarely occurs in organizations unless shared values and beliefs inhibiting progress are altered (Schein, 1985).

## Principal as Administrator

Administration is a third role conceptualization you need to understand. This term too has been defined and used in various ways. Some authors (e.g., Hanson, 2003; Sergiovanni, Kelleher, McCarthy, & Fowler, 2009) have treated it as a contemporary synonym for management. Nevertheless, many books on school administration, including this one, define it as a comprehensive concept that encompasses both management and leadership functions as depicted in Figure 2.1. Based on the conviction that effective principals must lead and manage, principals are viewed as administrators who continuously transition between and coordinate their leadership and management functions.

*Figure 2.1* Conceptualization of the Principal as an Administrator.

Intense efforts to improve schools understandably have affected principals. Rather than reordering priorities in their work, reform initiatives essentially broadened role expectations based on the assumption that principals had the capacity to assume added responsibilities (Hallinger, 1992). In fact, the major challenge for today's principal is not deciding whether to lead or to manage; rather it is acquiring the essential acuity and time to do both effectively. In addition to understanding differences between managing and leading, a principal must have a positive attitude toward performing both roles. Adapting the often cited distinction between management and leadership developed by Bennis and Nanus (1985), ideal principals are described here as administrators who do things right when they manage and do the right things when they lead. A comparison of these two roles is shown in Table 2.1.

*Table 2.1* Comparison of Management and Leadership in the Administrative Role of Principals

| *Variable* | *Management* | *Leadership* |
|---|---|---|
| Time dimension | Focusing on present operations | Focusing on future vision |
| Material resources | Allocating and controlling | Acquiring additional as needed |
| Human resources | Monitoring, supervising, and evaluating | Motivating and collaborating |
| Direction | Enforcing laws, policies, and rules | Recommending new policy and rules |
| Influence | Relying on position, rewards, and punishment | Relying on expertise and relationships |
| Objective | Organizing and ordering | Creating, building, and improving |
| Guidance | Relying on objective evidence | Relying on evidence and values |
| Conflict | Preventing and managing | Capitalizing to pursue change |
| Risk | Preventing and minimizing | Accepting to pursue change |

# LEADERSHIP: A DIFFICULT AND ESSENTIAL ROLE

Describing the extent to which principals actually lead is difficult, both because of multiple definitions of leadership and because conditions surrounding practice are inconstant. Generally, protracted efforts to reform schools have resulted in obvious demands for principals to exert greater leadership. Less obviously, this enhanced expectation has not diminished demands for principals to manage human and material resources. Consequently, many principals experience role conflict (Catano & Stronge, 2006), a condition typically stemming from tensions produced by incongruent stakeholder expectations (Hanson, 2003). For example, community members may expect a principal to initiate needed change whereas teachers expect him or her to protect the status quo. Though both leadership and management are essential roles, the former clearly is the more difficult and daunting assignment.

## Uncertainty and Risk

Historically, public schools have been shaped as institutions of stability and not agencies for social change. As such, educators were directed to instill in their students society's prevalent values and beliefs rather than preparing them to engage in social reconstruction (Spring, 2000). Over time, educators also learned that avoiding possible failure was preferable to taking risks (Kowalski, Lasley, & Mahoney, 2008)—a mindset that helps us understand why many administrators and teachers have been reluctant to experiment with new ideas or to initiate structural changes in schools.

Making decisions about what should be done to improve schools is more difficult and risky than making decisions about how to do things correctly. The primary reason is that leadership decisions usually entail higher levels of uncertainty. Decision uncertainty is a condition that arises when a person cannot predict the future accurately, either because he or she lacks critical information or because the types of information required cannot be accessed (Nutt, 1989). Uncertainty can be centered externally (i.e., outside the school) or internally (i.e., inside the school). Both types of uncertainty may occur in three dimensions: (a) not knowing future conditions, (b) not knowing the effects of future conditions, and (c) not knowing responses to future conditions (Milliken, 1987). Assume as a principal you are considering three new approaches to teaching reading because you want to improve the academic performance of students on the state achievement test. The uncertainty surrounding your decision is demonstrated by examples provided in Table 2.2. The less certain you are about conditions at each of these levels, the more difficult and risky your decision becomes.

Principals have dissimilar levels of tolerance for uncertainty, and those with a low level usually make subjective decisions (Kowalski et al., 2008). Those who do this are prone to selecting the option they personally favor rather than the option that has been found to have the greatest utility for the school and society. If you behaved in this manner in relation to the example in Table 2.2, you would select the program you prefer even though you have no evidence validating its superiority. When you act intuitively, you increase the probability of organizational and individual risk; that is, you make it more likely that your decision will affect the school, the community, or you negatively.

*Table 2.2*  Examples of Environmental Uncertainty Related to Adopting a New Reading Program

| Uncertainty Condition | Examples |
|---|---|
| Not knowing future environmental conditions | You do not know if the state will continue testing or using the same achievement test; you do not know if the community will change demographically |
| Not knowing the effects of future environmental conditions | If the state changes its testing policy or if the community changes, you do not know if these alterations will affect the potential value of any or all of the three programs you are considering |
| Not knowing response to future environmental conditions | If the state changes its testing policy or if the community changes, you do not know how the alterations will affect the performance of any or all of the three programs you are considering |

## Ambiguity

Decision ambiguity occurs when elements of a decision are "unclear or unknown, as contrasted with uncertainty, in which important factors are clear but making prediction using a factor is not" (Nutt, 1989, p. 6). In the case of public education, ambiguity has been produced primarily by philosophical dissonance—that is, competing values and beliefs. Some societal groups, for instance, believe that the primary mission of public schools is preparing students for the workforce; others believe that it is preparing good citizens; and still others believe it is preparing students for college. As a result of these different and often competing preferences, principals often are unclear as to their primary objectives and the preferred strategies for achieving them. And the greater the level of ambiguity, the more employees question the organization's motives and the value of their own work (March & Simon, 1958).

## School Reform and Leadership

School reform scholars (e.g., Fullan, 2001; Hall & Hord, 2006) agree that principals should lead the process of school improvement; and, from a prescriptive perspective, almost everyone agrees with them. The extent to which principals are doing this and explanations for their behavior are less defined. Since the early 1980s, many reform initiatives have called for principals to exert leadership, but in reality they forced them into a managerial role. That is, principals were relegated to implementing change that they had little or no part in developing. In his study of principals and school reform, Portin (1998) concluded that national and state reforms actually have "constrained principals to a largely managerial role—a role which leaves decreasing amounts of time to lead" (p. 344).

The ineffectiveness of centralized, coercive change strategies has resulted in new perspectives about school improvement. Namely, many policymakers now concede that reform is more likely to succeed if it is developed and guided locally, increasing the probability that intentional changes are relevant to the real needs of students. In this more enlightened view, the calls for principals to exert leadership are louder than at any point in the past.

## ADMINISTRATIVE RESPONSIBILITIES

Within their two broad role conceptualizations, principals assume many specific responsibilities. Their order of importance and the extent to which they require attention depends on several variables such as level of schooling (e.g., elementary versus secondary), the quantity and quality of human and material resources, school size, employer–community expectations, and the nature of the community and students served. Collectively, these primary responsibilities, listed in Figure 2.2, present both leadership and management challenges.

### Visioning

Effective administrators are often described as visionaries—leaders who know what schools should look like in the future. In the absence of this image, school personnel are likely to be reactive rather than proactive; that is, they will continuously respond to contextual conditions rather than taking a proactive stance to shape the future (Kowalski, 2008). Properly sculpted, a school's vision should provide a destination known to and supported by all or at least most stakeholders. Having such a mental image and articulating it to others, however, does not ensure that a school will improve continuously. If a principal forges a vision independently, relying on personal intuition and philosophy, he or she increases the probability that the image will not serve its intended purpose.

Properly constructed, a school's vision statement is a one- or two-page narrative painting a picture of what the school is intended to look like at a designated point in the future (Winter, 1995). It provides the basis for school improvement and is developed prior to a strategic improvement plan (Cunningham & Gresso, 1993). Moreover, it constitutes a symbolic statement that helps stakeholders to give meaning to action (Conger, 1989) and serves as a sociological force generating shared commitment essential to carrying out intended changes (Björk, 1995). Overall, a school's vision focuses on creating the ideal school rather than perpetuating traditional deficit models that simply focus on correcting existing problems (Cunningham & Gresso, 1993).

Visioning is a course of action that entails developing and periodically adjusting a school's vision. It is a generative process, enhancing and enlarging a school's capacity to shape its future by providing richer meaning to the collective experiences of exploring problems, needs, strengths, and values. In essence, visioning provides a reference point against which day-to-day activities can be tested against shared future directions (Senge, 1990). Rather than dictating a vision statement, the principal's role should be to initiate, facilitate, and sustain democratic discourse that results in a collective vision.

### Planning

In simple terms, planning entails the development of goals deemed essential to achieving a vision and the adoption of implementation strategies for them. Though the No Child Left Behind Act and related state accountability requirements have made planning an essential responsibility for principals, some practitioners have not been enthusiastic

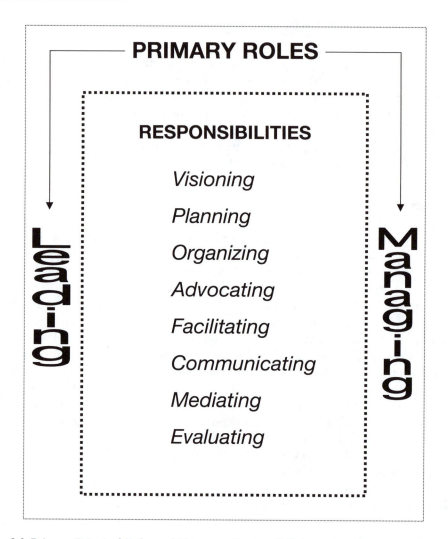

*Figure 2.2* Primary Principal Roles and Common Responsibilities.

about assuming this complex assignment. Available evidence suggests, however, that mandates for school planning are defensible. As examples, authors summarizing research on effective schools (e.g., Johnson, Livingston, & Schwartz, 2000; Purkey & Smith, 1982, 1983; Wimpelberg, Teddlie, & Stringfield, 1989) have reported that principals and colleagues in these institutions collaboratively develop and use clearly stated goals.

## Organizing

Principals organize by bringing together and arranging people, materials, and other resources to ensure attainment of the school's goals. As examples, they decide how grade levels or departments are shaped, employees are assigned, daily classes and extracurricular events are scheduled, and resources are allocated. Frequently, they also determine when and under what circumstances facilities can be used outside the regular school day. Organizational decisions almost always influence organizational efficiency, safety, operational costs, and overall effectiveness (Robbins & Coulter, 2007; Schermerhorn, 2008). Ultimately, however, organizational decisions center on creating an environment that simultaneously enhances student learning and progress toward the established vision.

## Advocating

As professional educators and the official representatives of their schools, principals have a responsibility to be vocal advocates for students and school improvement. They fulfill this obligation by first creating positive relationships with parents, students, staff, and other stakeholders—associations that allow them to lead in the community as well as in the school (National Association of Elementary School Principals, 2009). Once trust and credibility are established, principals are better able to assume an active role in educating the community about existing needs and urging citizens to participate in and support needed school reforms.

## Facilitating

In simple terms, facilitation involves making it easier for school employees to accomplish their responsibilities individually and for them to meet school goals collectively. For example, a principal may ensure that teachers have access to necessary materials, equipment, and staff development. One of the most important aspects of facilitation is creating opportunities for staff to interact so that they can be part of a learning community (Protheroe, 2004). Another is to provide assistance to teachers individually so that they can grow professionally and become more proficient instructors. Facilitative principals typically gain the respect and admiration of school employees, outcomes that enhance their ability to influence employee behavior (Nyberg, 1990).

## Communicating

New normative standards for administrator communicative behavior have evolved over the past three decades (Kowalski, Petersen, & Fusarelli, 2007). Historically, many principals protected information and disseminated it to employees and other stakeholders on a "need-to-know" basis. This mindset, embedded in the bureaucratic notion of the ideal organization, led organizational managers to believe that they shared information only when they had to (a) provide job instructions and rationale, (b) explain established policy, procedures, and practices, (c) provide performance feedback, and (d) inform others of the organization's mission and objectives (Katz & Kahn, 1978). This perception of effective administrative communication is no longer acceptable in a society in which most data can be accessed independently and without administrative approval.

Today, principals are expected to be relational communicators (Kowalski et al., 2007); that is, they exchange information in an effort to erect and maintain positive relationships with stakeholders (Bruning & Ledingham, 2000). They do this in a manner that minimizes the effects of authority and actual power differences between and among the communicants (Burgoon & Hale, 1984) and ensures that the exchanges benefit all parties (Grunig, 1989). Principals who behave in this manner are better able to identify and address unmet needs (Conrad, 1994) and they are more likely to persuade others that schools are public assets rather than liabilities (Bruning & Ledingham, 2000).

## Mediating

Conflict in schools, and in all other organizations, is inevitable because individuals and groups bring competing values and beliefs into schools (Hoy & Miskel, 2005). In the past, most principals were taught and socialized to treat conflict as a counterproductive and unwelcome circumstance. Therefore, they attempted to avoid it; and when that was impossible they were inclined to eradicate it as quickly as possible. The two recurring preferences were either to refuse to deal with the underlying tensions or to surrender to them—both options constituting poor managerial choices that merely deferred negative consequences (Hanson, 2003). Principal reactions to collectively bargaining with teachers in the past provide quintessential examples: when confronted with demands from employees, many principals either ignored them (based on the belief that they would eventually dissipate) or acquiesced (based on the belief that mollifying teachers provided a quick and politically advantageous solution). Addressed appropriately, mediation requires more than retreat, surrender, or simply choosing one side over the other. Managing and resolving conflict is a complex and challenging responsibility that requires principals to diagnose situations accurately and to subsequently apply relevant tactics to manage the situation.

Modern perspectives of school conflict differ substantially from those prevalent just a few decades ago. Now, enlightened administrators realize that conflict is a potential catalyst for organizational improvement because the tensions underlying it often make change more palatable to many stakeholders (Hanson, 2003). Moreover, a principal's performance as a mediator is now commonly judged by the degree to which he or she is able to maintain harmony among a school's stakeholders (Yukl, 2005).

## Evaluating

Principals are supposed to evaluate overall school performance, the success of individual school programs, and employee performance. Accurate evaluations across these areas are critical for at least three reasons: they provide a guide for decisions; they are indispensable with respect to institutional accountability; and they provide essential insights regarding organizational behavior (Stufflebeam & Webster, 1988). Unfortunately, evaluation has often been ignored or applied haphazardly, either because principals did not comprehend its purposes or because they applied the process narrowly.

There is a distinct difference between assessment and evaluation; and in the past the former has received much more attention. Assessment entails measurement—such as determining a student's test score or the number of times a teacher praises her students. Evaluation, by comparison, entails judgments about assessments. In order to draw accurate conclusions, principals must possess essential knowledge pertinent to the assessments or at least know how such knowledge can be accessed. Consider for example an elementary school in which 5 percent of the students fail to reach the benchmark on the state's mandated achievement test. Based solely on this outcome, many stakeholders would most likely conclude that the school's performance is poor. A comparison with other schools having similar demographic profiles, however, reveals that the school's test scores are better than 97 percent of the schools in the comparison group. Given present demands for school improvement and accountability, principals are expected to be proficient evaluators.

Likewise, there is a distinct difference between formative and summative evaluations; and, in the past, principals were primarily concerned with the latter. Summative conclusions determine performance levels—for example, determining if an employee or a program should be retained. Formative conclusions are intended to provide guidance for improvement—for example, assessing teacher performance and making judgments regarding ways that the teacher can become more effective. In the context of school reform, greater emphasis has been placed on balancing the formative and summative evaluations (Natriello, 1990).

## REFLECTIONS

Are principals leaders, managers, or administrators? The position articulated here is that they are administrators who assume both leadership and management roles. Leadership entails decisions about what needs to be done to improve a school; management entails decisions about how things should be done. Though the former role is clearly more demanding, risk-laden, and popular, the latter role also remains crucial. Therefore, contemporary principals are administrators who lead and manage. Moreover, principals assume more specific responsibilities requiring leadership, management, or both. Those discussed here include visioning, planning, organizing, advocating, facilitating, communicating, mediating, and evaluating.

As you think about responsibilities given to principals, you should understand the reasons why leadership has emerged as a popular and presumably more essential role. Likewise, you should comprehend why many persons view management negatively and why this perception is misguided.

Finally, consider the effects of expanding the responsibilities given to principals. As examples, leadership functions, such as visioning and planning, and management functions, such as allocating technology and protecting databases, require knowledge and skills that were rarely discussed 30 years ago. Yet some critics believe that any person with basic managerial skills can perform adequately in this difficult and demanding position.

## Knowledge-Based Questions

1   What factors have contributed to the growing need for principals to function as leaders?
2   How would you respond to those who believe that principals should be leaders, not managers?
3   How would you respond to those who believe that principals should be managers, not leaders?
4   Why do leadership decisions usually entail more risk than management decisions?
5   What is the nexus between visioning and planning?
6   What are the differences between mediating and facilitating?
7   What responsibility should a principal have for educating the public about school performance and school improvement?

## Skill-Based Activities

1   In the vignette at the beginning of the chapter Judy Carrigan questions her decision to become an assistant principal. Assume you are her friend and colleague. Applying the content in this chapter, determine what advice you would give to her.
2   Identify what you would do as a principal to develop positive relationships with stakeholders.
3   Based on your personal experiences as an educator and the content in this chapter, identify what you would do as a principal to resolve conflict between teachers and parents.
4   Some persons believe that school improvement initiatives should be determined by state officials and local school boards acting on behalf of stakeholders. They see educators, including principals, as instruments for carrying out these decisions. Based on what you read in this chapter, develop a position statement in favor of or against this line of thinking.

## CHAPTER 3

# Effective Schools for All Students

*Meet Eduardo Gomez, principal of Hamilton Lincoln High School. A year ago when he assumed the position, his closest friends told him he had made a big mistake. Hamilton is a city in decline. The economy has been devastated by the loss of industry, taxable property, and population. As a result, many middle-class families have left the community; in the past 25 years, the school district's enrollment has declined 32 percent. Over 50 percent of the district's students qualify for free and reduced-price school lunches.*

*Lincoln's previous principal lasted just 2 years. He was the school's third principal in 9 years. Employed primarily because of his reputation as a stern disciplinarian, his "honeymoon" in Hamilton ended abruptly after just 18 months. Local media and the teachers' union criticized his heavy-handed tactics and contended that conditions at the school had deteriorated under his leadership. Most notably, they pointed out that student suspensions and expulsions had increased while the percentage of students passing the state's mandated high school graduation test decreased. Sensing little political support for the principal, the superintendent and school board made no effort to protect him politically. Angered by their passive behavior, he resigned.*

*The search for a new principal yielded only four applicants—one of whom had been dismissed twice previously as a high school principal. Among the remaining applicants, Eduardo Gomez clearly had the best credentials. He was then a successful high school principal in Texas and was completing his dissertation requirement for a doctorate in school administration. His primary motive for seeking the position at Lincoln, which he candidly shared with district officials, involved his wife's family. Her parents owned a restaurant in a small town 22 miles from Hamilton, and they wanted to retire and have her assume management of the business.*

*During his employment interview, Mr. Gomez outlined his education philosophy. The superintendent and board members quickly realized that his values and beliefs were dissimilar to those held by his predecessor. Rather than focusing on student discipline and close supervision of teachers, he talked about building a learning community in which administrators, teachers, parents, and students could collaborate to build a more effective learning environment. He expressed confidence that the school could become more effective if the right circumstances could be established.*

*His comments did not exactly instill confidence in several skeptics convinced that the school's primary problems remained unruly students, militant teachers, and biased media coverage. Yet the superintendent and board did not have more attractive options. Of the remaining two candidates interviewed, one had no previous administrative experience and the other expressed beliefs that matched those of the previous principal. Given these options, a majority of the board members decided to roll the dice and offer the position to Mr. Gomez. The two dissenters warned the others that he was an idealist who would probably resign in a few years after he learned the brutal truth about Lincoln High School.*

## INTRODUCTION

The sustained pursuit of school reform has taught us many lessons. One of them is that stakeholders in most school systems disagree over the primary purposes of education and over what should be done to improve school performance. At one end of the spectrum, there are persons who believe that the primary problems in low-performing schools are lazy students and incompetent teachers; in their eyes, school improvement will only occur if principals force students and teachers to perform at higher levels. At the other end of the spectrum, there are persons who believe the primary problems in low-performing schools are ineffective structure and inadequate resources; in their eyes, school improvement requires principals to mobilize stakeholders to reshape schools and to take advantage of all community resources.

As an assistant principal or principal, you will encounter persons at both ends of this spectrum. When this occurs, one alternative is to act politically; that is, you simply decide to embrace the perspective held by those possessing the most power. Though this decision may be expedient, it is not prudent in the context of professional practice. As an educator and administrator, you should be able to analyze opposing views and attempt to build consensus in the context of the community and school in which you practice.

The primary purposes of this chapter are to examine emerging perspectives on school improvement and the principal's role as a change leader. Content is divided into three sections: success for all students, framework for successful schools, and school climate. After reading the chapter, you should be able to demonstrate the ability to do the following tasks correctly:

• Articulate why evolving world and societal conditions have changed the social and personal consequences for student failure
• Define a school's mission, philosophy, vision, and plan
• Describe the concept of organizational climate and identify its components
• Explain how school climate, and especially school culture, affect student learning
• Detail the difficulty associated with changing each element of school climate

# SCHOOL REFORM AND THE PRINCIPAL

## Why Change is Essential

More than a quarter of a century ago, the report *A Nation at Risk* (National Commission on Excellence in Education, 1983) blamed the ineffectiveness of the education system for jeopardizing the nation's status as the world's eminent economic power. Despite intense and sustained reform efforts in the aftermath of this report, statistics indicate the overall effectiveness of the country's education system has not improved appreciably. Among every twenty children born in 1983 and entering kindergarten in 1988, fourteen graduated from high school on time in 2001, ten started college in the fall of the same year, and only five earned a degree in the spring of 2005 (U.S. Department of Education, 2008). Nationally, about two-thirds of all students graduate from high school; and, as troubling as that figure is, it does not reveal the depth of problems in selected school districts. In Cleveland, for example, only 30 percent of the freshman class in 2001 graduated from high school 4 years later (Swanson, 2004). In an information-based society, even single-digit failure rates are troubling because employment opportunities for persons lacking basic academic skills keep shrinking.

Acknowledging data showing that a considerable number of high school graduates have lacked basic academic skills, over half the states have enacted laws requiring students to pass high school exit examinations (*Do High School Graduation Tests Measure Up?*, 2004). In the minds of most citizens, however, a high school diploma is no longer sufficient evidence that students are prepared to be productive members of an information-based society. Today, success is also defined by requisite skills allowing persons to extend their education or to apply their knowledge in ways that meet personal and societal needs. As examples, young citizens are expected to "think independently, solve problems, work as members of teams and use a variety of technologies" (*A Framework for Success for All Students*, 2006, p. 16).

## Why Principals Must Lead

Those preparing to be principals need to understand the nexus between sustained social demands for excellence and evolving expectations for school leadership. In the past, directives for elementary and secondary schools came primarily from state and federal laws; and educators, including principals, merely had the responsibility of implementing them (Schlechty, 2008). Over time, administrators learned to be reactive rather than proactive; and consequently, they often lacked a vision of an ideal future and their methods and goals for improving schools were unconnected (Haberman, 1994). Recognizing that centralized mandates and their effects on individual schools had failed to produce the anticipated level of improvement and concurrently had limited democratic localism (i.e., the political right of citizens to participate in shaping school reform policy in districts and schools), policymakers and other stakeholders turned to deregulation and decentralization strategies (Bauman, 1996). That is, states often relaxed mandates allowing local districts to determine how they would meet broad state goals and local districts gave individuals schools greater autonomy to do the same (Weiler, 1990). Noting this history and then looking forward, Schlechty concluded that most citizens now want principals who can tailor reforms to specific academic needs, personal student development, and overall improvement of local communities.

Acceptance of the principal's role as reformer, especially among educators, has been attenuated by erroneous assumptions and misperceptions. Four stand out as having been especially detrimental:

- *Erroneously assuming that schools cannot be restructured.* Persons guided by this assumption believe that schools are intractable institutions and that the public neither seeks nor tolerates substantial restructuring.
- *Erroneously assuming that schools do not need to be restructured.* Persons guided by this assumption believe that causes of low productivity lie outside of schools—variables such as poverty, family structure, and student indifference. They believe that demands for school reform are basically a political ploy intended to divert public attention from fundamental social problems.
- *Interpreting the principal's role as change leader incorrectly.* Persons exhibiting this problem believe that role conceptualization calls for principals to behave autocratically, dictating changes and forcing others to implement them.
- *Interpreting school-based reform incorrectly.* Persons exhibiting this problem believe that decentralized approaches to school improvement are unrealistic and possibly counterproductive (e.g., allowing schools to chart their future would exacerbate inequalities in educational opportunities).

Such views, however, are not supported by effective schools research. In fact, some poorly performing schools have improved substantially and principals in highly effective schools commonly exhibit transformational and democratic leadership styles. Specifically, principals who effectively lead change (a) ensure that new ideas are guided by a shared vision of the future, (b) work with others to plan and establish environments that permit educators to collaborate and communicate effectively, (c) encourage experimentation, and (d) consistently evaluate outcomes (Protheroe, 2005). Equally notably, they have proven that it is possible and advantageous to pursue school-based improvements within the parameters of nonnegotiable district goals (Marzano & Waters, 2009).

## FRAMEWORK FOR SUCCESS

All decisions entail some risk because choices we make may have negative consequences for schools or for us. As leadership decisions normally involve greater uncertainty (i.e., the extent to which the consequences of alternatives are precisely known), they usually give rise to greater risk than do managerial decisions (Kowalski, Lasley, & Mahoney, 2008). Principals can reduce risk, however, by acquiring and applying essential knowledge, skills, and dispositions. Specifically in the context of school reform, the contemporary principal relies on these attributes to forge a framework for continuous improvement. This structure, developed collaboratively with teachers and other relevant stakeholders, has four cornerstones—mission, philosophy, vision, and plan—as illustrated in Figure 3.1.

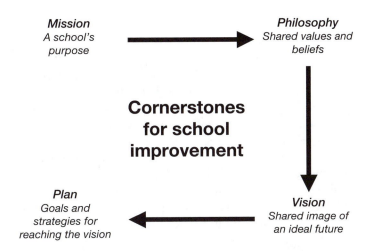

*Figure 3.1* Cornerstones for Creating Schools that Allow Success for All Students.

## Mission

The literature contains hundreds of definitions of an organization's mission, and not all of them are compatible. Here, mission is defined as a statement that describes a school's purpose. Properly developed, it should answer the question: Why does the school exist? In order to serve its intended purpose, the statement should be written in the present tense using succinct language that can be understood by stakeholders. Ideally, it reminds stakeholders of what the school is expected to accomplish and guides employees as they make decisions that affect outcomes.

In the case of public elementary and secondary schools, a core mission is determined by a state's constitution and related laws or policy. For example, a public school is required to provide free and reasonably equal educational opportunities to eligible students. Though district and school officials cannot reduce the core mission determined by the state, they can extend the mission (e.g., provide a broad curriculum) or refine it so that it addresses the specific needs of the local community being served (e.g., provide effective school-to-work programs). In the past, administrators in colleges and pre-collegiate private schools have paid greater attention to mission statements than have public elementary and secondary school administrators. This is because the missions for schools in the latter category have been determined largely by states. Increasingly, however, states are encouraging schools to customize their missions so that they are more relevant to the real needs of students served. At the same time, local school officials are being held accountable for meeting their approved missions (Kowalski et al., 2008). Accordingly, principals should consider two issues regarding mission statements: the extent to which they have measurable components and the types and sources of data available to verify the extent to which the mission is accomplished (Guthrie & Schuermann, 2010).

## Philosophy

Properly constructed, a school's philosophy statement conveys shared values and beliefs that give meaning to the school's mission and vision, especially in the areas of teaching and learning. At first glance, developing the document may seem simple. In fact, the process can be exceedingly contentious and difficult for principals, especially if they approach the task democratically in public schools where parents hold dissimilar and often competing values. Yet having the correct values and a commitment to shared guiding principles are key factors that distinguish a productive learning community from an ordinary school (DuFour & Eaker, 1998).

Compared with mission statements, philosophy statements are typically lengthier because they may address many facets of education. Consider the following examples of dispositions that could be dealt with in this document:

- Student responsibility for learning
- Teacher responsibility for individualizing instruction
- Teacher collaboration
- Parental involvement
- Extracurricular activities
- Pupil conduct
- Testing and other forms of evaluation
- Ability grouping
- Scope of the curriculum

Shared values and beliefs concerning these and other facets of schooling are critically important to school effectiveness.

Private schools, and especially parochial schools, have tended to emphasize philosophy statements and to rely on them in structuring school climate. Some fundamentalist Christian schools, for example, require parents (and students of sufficient age) to sign a statement indicating that they accept and agree to abide by the school's philosophical tenets. Public schools, obviously, could not do this. Nevertheless, public schools also should be guided by philosophical principles that shape the school and daily activities.

## Vision

Whereas a school's mission describes institutional purpose, a school's vision describes what the school is expected to look like in meeting its mission at some designated point in the future. Essentially, it is a coherent picture of how a school will appear and operate after core beliefs, articulated in the philosophy statement, have been actualized (Zmuda, Kuklis, & Kline, 2004). Thus, a vision statement expresses "an ideal, a dream that is grounded in those fundamental meanings and values that feed a sense of human fulfillment" (Starratt, 1996, p. 14). At the same time, however, it should (a) be realistic, (b) be credible, (c) be attractive to most stakeholders, and (d) clearly state how the intended future is better than prevailing conditions (Bennis & Nanus, 1985).

The history of American public education demonstrates that there are many routes schools can take into the future, but many of them end up at undesirable destinations.

A vision is intended to change the mindset that educators and local communities have little or no control over roads they take. A vision provides criteria for making the right choices; and therefore its merit is determined by its potential for shaping an improved future state (Chance, 1992). In order to meet this standard, a vision statement should (a) attract commitment, (b) energize stakeholders, (c) define excellence, and (d) bridge the present to the future (Nanus, 1992). These qualities are much less likely in visions developed solely by principals. A communicative approach to visioning is a more productive alternative; it encourages stakeholders to state and test their individual visions and then to collaborate in building a shared vision (Kowalski, 2008).

## Plan

Research by Elmore (2003) casts doubt on the popular belief that school ineffectiveness is largely a product of incompetent or unmotivated employees. He found educators and students in low-performing schools often worked hard; however, they made poor decisions about what to do next to elevate their performance. This finding illuminates the critical nature of the four cornerstones of effective school improvement. Not knowing what to do next may stem from ambiguity of purpose, vague or unknown values and beliefs, an unawareness of an ideal future, and absence of a plan to control the future.

Whereas vision provides a destination, planning provides goals and strategies for reaching the destination. When a plan is developed to achieve the school's shared vision, data are analyzed and then integrated with mission, philosophy, and evolving social conditions, allowing principals to make informed resource allocation decisions (Cunningham & Gresso, 1993). Consensus in planning, just as in visioning, makes it more probable that stakeholders will have a sense of ownership in a change process (Fullan, 2004). A school plan has two distinguishable but interrelated dimensions: process and technique. The former details the sequence of the stages (i.e., ordering what is to be accomplished); the latter identifies approaches to be used at each stage (i.e., methods for reaching goals) (Nutt, 1985). Thus, an effective school plan includes goals and strategies for meeting them. A collaboratively developed school plan has several notable attributes as demonstrated by the following examples:

- The scope of information is broadened by having internal (e.g., teachers) and external (e.g., community residents) participants.
- Real needs are more likely to be diagnosed accurately.
- Needs are more likely to be analyzed and aligned with school and community philosophies.
- Participants are exposed to data that increase their knowledge of the school allowing them to make informed decisions.
- Participation makes it more likely that a broad base of stakeholders will support the plan.

Reaching a shared vision depends on making the correct decisions and having support and cooperation from those affected (James, 1995). Both conditions are less probable when principals fail to plan, plan in isolation, and fail to secure broad support for their initiatives.

## SCHOOL CLIMATE

The importance of cornerstones for school improvement becomes clearer when they are evaluated in the context of school climate. A school's climate is often compared to an individual's personality. When interacting with a person, we are affected by the way he or she looks, acts, and otherwise treats us. Our feelings toward a school evolve in much the same way. How you think about a school, especially the one in which you are employed, is critically important because there is a nexus between sentiments and behavior (Hoy & Miskel, 2005)—a connection that may not be recognized by employees or by those who seek to change employee behavior. For this reason, school climate is a fundamental issue in restructuring schools so that all students can succeed in them.

### What is Climate?

Organizational climate is a descriptive metaphor that provides a conceptual framework for understanding a school's distinguishing characteristics (Miskel & Ogawa, 1988) and employee perceptions of role expectations, that is, perceptions of what they are expected to do and how they should behave in meeting these responsibilities (Hoy & Miskel, 2005). Though myriad definitions of organizational climate are found in the literature, the one applied here was originally developed by Tagiuri (1968) and adapted to schools by Hanson (2003). It posits that climate has four components:

- *Physical frame.* The physical attributes of a school are part of *ecology* and they include factors such as the campus, classroom, equipment, and furniture.
- *Social frame.* The social attributes of a school are part of *milieu* and they include aspects of social behavior (e.g., how employees treat each other, students, and visitors).
- *Structural frame.* The structural attributes of a school are part of *system organization* and they include factors such as lines of authority, an annual calendar, a daily schedule, sub-system design (e.g., grade levels or departments), and curriculum.
- *Symbolic frame.* The symbolic attributes of a school are part of *culture* and they include factors such as shared values, beliefs, and norms.

School climates are often measured in two important ways: disposition toward interactions and effects on student learning. With respect to the former, climates fall on a continuum ranging from "closed" to "open" (see Figure 3.2). The quality of openness has been applied to two associations: those occurring inside the school among educators and those occurring between educators and the external environment (e.g., parents, community officials, and pressure groups). Internally, open climates are characterized by "cooperation and respect within the faculty and between the faculty and principal" (Hoy & Miskel, 2005, p. 187); externally, they are characterized by a desire to have continuous information exchanges with the external environment (Hanson, 2003). In an open climate, teachers are encouraged to collaborate (Timperley & Robinson, 1998) and parents and other community members are encouraged to participate (Sheldon & Epstein, 2002). Conversely, in a closed climate, employees attempt to insulate themselves from each other and from community interventions.

# School climate

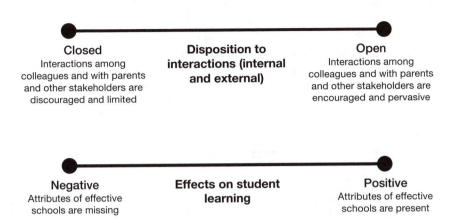

*Figure 3.2* Qualities of School Climate.

With respect to effects on learning, climates fall on a continuum ranging from "negative" to "positive" (see Figure 3.2). A positive climate includes attributes commonly found in highly effective schools (Kowalski, 2003)—conditions identified in the previous chapter such as collegiality, adequate resources, trust, and high expectations. In a negative climate, educators have inadequate resources, function independently, and are guided by counterproductive convictions. For example, they may believe that a certain portion of students can never succeed academically or that instruction should be teacher-centered rather than student-centered.

## Changing Climate

Restructuring a school is an immense challenge for principals and district administrators, especially when the existing climate is closed and negative. Public schools generally have been resistant to change because they historically have been expected to promote social stability rather than social reconstruction (Spring, 2008). Correspondingly, most educators have learned that it is more advantageous to avoid failure than to take risks. For example, though teachers and principals are now often encouraged to experiment with new ideas and methods, the reward systems established by their employers often contradict this expectation (Kowalski et al., 2008). Risk taking and the opposite behavior, failure avoidance, are embedded in a school's climate (Schein, 1996); and, as school improvement entails change and change entails risk, altering climate is an essential part of school reform.

When sufficiently pressured politically or legally to improve schools, schools boards and administrators often have intuitively elected to change that which is easiest to change. For example, improving facilities or implementing block scheduling, though not necessarily effortless tasks, are easier to accomplish than is changing school culture. Though ecological and structural alterations often improve a school's image, their effects on student learning may be negligible if the prevailing culture is unaffected (Fullan, 2001; Hall & Hord, 2006). This is because educators usually revert to shared underlying assumptions about teaching and learning after pressures for change subside (Sarason, 1996).

Table 3.1 provides examples of changes across the four dimensions of climate, and comments regarding implementation difficulty and potential effects on student learning. The intent of this material is to reinforce two widely accepted conclusions. First, the persisting effects of a closed, negative climate almost always outweigh changes in the other dimensions (Sarason, 1996). Simply making stakeholders feel better about a

*Table 3.1* Difficulty Associated with Changing Dimensions of School Climate

| Dimension | Examples of attempted improvement | Comparative difficulty | Potential for school improvement |
| --- | --- | --- | --- |
| Ecology | Renovating or replacing a school building | Typically, change is easiest to accomplish in this dimension, especially if required resources are available or accessible | Though improving ecology is often essential, this change alone may have the least effect on overall school performance. Greatest influence is likely to occur in situations where existing facilities and material resources are very poor |
| Milieu | Having staff engage in staff development in an effort to improve collegiality and cooperation or replacing existing faculty | Typically, change in this dimension is difficult, because it requires behavioral alterations or staff replacements | Collaboration and trust have been found to be critical variables in effective schools. Thus, changing social interaction or personnel, especially in schools where faculty are loosely coupled and non-collegial, can have a positive effect on student learning |
| Organization | Adopting a year-round school calendar or adopting block scheduling | Typically, change in this dimension is moderately difficult, especially if the alterations occur in areas controlled by administrators | Evidence related to the effects of structural changes on student learning is quite mixed. This is especially true with respect to the two examples cited here |
| Culture | Changing teacher beliefs about the ability of all students to succeed academically or altering beliefs about the extent to which teachers can motivate students from low-income families | Typically, change in this dimension is very difficult, in part because identifying shared values and beliefs and diagnosing their effect on learning requires trust, open communication, and time | Respected school reform scholars (e.g., Duke, 2004; Fullan, 2001, 2007; Sarason, 1996) consistently have concluded that culture has the greatest influence on school effectiveness. Moreover, they posit that changes in other aspects of climate may be temporary or otherwise inconsequential if a counterproductive culture remains intact |

school does not ensure that student learning will improve. Second, elements of climate that are easiest to change tend to have the least amount of influence on a school's overall effectiveness (Kowalski, 2003).

## Critical Effects of School Culture

Distinctions between climate and culture in the literature have been neither crisp nor clean and, understandably, students often ask: What is the difference between school climate and school culture? Whereas climate is about feelings and behavior, culture is more focused on values, beliefs, and assumptions underlying feelings and behavior (Martin, 2002). In schools, shared fundamental assumptions guide employees as they make decisions pertaining to problems (Schein, 1996; Trimble, 1996) and to promoting and accepting change (Duke, 2004; Leithwood, Jantzi, & Fernandez, 1994).

Organizational cultures are commonly described in relation to two qualities: *unity of beliefs* and *appropriateness of beliefs*. The former pertains to the extent that school employees share the same beliefs; this quality is described along a continuum from weak to strong. In a weak culture, for example, employees hold dissimilar and possibly competing beliefs (see Figure 3.3). The latter pertains to the extent that held beliefs are congruent with the prevailing knowledge base and best practices; this quality is described along a continuum from destructive to constructive (Kowalski, 2003). In a destructive culture, for example, employees are guided by beliefs contradicted by empirical evidence (see Figure 3.3). Research on effective schools generally indicates that productive schools have strong constructive cultures and that unproductive schools have strong destructive cultures.

Culture is difficult to diagnose accurately because it exists at different levels. The most widely referenced characterization, developed by Schein (1992), portrays it as a three-layer iceberg, with two layers above and one layer below the water line. The invisible layer is much more difficult to understand and assess. Culture's highest and most discernible level contains physical *artifacts*—symbolic representations of a school's values

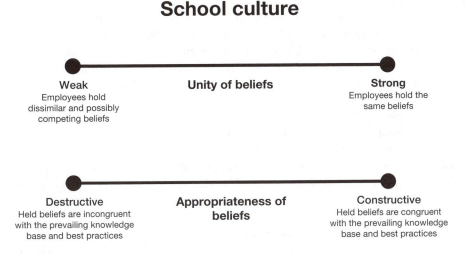

*Figure 3.3* Qualities of School Culture.

and beliefs. Displays located in the main entry, along the hallways, and in classrooms are examples. The prevalence of trophies in these areas implies that athletics and competition are an important aspect of the school's culture. Culture's middle layer contains *espoused beliefs*, convictions that are communicated or intended to be communicated publicly. They typically are found in official documents, such as philosophy statements, school handbooks, policy manuals, and vision statements. Such statements detail what school officials and employees say they believe in relation to important issues such as curriculum, student discipline, and teacher responsibilities. The bottom layer is largely invisible and contains *underlying assumptions*—postulates regarding fundamental issues of practice. Unearthing them is usually complex and time-consuming because educators are reluctant to discuss them or admit that they are influenced by them (Firestone & Louis, 1999).

Hoy and Miskel (2005) also describe school culture as having three layers. Their top layer includes *norms* (e.g., working closely with parents, supporting the principal); the middle layer includes *values* (e.g., collegiality, trust, teamwork); and the bottom layer includes *abstract premises* (e.g., about student learning, about human relationships). In both their and Schein's depictions, elements of culture become increasingly intangible and difficult to diagnose as you move from the top to the bottom layers. Though the upper two levels of culture convey important information, they frequently are misleading. Consider an elementary school in which nearly 15 percent of first-grade students are retained annually. Despite this statistic, the principal and teachers proclaim publicly that "all our students can and will succeed academically." The slogan is found on bulletin boards and appears on the cover of the student handbook. In truth, most faculty members accept an underlying assumption that many students attending the school are predestined to fail because they live in poverty, are being reared in dysfunctional homes, or have limited intellectual capacity.

School culture is sustained and protected through socialization—a process in which shared values and beliefs are passed to each new employee and subsequently get transformed into routine behaviors (Schein, 1992). When you first began teaching, experienced teachers and possibly the principal shared with you "how things really get done in this school." Such conversations were critical to your socialization, especially if the way things got done differed from espoused beliefs communicated to you during official orientation experiences. New teachers quickly learn that they are expected to conform to norms expressed by their peers, even if those norms contradict official district and school positions. Thus, socialization is a process designed to draw new members into the existing culture. Three outcomes are possible:

- *A new employee fails to be socialized*. If this occurs, the employee may resign, he or she may be dismissed, or he or she may survive but be ostracized.
- *The new employee is moderately socialized*. If this occurs, the employee may adopt some of the underlying assumptions and reluctantly abide with others.
- *The new employee is completely socialized*. If this occurs, the employee embraces the culture enthusiastically.

Even when moderately or completely socialized, educators may be reluctant to discuss abstract premises about human nature and schooling. Their unwillingness to do so may stem from awareness that their underlying beliefs are unacceptable or at least controversial professionally or politically. Moreover, persons may suppress such beliefs and values in order to reduce the internal conflict they are experiencing (Schein, 1992). Consider, for instance, a first-grade teacher convinced that a percentage of her students cannot succeed academically. As a result, she complies with prevailing practice in the school and retains several students annually. At the same time, however, she is aware that her action is not supported by a preponderance of the research on student retention. Thus, either she is reluctant to discuss her belief or she has suppressed it and thus is fundamentally unaware of how it is affecting her behavior.

## REFLECTIONS

Why has it become critically important to restructure schools so that all students have improved opportunities for success? How have demands for school reform affected the role conceptualization for principals? What is the principal expected to do in restructuring schools? After reading this chapter, you should have insights that allow you to address these fundamental questions.

In an information-based and reform-minded society, demands for principals to be knowledgeable, transformative, and democratic leaders have steadily increased. This is because traditional approaches, namely centralized mandates, have simultaneously failed to change most low-performing schools and alienated stakeholders, who feel they no longer have a voice in education policy. As a result, policymakers in most states have adopted directed autonomy as a preferred strategy—an approach in which (a) states set broad non-negotiable goals, (b) local officials are given leeway to determine how they will be met, and (c) local officials are held accountable for outcomes (Weiler, 1990). As a result, the expected role for principals has shifted from reform implementer (a managerial responsibility) to reform designer (a leadership responsibility).

Research on effective schools demonstrates that four documents—mission statement, philosophy statement, shared vision, and effective plan—are pivotal to creating schools in which all students can succeed. These school-improvement cornerstones are especially vital in relation to altering counterproductive school climates. Intensification mandates, the prevalent reform strategy during the 1980s, failed because they ignored the fact that climate, and especially school culture, influenced teaching and learning. When governmental agencies enacted mandates, educators who disagreed with them masked their feelings and spitefully obeyed, especially if non-compliance resulted in legal penalties. But once the pressure to enact the mandates subsided, they reverted to the tried and true approaches because these behaviors were nested in cultural assumptions (Fullan, 1999).

As an aspiring principal, you need to understand evolving conditions that require administrators to be effective and democratic leaders. Equally important, you need to comprehend why it is essential to restructure the climate of unproductive schools and why the four cornerstones described in this chapter are integral to that goal.

## Knowledge-Based Questions

1   Various studies demonstrate that approximately one-third of all students in America during the past century failed to succeed academically (i.e., they either did not graduate from high school or did so without requisite skills). Given this history, why should we now be concerned that this failure rate persists?

2   What are the fundamental differences between a centralized approach to school reform and a directed autonomy approach to school reform?

3   Are mission, philosophy, vision, and planning interrelated? If so, in what ways?

4   Why is it advantageous to use a communicative approach to developing the four cornerstones identified in this chapter?

5   Why is school climate a critical factor in school improvement?

6   Which element of climate is easiest to change? Which is the most difficult to change?

7   What factors have made educators skeptical about principals being change leaders?

## Skill-Based Activities

1   In the vignette at the beginning of the chapter, some board members consider Mr. Gomez to be an idealist. Applying the content in this chapter, evaluate the decision to employ him as principal of Lincoln High School.

2   Assume you have been employed as a principal for a middle school enrolling 350 students. The school has never had a vision statement. The superintendent recommended and the board approved your employment on the premise that you were a "visionary leader." Detail how you would proceed to develop a vision for the school.

3   Evaluate the difficulty of developing a vision statement and school plan for achieving the vision based on two criteria: risk and uncertainty.

4   Assume you are the new principal of either a 700-student high school or a 400-student elementary school. In the context of the role you selected, detail the following:

   •   the difficulty you would encounter in diagnosing the existing school culture;
   •   the factors that would determine your evaluation of the existing culture;
   •   the difficulty you encounter in changing the school culture if that were necessary.

# PART II

# Leadership Expectations

## CHAPTER 4

# Principal Behavior and Instructional Leadership

*Walnut Grove Elementary School is located adjacent to a subdivision in a large suburban community. Three years ago, Denise Brown was promoted to become the school's principal after having served as the assistant principal for 6 years. Her predecessor and mentor, Peter Eton, had been principal for 12 years. After she replaced him, she did her best to emulate his administrative behavior.*

*Despite experiencing two teacher strikes during his tenure, Principal Eton maintained political support from nearly all of the school's forty-seven employees. In fact, his relationships with the school's employees were more resilient than his relationships with the district's other administrators. He often told teachers privately, "I'm really on your side but I have to be careful how I express my support." Teachers in particular appreciated that Principal Eton never expected them to do extra work unless they were rewarded. As examples, teachers who volunteered for special duties (e.g., helping organize special events) were given preferential treatment in securing travel funds. Before retiring, he gave his protégé, Mrs. Brown, the following advice. "Treat staff members fairly, especially when you ask them to do extra work. They are just like us. They'll do extra work if they receive something in return."*

*Shortly after Mrs. Brown became principal, the school district incurred a significant decline in state funding. Subsequent budget cuts imposed by the superintendent affected nearly every aspect of Walnut Grove Elementary School. For example, funds for travel, supplies, and equipment were reduced by 35–50 percent. At the same time, however, schools in the district were being pressured to elevate their effectiveness. Denise no longer had the level of resources she could use to reward staff members. Teachers, already angered by the budget cuts, candidly informed Principal Brown that they would not serve on committees or help with special projects unless they received some form of acceptable compensation.*

*Without the adequate resources enjoyed by her predecessor, Mrs. Brown was in a difficult position. She attempted to reason with staff members, explaining why their assistance was essential and why she could no longer reward them for assuming extra assignments. The fact that she was asking employees to do additional work without compensation angered several of the more militant teachers who began criticizing her openly. Mrs. Brown felt that she was being treated unfairly not only by the teachers but also by the superintendent, who expected her to do more with less.*

## INTRODUCTION

Principals exhibit recurring patterns of behavior that reveal their "style" as an administrator. The extent to which a leader's style is deemed acceptable depends on role expectations—that is, the behaviors persons expect from a principal. Conflict emerges when administrators are confronted with multiple and possibly incompatible expectations. Principal Brown, for example, faces such a dilemma. On the one hand, staff members demand that she emulate her predecessor. On the other hand, the superintendent expects her to motivate the staff to pursue needed changes even though resources available to the school have been reduced substantially.

At least since the 1960s, the literature on school administration reveals that principals have been expected to be instructional leaders. This role basically has entailed identifying problems that limit academic achievement, initiating changes to eradicate or minimize these problems, and directing teachers to implement the changes. Though the demand for instructional leadership continues, the conceptualization of this role has been modified substantially over the past two decades (Marks & Printy, 2003, 2006) and consequences for poor principal performance are more punitive than in the past (Sunderman, Kim, & Orfield, 2006).

The first purpose in this chapter is examining principal behavior in relation to formal role expectations, personal dynamics, and work environment. The second purpose is to discuss contemporary perspectives of instructional leadership and to demonstrate how behavior determinants influence principal performance in this critical function. After reading this chapter, you should be able to demonstrate the ability to do the following correctly:

- Explain why principal behavior affects school performance
- Identify the primary determinants of principal behavior
- Differentiate between the traditional conceptualization of principal as instructional leader and the principal's role in shared instructional leadership
- Differentiate between administrative strategies and administrative style
- Differentiate between autocratic, democratic, and delegative leadership styles
- Differentiate between transactional and transformational leadership styles
- Differentiate between ineffective and effective assumptions and behaviors related to instructional leadership
- Identify basic characteristics of principals who are effective instructional leaders

# PRINCIPAL BEHAVIOR

Common principal roles and responsibilities, discussed previously in chapter 2, demonstrate the complexity of this administrative position. The ways in which principals respond to this complexity, however, are dissimilar. As examples, some principals are dictatorial whereas others are highly collaborative; some treat employees as subordinates whereas others threat them as peer professionals; some spend a great deal of time working directly with teachers to improve instruction whereas others immerse themselves in other duties. Given this disparate behavior, you should understand the determinants of school administrator behavior and implications of behavior on teaching effectiveness and student learning.

## Why Principal Behavior Matters

Among factors known to influence school improvement, the performance of a principal has long been touted as a critical variable (e.g., Harris & Willower, 1998; Leithwood & Montgomery, 1982). Today, however, there is mounting evidence validating the association between principal leadership and student achievement. Marzano, Waters, and McNulty (2005), for example, found a moderate but significant relationship between these variables. They concluded that administrative actions related to academics influence policy, teacher behavior, and possibly student behavior. They posit that even minor levels of principal influence can make a critical difference in school effectiveness.

If principal behavior matters, you need to understand behavioral determinants and to distinguish between productive and counterproductive behavior. If asked, you could probably develop a long list of reasons why schools need principals. All or most of them are likely to have a common thread—the expectation that *principals need to lead and manage in ways that ensure institutional effectiveness.* To meet this benchmark, principals must not only behave in ways that elevate student achievement; they must influence others to do likewise. Explaining how principals are able to do these things is more difficult than explaining that they are necessary.

## Determinants of Principal Behavior

For well over a century, scholars have sought to explain why administrators occupying the same role in similar social systems exhibit divergent behavior. Scholars in most disciplines have relied on a general formula provided by Getzels and Guba (1957) decades ago to explain this condition. The formula identifies behavior as a function of the intersection of organizational role (a sociological dynamic) and personality (a psychological dynamic). As an example, role expectations for elementary school principals employed in the same district are almost certainly identical. Accurate observations of their practice, however, reveal less than uniform behavior. Why? Principals bring unique personal characteristics to schools and the extent to which they integrate these characteristics with formal role expectations varies. More recently, scholars also have recognized that work contexts affect behavior. For example, each elementary school in the district has its own climate and the extent to which elements of climate affect principal behavior is inconstant. Thus, three categories of behavior determinants are addressed here as illustrated in Figure 4.1.

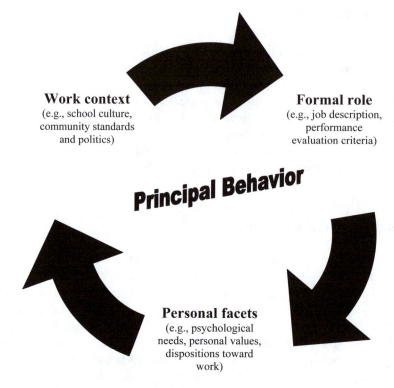

*Figure 4.1*  Forces Influencing Principal Behavior.

## Formal Role Expectations

Formal role expectations are conveyed to principals by the school board through the superintendent (or designee). They are typically detailed in official documents, such as job descriptions and policy statements, and reinforced through formal procedures, such as annual performance evaluations and compensation programs. Principal role expectations were addressed previously in chapter 2.

## Personal Dynamics

A principal enters the position with personal characteristics, such as psychological needs, philosophical dispositions, and relevant knowledge. As noted, these qualities often do not comply completely with formal role expectations, resulting in both personal and institutional tensions (Getzels & Guba, 1957). As an example, a school board and superintendent may direct a novice principal to supervise teachers closely and to deal with unsatisfactory performance swiftly and sternly; however, the principal has a need to be accepted and liked by school employees and thus he is reluctant to comply.

A principal also may struggle with formal role expectations because he or she lacks the knowledge and skills essential to comply with them. Today, for example, principals and teachers are supposed to consider data and other evidence when making critical decisions affecting schools and individual students. Many educators, however, lack the knowledge and skills to do this (Kowalski, 2009). Skills required for administrators are commonly divided into three categories construed by Katz (1974):

- *Technical skills.* These pertain to the proficiency to complete an activity successfully, particularly an activity that has prescribed methods, processes, procedures, or techniques. An example is a principal possessing skills required to apply computer software to create a school master schedule.
- *Human skills.* These pertain to the ability to work well with others, especially in terms of understanding behavior, engaging in collaboration, and motivating others. An example is a principal possessing the human skills necessary to adjudicate conflict between two faculty factions.
- *Conceptual skills.* These pertain to abstract abilities, such as understanding a school as a social and political system or schools as open systems. An example is a principal possessing the conceptual skills to engage in visioning and planning.

The extent to which a principal possesses requisite knowledge and skills is often apparent in overt behavior. Those with limited expertise may be defensive and indecisive when confronted with difficult decisions.

Principal behavior also is affected by personal dispositions toward work, such as the extent to which goal attainment and relationship building are emphasized. Research conducted during the 1950s at Ohio State University (Halpin, 1966), for instance, sought to determine behavioral differences based on such general dispositions. Findings revealed that effective administrators ranked high in both dimensions whereas ineffective administrators ranked low in both dimensions.[4] Other studies have focused on the effects of administrator dispositions. As examples, high initiating structure leaders have been found to achieve greater group productivity than high consideration leaders (e.g., Schriesheim, House & Kerr, 1976), but they were more likely to generate grievances and their turnover rates were higher (e.g., Fleishman & Harris, 1962). Conversely, high consideration leaders have been found to have more satisfied subordinates (e.g., Fleishman & Harris, 1962) but their influence on organizational effectiveness was inconclusive (e.g., House & Baetz, 1979). Overall, research has not established the superiority of either orientation, in part because definitions of success and conditions in organizations are inconstant. However, principals who rank high in both consideration and initiating structure appear to be best suited to engage in collegiality, democratic decision making, and other productive aspects of school improvement.

Beliefs, values, and assumptions are other aspects of personal dynamics that influence administrative behavior. Principals, for example, have dissimilar beliefs about worker and student motivation; some believe most people are lazy and must be closely supervised whereas others believe that most people are industrious and will be highly productive if given autonomy. The need for schools to change and the manner in which change should be pursued are other examples of disparate beliefs held by principals.

## Work Environment

Principal behavior also is affected by political and cultural forces both in schools (Hoy & Miskel, 2008) and in the environment surrounding schools (Langer & Boris-Schacter, 2003). As discussed in the previous chapter, school culture consists of shared values, beliefs, and assumptions, especially about the manner in which educators should deal with problems of practice. These cultural components are reinforced by norms—social group standards that guide and control behavior. In some schools, cultural norms are incongruent with formal role expectations. For example, employees may share the assumption that principals should be passive and not intrude into classroom activities whereas the principal's job description specifies active and continuous involvement in instructional programs.

Community politics and culture impinge on principal behavior because principals spend time working with parents and other community leaders (Jackson & Peterson, 2004) and community stakeholders are able to exert political influence over administrators (Levin, 1999). Consider the following two examples demonstrating how external forces can influence principal behavior"

- In a small rural community, a principal was chastised after several parents reported seeing him drinking a beer while having dinner with his family at a local restaurant. In issuing a formal reprimand, the superintendent wrote, "Drinking in public is not acceptable behavior for administrators in this community."
- The relatively new principal of an urban high school, speaking to the local Rotary Club, told the audience that "students with less than a 'C' average should not be allowed to participate in athletics." His comment was reported and criticized the next day by a sports reporter who had heard his speech. The newspaper column spawned more than a dozen letters from angry parents indicating that the school district did not have and should not have such a policy. Directed by the school board, the superintendent issued a formal warning to the principal indicating that in the future he should refrain from offering personal opinions that were incongruent with established policy.

There is a fine line separating a principal's private life and personal freedoms from his or her capacity as a school official—and what is acceptable in one setting may be grounds for dismissal in another. Moreover, various groups in schools and communities commonly expect different behaviors from a principal. In dealing with student discipline, for example, parents may expect her to provide counsel and direction; students may expect her to be understanding and compassionate; and teachers may expect her to enforce policy and rules without exception. Pleasing everyone under this condition is difficult if not impossible.

Despite a myriad of forces potentially influencing principals, persons in this position generally exhibit behavioral consistencies, especially with respect to problem-solving and decision-making behavior (Kowalski, Lasley, & Mahoney, 2008). Research conducted across schools indicates that administrator behavior usually does not change significantly even after job descriptions and performance evaluation are adjusted to support "new approaches, new structures, and new challenges" (Jackson & Peterson, 2004, p. 83).

## ANALYZING PRINCIPAL BEHAVIOR

### Strategy and Style

Consistencies in principal behavior may reflect prevailing administrative strategies and personal styles. A strategy is a broad, long-term, comprehensive, and collective pattern of behavior (Bassett, 1970). In a school district, an administrative strategy typically is determined by the superintendent and in schools it is determined by the principal. The tactics deployed are characteristic of personal philosophical dispositions and shared assumptions embedded in a district or school culture. The two most common strategies applied in education involve the distribution of authority (centralization versus decentralization) and employee relations (competition versus collaboration). Table 4.1 provides details regarding these strategies.

Administrative style, by comparison, involves individual behavior, and in the literature, it typically is called leadership style. Style has been defined as an action disposition, or pattern of behaviors, displayed by an administrator (Immegart, 1988); it describes the way an administrator usually handles work responsibilities, such as human relations, supervision, and power sharing (Bassett, 1970). Style is especially relevant to understanding how a principal provides direction, implements plans, and motivates others.

## Style and Influencing Others

The administrative style of principals is commonly discussed in terms of supervision and approaches to influencing behavior. From a supervisory perspective, the following typology developed by Lewin, Lippitt, and White (1939) describes three distinct styles and it remains prevalent in the literature:

*Table 4.1* Examples of Administrative Strategies Applied by School Districts

| Strategy | Description | Examples of underlying assumptions | Examples of effects |
| --- | --- | --- | --- |
| Centralization | Authority is concentrated: the superintendent (or designees in larger districts) makes all consequential decisions | Principals either cannot or will not make important decisions; the superintendent is more knowledgeable and skillful than principals | Principals feel disempowered; they are relegated to managing the superintendent's decisions |
| Decentralization | Authority is dispersed among district-level administrators and principals | Needs and conditions vary among schools; principals can and will make effective decisions based on the needs and conditions in their schools | Principals are empowered and required to lead; they also are held accountable for outcomes |
| Competition | Principals are encouraged to compete with each other | Principal performance is elevated by competition; high-level performers should be rewarded | Principals are reluctant to share information and resources; district schools compete with each other |
| Collaboration | District administrators and principals function as team | Collaboration produces synergy; system performance is more important than individual performance | Principals are inclined to share information and resources; district schools help each other |

- Autocratic (or authoritarian) style
- Participative (or democratic) style
- Delegative (or laissez faire) style

Autocratic style is nested in the assumption that employees, if allowed to function autonomously, cannot or will not contribute to school effectiveness (Hanson, 2003). Principals embracing this belief restrict teacher decision making, even in core technical areas such as allowing them to determine homework requirements. Principals exhibiting a democratic style are guided by two opposing beliefs: stakeholders, including school employees, have a fundamental right to participate in important decisions; and shared decision making is generally more effective than autocratic decision making—in terms of both decision quality and political acceptance (Kowalski et al., 2008). Delegative principals believe that employees should be given free reign; they intervene only when problems or their supervisors force them to do so. Figure 4.2 illustrates differences among these three leadership styles.

From an influence perspective, principal behavior is commonly described as being either transactional or transformational. Transactional behavior stems from the belief that most persons are self-centered and do things only when they are apt to benefit or suffer if they refuse (Burns, 1978). Sergiovanni (2001) describes transactional behavior as a political quid pro quo: "The wants and needs of followers and the wants and needs of the leader are traded and a bargain is struck" (p. 136). In transactions involving a principal and an employee, each party is usually aware of each other's motives (Leithwood & Duke, 1999). A principal, for example, may convince a teacher to serve on a textbook adoption committee by providing travel funds so she can attend a national reading conference. Coercion also can be used in transactions. For example, a principal may threaten to punish the teacher (e.g., recommend that she be involuntarily transferred to another school) if she refuses to serve on a textbook adoption committee.

Transformational behavior, by comparison, appeals to psychological needs for esteem, autonomy, and self-actualization (Sergiovanni, 2001) and to moral values such as liberty, justice, equality, peace, and humanitarianism (Yukl, 1989). This style is predicated on the belief that, by being inspirational, administrators elevate motivation and morality across the organization (Burns, 1978) and induce employees to transcend their self-interest for the sake of the organization (Bass, 1985). Transformational behavior is also outcome-oriented. Constructing a shared vision, setting goals and priorities, providing support, modeling effective behavior (Leithwood, Jantzi, & Steinbach, 1999), and remaining passionate about the vision (Bennis & Nanus, 1985) are recognized characteristics.

Often, leadership styles are viewed as being mutually exclusive; that is, a principal is thought to be either transactional or transformational. In fact, these are distinct behaviors. Effective leaders use a combination of both styles, but they skillfully determine when each is appropriate (Bass, 1985). In the context of school reform, transformational styles have become more essential. Figure 4.3 provides a comparison of transactional and transformational styles.

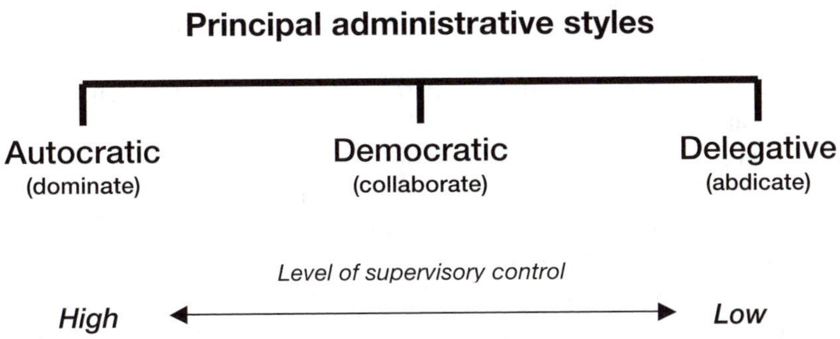

## Principal administrative styles

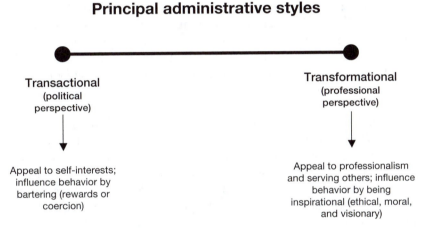

Figure 4.2  Principal Administrative Styles Based on Supervisory Control of Employees.

Figure 4.3  Principal Administrative Styles Based on Influencing Behavior.

## EXERCISING POWER

Power is defined here as the ability to influence individuals and groups. In their seminal work on social systems, French and Raven (1960) identified five types of power observed in social systems:[5]

- *Legitimate power.* This form of power derives from a person's official position. As an example, a principal's legitimate power is granted by the school board through the superintendent. Legitimate power is often referred to as authority. A principal who relies on authority to change a teacher's behavior might say, "As principal, I am directing you to change the way you test your students."
- *Coercive power.* This form of power is based on the assumption that a person responds to punishment or threat. Therefore, a principal must have the capacity to punish others. Coercive power is often applied as a support for legitimate power. A principal who relies on coercion to change a teacher's behavior might say, "As principal, I am

directing you to change the way you test your students; and if you refuse, I will officially issue a reprimand for your disobedience."

- *Reward power.* This form of power is based on the assumption that a principal can provide positive outcomes for others. Reward power, like coercive power, often is applied as a support for legitimate power. A principal who relies on rewards to change a teacher's behavior might say, "As principal, I am recommending that you change the way you test students; and if you comply, I will write a positive letter to support your application for tenure."
- *Expert power.* This form of power is based on a principal possessing special information or expertise that others need or value. The depth of this form of influence depends on the extent to which a principal's expertise is atypical and crucial to the school. A principal who relies on expertise to change a teacher's behavior might say, "Based on my experiences dealing with this problem, I advise you change the way you test students."
- *Referent power.* This form of power results from charisma or fame. In order to exercise it, a principal must possess characteristics admired by others. Those being influenced are prone to seek the principal's approval and to ignore his or her shortcomings. A principal who relies on referent power might try to change a teacher's behavior by saying, "I think you have great potential; and if you alter the way you test students, I think you will be more successful."

To acquire and effectively exercise power, principals need to know the advantages and disadvantages of power alternatives. For instance, position authority is convenient and universally recognized (especially in schools where teachers commonly respect authority), but it tends to decrease in effectiveness when used repeatedly. Coercion and rewards can produce desired results if applied judiciously, but these options almost always alter personal relationships between the principal and employee (either positively or negatively), making their effects in the future less predictable. As exemplified in the vignette at the beginning of the chapter, contextual changes (e.g., a reduction of resources) may restrict a principal's ability to use rewards or coercion. Among the five types of power, referent is the most enduring and broadest; but not all principals possess it and they may be unable to acquire it. Moreover, charismatic leaders may be divisive figures who demand unquestioning obedience.[6]

Effective principals deploy several forms of power, but they do so selectively after analyzing contextual variables. In the realm of school improvement, though, expert power arguably has become most valued. Consider the following conditions supporting this conclusion.

- In two studies of public schools spanning several decades, Sarason (1996) found that low-performing institutions had negative cultures promoting and sustaining ineffective practices. Educators in these schools, however, were incapable of improving the situation independently because they understood neither institutional culture nor its effects on student learning (Sarason, 1996). In such schools, a principal who understands school climate, institutional change, and instructional improvement has become an essential asset.
- Administrators who lack credibility as instructional leaders rarely influence academic improvements. Conversely, teachers usually listen to principals whom they view as

credible sources with respect to curriculum, instruction, and evaluation (Marzano et al., 2005).

- Sustained pressures placed on low-performing schools have made principal expertise a crucial commodity (Hallinger & Heck, 1996).
- Expertise also is symbolically important. By demonstrating that knowledge of social systems, institutional change, curriculum, and instruction matters, principals encourage others to broaden their expertise and rely more heavily on knowledge, skills, and evidence to make important decisions (Kowalski et al., 2008).

## INSTRUCTIONAL LEADERSHIP

The idea that principals must be instructional leaders is not new. Until the 1990s, however, this aspect of school administration was conceptualized in a hierarchical manner; that is, principals were identified as the primary or sole source of expertise. As designated experts, they were supposed to observe teachers, evaluate their effectiveness, and when necessary, direct them to change teaching practices (Marks & Printy, 2003). In his review of supervision textbooks published between 1985 and 1995, Reitzug (1997) found four prevalent images that support this conceptualization: (a) principals were cast as being expert and superior, (b) teachers were cast as being deficient and voiceless, (c) teaching was treated as fixed technology, and (d) supervision was described as a discrete intervention. These images marginalized teacher knowledge and minimized concerns about teachers being isolated from each other. The traditional conceptualization of instructional leadership was attenuated by three prevalent conditions affecting many principals: (a) they did not understand the role, (b) they understood the role but philosophically rejected it, or (c) they understood and accepted the role but lacked the resources essential to fulfill it.

Lessons learned from failed reforms over the past few decades have contributed to more enlightened perspectives of instructional leadership. One of the most prevalent is the concept of shared instructional leadership described by Marks and Printy (2003, 2006). In this conceptualization, principals delegate authority to teachers, especially in core technical areas; they collaborate and facilitate to ensure that the authority is used properly; they involve teachers collectively in problem solving and decision making at the school level.

As in all aspects of administrative behavior, underlying assumptions determine the quantity and quality of principal engagement in instructional leadership. Because administrators do not share common assumptions, the extent to which they involve themselves in curriculum and instruction predictably varies. Table 4.2 includes a comparison of ineffective and effective assumptions relevant to instructional leadership. Table 4.3 includes a comparison of ineffective and effective behaviors.

Despite a discernible shift in conceptualizations of instructional leadership since the early 1990s, and despite recurring calls for schools to function as learning communities, some principals continue to view instructional leadership in the traditional hierarchical perspective. Studying how a group of principals connected their work to school improvement, Reitzug, West, and Angel (2008) found that these school administrators articulated multiple conceptualizations of instructional leadership—another piece of evidence that helps us to explain divergent principal behavior.

*Table 4.2* Comparison of Ineffective and Effective Assumptions Related to Instructional Leadership

| Factor | Ineffective assumptions | Effective assumptions |
|---|---|---|
| School vision | Educators have little or no power to determine the future; therefore, a vision is basically unimportant | Educators can and should shape a school's future, and a shared vision is essential to this task |
| Planning | As most decisions are made outside the school and imposed on educators, planning is basically unimportant | Planning provides essential goals and strategies for pursuing a shared vision |
| Curriculum | Curriculum is imposed by government (state and federal) and implemented by educators | Though curriculum is shaped by government, educators have a responsibility to ensure that it is relevant for all students and local communities |
| Instructional focus | Schools should be teacher-centered (i.e., based on what teachers need and want) | Schools should be student-centered (i.e., based on what students need and want) |
| Instructional supervision | Teachers are subordinates requiring close supervision and constant direction | Teachers are peer professionals who should have autonomy in core technical areas and be involved in major decisions |
| Motivating employees | Most persons are selfish; therefore, they must be bribed or coerced to do things they would not do independently | Most persons seek to serve others and to be successful; if given opportunities, they will be creative and productive |
| Evaluation | Only summative evaluation (i.e., determining if a program or employee performance is adequate) is essential | Both summative and formative evaluation (i.e., seeking to improve programs and employee performance) are essential |
| School culture | Culture is imposed by external forces; thus, it is beyond the control of administrators and teachers | Culture is the most critical variable in school improvement; educators must replace or modify negative cultures |
| Low student performance | Student failure stems solely from social (e.g., poverty) or personal (e.g., laziness) problems; thus, some students fail regardless of the experiences they are offered | Though many low-performing students are hindered by social and personal problems, the experiences they are offered in school make a critical difference in academic success |
| Low school performance | Social and political forces cause schools to underperform and educators cannot ameliorate these problem | Though social and political forces affect school performance, educators have the power to improve school performance |
| Parental involvement | Parents of low-performing students are incapable or unwilling to become involved in education; forced participation only generates conflict | Parental involvement is a critical factor in student performance; educators have a responsibility to seek the active involvement of all parents |

*Table 4.3* Comparison of Ineffective and Effective Instructional Leadership Behavior

| Factor | Ineffective behavior | Effective behavior |
| --- | --- | --- |
| School vision | A vision is not developed or it is developed unilaterally and imposed on others | A vision is established collaboratively and then pursued passionately |
| Planning | Planning is not conducted or it is conducted in an exclusive (alone or with a few others) and perfunctory manner | Planning is conducted inclusively (with myriad stakeholders) and the results evaluated and revised periodically |
| Curriculum | Curriculum is managed but rarely developed, coordinated, or evaluated | Curriculum is coordinated and evaluated periodically to determine effectiveness and modifications are based on evaluation outcomes |
| Instructional focus | Principal evaluation and interventions focus largely on teacher behavior | Principal evaluation and interventions focus on both teacher and student behavior |
| Instruction supervision | Interventions are sporadic and intended to improve the performance of the most ineffective teachers | Interventions are pervasive and intended to improve the performance of all teachers |
| Motivating employees | Transactional approaches are used | Transformational approaches are used |
| Evaluation | Summative evaluations of programs and employee performance are conducted only as required by policy | Summative and formative evaluations of programs and employee performance are conducted as needed to produce evidence relevant to school improvement |
| School culture | Culture is ignored or the principal conforms to and protects a negative culture | Culture is diagnosed and evaluated with respect to school effectiveness; negative values, beliefs, and assumptions are replaced or modified |
| Low student performance | Student failure is blamed on external variables (social, political, and economic issues) or students themselves; thus, little or no effort is made to restructure curriculum and instruction | Student failure is recognized and efforts are made to restructure curriculum and instructional approaches |
| Low school performance | School ineffectiveness is blamed on external variables (social, political, and economic issues) and students; thus, little or no effort is made to restructure school climate | School ineffectiveness is recognized and efforts are made to restructure school climate |
| Parental involvement | Parental involvement is either discouraged or reluctantly tolerated | Parental involvement is encouraged |

## REFLECTIONS

Myriad factors influencing principal behavior were discussed here in three categories: those pertaining to formal role expectations; those pertaining to personal dynamics; and those pertaining to work environments. Variability in principal behavior has become a highly relevant issue in relation to school performance, because there is growing evidence of a nexus between principal interventions and student learning. After reading this chapter, you should reflect on principals you know. Consider their behavior and think about variables and assumptions that may have influenced them.

Relying on what is known about administrative behavior generally and effective instructional leadership specifically, an image of the principal as a competent instructional leader emerges. For example, they tend to be democratic, collaborative, supportive of change, and inspirational. Though they use a mix of transformational and transactional styles, they are primarily transformational leaders—especially in relation to seeking school improvement. As you look forward in your career, consider how your beliefs, values, and assumptions will affect your behavior as a principal generally and instructional leader specifically.

## Knowledge-Based Questions

1   What personal dynamics affect a principal's behavior?
2   What work environment factors affect a principal's behavior?
3   What occurs when formal role expectations are incompatible with personal dispositions or work environment factors?
4   What is the difference between administrative strategy and administrative style?
5   How was instructional leadership conceptualized prior to the 1990s?
6   What is the fundamental difference between transactional and transformational leader behavior?

## Skill-Based Activities

1 Assume that you are one of three middle school principals employed in the same district. Though you have identical job descriptions, the superintendent recognizes that each of you has a different leadership style. Identify possible reasons for this condition and take a position as to whether the differences constitute a problem that the superintendent and principals should address.

2 As a principal, you are trying to help a teacher who has difficulty controlling disruptive pupils in her class. Using the forms of power discussed in this chapter, select the one you would use to influence her and defend your choice.

3 Explain the effects of assumptions on principal behavior, especially in relation to functioning as an instructional leader.

4 Describe what you consider to be the ideal role of the principal as instructional leader.

5 Identify principal behaviors that have a negative effect on teaching, student learning, and overall school effectiveness.

## CHAPTER 5

# Organizing and Evaluating Instructional Programs

"Only organizations that have a passion for learning will have an enduring influence."

Steven Covey (Covey, Merrill, & Merrill, 1996, p. 149)

*Grant High School, located in a suburb of a major city in the southeast, serves approximately 1,100 students enrolled in four grade levels. Last year, just over 70 percent of the graduates enrolled in a college or university. Donald West, the principal, is a veteran administrator, having served as the principal in two smaller high schools prior to his current position. After he arrived at Grant 2 years ago, his first major initiative was to promote block scheduling.*

*Initially, some faculty members were dubious about moving from a traditional seven-period school day; but Mr. West was persuasive and, after a few months, all but three of the school's fifty-seven teachers voted to adopt a block schedule the following school year. The superintendent and school board supported the change, though they devoted little time to examining the issue.*

*The decision to adopt a block schedule at the high school was reported in the media and, 5 months prior to actual change, Principal West sent a letter to parents informing them of the change and explaining the benefits of the new scheduling paradigm. Only a few parents and students voiced concerns about the change or asked questions pertaining to it.*

*To ensure a smooth transition, the principal and counselors began building the master schedule for the following school year in May. At that point, students realized that they would be unable to enroll in all the courses they intended to take. Those seeking admission to highly selective colleges were the most concerned; they feared that not taking certain one-semester elective courses would be detrimental to their applications. By mid-May, data revealed that enrollment in elective courses, especially in art, music, and physical education, would drop considerably. Noting the changes, Principal West informed several teachers that they almost certainly would have to teach classes that they had not taught previously.*

*By June 1, opposition to block scheduling had become organized and was being led by Catherine Myer, a parent and professor at the local college. Opponents began paying for advertisements in the local media urging the superintendent and school board to rescind approval of block scheduling at the high school. Professor Myer and several other parents appeared at the July school board meeting in an attempt to convince the board to support their position. She listed several objections to block scheduling and summarized by saying that there was little or no empirical evidence supporting the principal's belief that block scheduling would have a positive effect on student achievement.*

*Initially, all seven school board members had voted to approve block scheduling, but after listening to opponents, two publicly stated that they would vote differently if given another opportunity. The remaining board members indicated they were standing firm—at least until there was evidence showing that block scheduling was not a more effective structure.*

*The mounting conflict over block scheduling strained the relationship between the superintendent and Mr. West. The superintendent, who had limited knowledge of block scheduling, relied on the principal's leadership. He had recommended approval of the concept based on confidence he had in Mr. West. But, in the aftermath of Professor Myers's criticisms, he was not sure he had been given proper counsel. Though Grant High School proceeded with block scheduling, the superintendent, with the support of the entire school board, announced publicly that the effects of block scheduling would be evaluated by an external consultant over the next 2 years. He added that, if student achievement did not improve, the school would return to its traditional seven-period schedule. Privately, the superintendent made it clear to Principal West that he was not pleased with how this issue had evolved.*

## INTRODUCTION

Principals, independently or collaborating with other school employees, determine how instructional programs are organized and delivered. Decisions in these areas clearly affect employees and students, but they also may have ramifications for parents, the school district, and possibly non-parent stakeholders. If affected groups disagree with an instructional programming decision, conflict typically ensues and almost certainly the following questions are asked: Who benefits from the decision? Who influenced the decision? Were all stakeholders given an opportunity to influence the decision?

This chapter addresses issues pertaining to organizing instructional programs. Content is reflective of four primary objectives:

- Describing why the organization of instructional delivery is important
- Identifying possible choices and procedures for organizing the school day
- Considering options for organizing the school year
- Applying the concept of the learning organization to schools

After reading this chapter, you should be able to demonstrate the ability to do the following correctly:

- Explain why organizational decisions for instructional delivery are important
- Identify options for organizing subsystems in elementary and secondary schools
- Identify options for daily school schedules

- Identify options for annual school calendars
- Explain the nature of a learning organization

## SCHOOLS AS SOCIAL SYSTEMS

An organization's climate is in essence its personality (Sargeant, 1967); it is an attribute that shapes a person's feelings about a school. Structure, or organization, is one of the four elements of climate and, as such, it partially determines how teachers and students feel about the school—and how they feel often affects how they perform. Therefore, restructuring can alter a school's climate; and ultimately it can influence student academic performance (Kowalski, Petersen, & Fusarelli, 2007).

Schools are complex social systems and, as such, they should be analyzed in relation to three qualities:

- *Boundaries.* Border lines among and within social systems are arbitrary but consequential. How a principal groups teachers and students, for example, is not inconsequential.
- *Subsystems.* Every social system is composed of interrelated subsystems. For example, in elementary schools what occurs at one grade level or in secondary schools what occurs in one academic department has some consequences for other grade levels and departments. Thus, subsystems operating autonomously often generate unintended consequences for other subsystems or possibly the entire school.
- *Multiple causation.* Problems and outcomes in a social system rarely have a single cause. In schools, for example, it is highly improbable that low student performance on state achievement tests is caused by one variable.

Interdependence among subsystems is usually described as *coupling*, a concept that was applied to schools by Weick (1976). If subunits have complete or substantial autonomy, a school is described as being *loosely coupled*; if subunits have little or no autonomy, the school is described as being *tightly coupled*. Long ago, Bidwell (1965) recognized that instruction in most schools was delivered independently among and within subsystems and even independently from administrators. Later, scholars (Fennell, 1994; Firestone, 1985; Wilson & Corbett, 1983) found that linkages among and within subsystems were important variables determining if planned change initiatives succeeded.

If one form of coupling was proven to be consistently superior, and if coupling were a fixed attribute, a principal would simply be trained to implement loose or tight coupling. In fact, however, linkages in schools are dynamic and effective change often requires a mix of the two conditions. In this vein, the noted scholar Michael Fullan (1991) postulated that centralization of authority, a strategy that favors tight coupling, errs on the side of too much control whereas decentralization, a strategy that favors loose coupling, often errs on the side of chaos. Consequently, principals should understand the importance of subsystem interdependence so that they can work with others to implement an effective mixture of loose and tight linkages best suited for the contextual variables in their work environment (Fennell, 1994; Meyer, 2002).

# ORGANIZING FOR INSTRUCTIONAL DELIVERY

Though education experts posit that philosophy, curriculum, and instructional strategies should determine the organizational pattern of a school, pragmatic considerations, such as funding and available facilities, and tradition often have trumped these considerations. How and why a district separates schools by grade levels and why principals structure the school day the way they do are not matters that capture the attention of many stakeholders—especially those who do not have children enrolled in the schools. Nevertheless, these should be treated as critical administrative decisions because they have the potential of affecting student learning.

## Elementary Schools

The structure of an elementary school is analyzed with respect to vertical and horizontal planning. Vertical planning (i.e., what occurs from grade level to grade level) has been premised on students progressing from one grade level to another until the school's entire program of study has been completed. This organizational approach is rooted in the assumption that students of the same chronological age benefit adequately from receiving a uniform instruction concurrently—a premise that has been frequently challenged. The dominant horizontal plan (i.e., what occurs at a given grade level) has been the self-contained classroom—that is, one teacher providing instruction in all basic subjects. This configuration is premised on two perceived advantages. First, students are presumed to adapt more readily to school if they are placed with a single teacher and a relatively small group of students for all or most of the school day. Second, the self-contained classroom configuration is efficient, orderly, easy to administer, and understood by parents. Many elementary schools have modified their horizontal plan by providing partial departmentalization in the upper grades; for example, two fifth-grade teachers may team together in that one teaches science and mathematics for both sections and the other teaches language arts and reading for both sections.

Over the last half century, traditional horizontal planning in elementary schools has been augmented by the following concepts:

- *The deployment of art, music, and physical education teachers.* This option provides students with exposure to instructors who have concentrated preparation in their specializations and it provides teachers in self-contained classrooms with preparation time during the school day.
- *Resource rooms.* These rooms provide students opportunities for individualized or small group instruction outside the self-contained classroom for a portion of the school day. Their development resulted primarily from legal requirements for serving special needs students (i.e., those with individualized education programs [IEPs] requiring inclusion). Today, resource rooms also may provide work areas for teacher aides who focus on supplemental instruction as prescribed by teachers operating self-contained classrooms.

Several other concepts have been applied less widely in an effort to improve vertical and horizontal planning. The following are notable ideas that have had varying degrees of success:

- *Non-graded schools.* During the 1960s and 1970s, some elementary schools experimented with non-graded plans in response to persistent concerns about graded vertical planning. The concept calls for students to be grouped based on ability levels rather than chronological age, and it focuses on a student's continuous progress rather than grade-level promotions (Goodlad & Anderson, 1987). Most experiments with non-graded elementary schools, however, suffered from inadequate planning and insufficient support from teachers and parents (Gaustad, 1992). Compared with teaching in a traditional vertical plan, teaching multiage groups requires more teacher preparation.
- *Looping.* The practice of looping is used to fortify the traditional vertical plan found in elementary schools and has been used predominately in Grades 1–4. A teacher remains with the same group of students assigned to a self-contained classroom for 2 or more years. Perceived advantages of looping include extending instruction time as a result of teachers not having to become familiar with a new group of students at the beginning of each school year and building stronger ties between teachers and parents (Denault, 1999). Also, the teachers develop a deeper understanding of student strengths and weaknesses (Hume, 2007). Looping has often been promoted as an especially effective practice for low-performing students (Bracey, 1999).
- *Parallel block scheduling.* The application of block scheduling in elementary and secondary schools is dissimilar. In the former, parallel block scheduling involves teacher teams. As an example, consider a third-grade team consisting of three base teachers and an enrichment lab teacher. During a time block on Monday, base teacher A works with her whole class; base teacher B sends the higher-achieving half of her class to the enrichment lab and works with the remaining students; and base teacher C sends the lower-achieving half of her class to the enrichment lab. On subsequent days, the assignments for base teachers rotate (Delaney, Toburen, Hooton, & Dozier, 1998). The concept is thought to have two specific advantages: allowing teachers to collaborate and providing increased opportunities for smaller group instruction (Canady, 1990). Cost related to employing an enrichment lab teacher is a primary concern.

## Secondary Schools

As defined here, secondary schools include middle schools, junior high schools, combined junior–senior high schools, and high schools. Schools in the middle are intended to provide a transition experience for students between the self-contained environment of elementary schools and the totally departmental organization in high schools. During the first half of the last century, junior high schools were common, but criticisms of them mounted in the 1950s and 1960s. As examples, traditional junior high schools, including Grades 7, 8, and 9, often did not provide transition experiences as intended and many teachers in these schools taught as if they were employed in high schools.

Circa 1970, the middle school concept had become popular. Middle schools usually serve no grade lower than 5 and no grade higher than 8; the most prevalent grade configuration is Grades 6, 7, and 8. Philosophically, they were supposed to provide a more meaningful transition experience than junior high schools. But some districts created middle schools in name only; that is, underlying principles such as integrating subject matter, exploration, socialization, and articulation were ignored (Alexander & Kealy, 1969).

Compared with high schools, middle school curricula provide limited opportunities for elective courses (which are called exploratory courses at this level). They usually offer interdisciplinary courses combining two or more subject areas; for example, social studies is combined with language arts and mathematics is combined with science. Interdisciplinary courses allow instruction to be based on relevant issues or problems rather than on subject matter.

Today, three organizational patterns are found in middle schools:

- *Traditional departmental structure.* In this configuration, teachers are assigned to academic departments and courses are offered through departments.
- *Interdisciplinary team structure.* An interdisciplinary team usually consists of two to five teachers and the students they teach. According to Thompson and Homestead (2004), this structure is intended to deepen teacher understanding of their students, permit team members to engage in collaborative planning, foster collegiality among team teachers, and establish a community of learners. Fundamentally, teaming is an effort to organize a school into smaller and collaborative instructional groups. In his study of instructional teams, Supovitz (2002) found three conditions to be empirically related to student performance: collaborative preparation for instruction, occasionally teaching together so that team members could observe each other, and purposefully regrouping students to take advantage of team member strengths.
- *Hybrid structure.* This configuration includes limited use of self-contained classrooms (typically at the entry grade level) with either a departmentalized structure or interdisciplinary team structure at the remaining grade levels. This option is not widely used and is most likely found in middle schools that include Grade 5.

From an academic perspective, high schools are viewed as barometers of student success. As examples, statistics such as dropout rates, Scholastic Aptitude Test scores, the percentage of students entering college, and the percentage of students passing state graduation tests are used by the public to judge a school system's academic effectiveness.

The modal grade configuration for high schools is 9–12. Combined junior–senior high schools, usually containing Grades 7 through 12, are relatively common in small-enrollment districts. Junior–senior high schools almost always are organized with a departmental structure.

Experimentation also occurred in high schools during the 1960s and 1970s. Concepts such as team teaching, mini courses, and open-concept schools emerged and then retreated after academic excellence resurfaced as a dominant value (Kowalski, 2003). Beginning in the early 1980s, considerable pressure was exerted on high schools to become more academically focused (Perrone, 1985). As examples, states increased graduation requirements and many now require students to pass a graduation proficiency test. Emphasis on performance in basic academic subjects has affected the balance between required and elective courses in many high schools. Today, most students have fewer opportunities to enroll in elective courses; and, as a result, enrollments in subjects such as art, music, and industrial education fell dramatically in the early 1980s (Roberts & Cawelti, 1984). The persistence of the subject-oriented curriculum stems primarily from two factors: tradition and ease of measurement. With respect to the former, the traditional high school schedule was adopted throughout the twentieth century without evidence of effectiveness simply because it had become the norm (Fullan, 1990). With respect to the latter, the use of the Carnegie unit[7] as the criterion for high school graduation provided a measurement standard congruent with traditional scheduling that could be applied across states (Kowalski, 2006).

An attendance day in a secondary school is organized around instructional periods. Middle schools may have shorter but more instructional periods compared with high schools. Figure 5.1 is an illustration of a traditional daily schedule for a high school with 450 pupils based on seven instructional periods, each lasting 50 minutes. Note that there is a homeroom period and 5-minute passing times, and students are scheduled for lunch in either the first or second half of period 5. In the other half of period 5, students could be scheduled into study halls or allowed to engage in planned activities. Developing a master schedule for larger secondary schools used to be a time-consuming and complex task for principals; however, virtually all schools now use computerized scheduling software.

Since 1970, many schools adopted or experimented with *block scheduling*. In simple terms, block scheduling is an organizational approach in which students take fewer courses in a semester but have longer class periods. For example, a course in American history could be completed in one semester with 95-minute classes instead of in two semesters with 50-minute classes. The assumption is that teaching and learning improve as a result of longer but fewer class periods in a day and in a semester. The following are examples of other advantages attributed to block scheduling:

- Longer periods allow teachers to engage students in more active and in-depth classroom instructional activities (Gullatt, 2006)
- Teachers have to spend less time with administrative activities (e.g., taking attendance)
- Teachers benefit from having more preparation time (Queen & Isenhour, 1998)
- Teachers have a greater opportunity to build relationships with students (Canady & Rettig, 1995)
- School safety improves and student discipline problems decline (Queen, Algozzine, & Eaddy, 1997)

Conversely, a number of disadvantages have been identified with block scheduling. The following are several recurring concerns:

- Problems emerge with student transfers; students entering a school with block scheduling from a school with a traditional schedule (and vice versa) face additional adjustment problems (Shortt & Thayer, 1995)
- Teachers fail to take advantage of longer class periods and continue to plan and teach much as they did in 50- or 55-minute periods (Skrobarcek, Chang, & Thompson, 1997; Zepeda & Mayers, 2006)
- Most textbooks were designed for traditional class periods (Canady & Rettig, 1995)

| Period | Start time | End time | Lunch |
|--------|-----------|----------|-------|
| Homeroom | 8:00 am | 8:15 am | |
| 1 | 8:20 am | 9:10 am | |
| 2 | 9:15 am | 10:05 am | |
| 3 | 10:20 am | 11:10 am | |
| 4 | 11:15 am | 12:05 am | |
| 5 Lunch | 12:15 pm | 1:05 pm | Group A (12:15 to 12:40 pm) Group B (12:40 to 1:05 pm) |
| 6 | 1:10 pm | 2:00 pm | |
| 7 | 2:05 pm | 2:55 pm | |

*Figure 5.1* Example of Traditional 50-Minute Period Schedule for a 450-Student High School.

Interestingly, several issues are viewed concurrently as assets and liabilities. Two notable examples are student absenteeism and allocation of time. When students miss a day of school, they need to do makeup work for fewer courses—but concurrently they have more to make up in the courses they missed. And, though students actually have fewer total minutes of instruction in a block schedule,[8] teachers spend less time on administrative functions such as taking attendance (Hackman, 1995).

Arguably, the critical issue is whether block scheduling improves student academic achievement. Research on this subject has been inconclusive, at least as measured by standardized tests. Some studies (e.g., Gruber & Onwuegbuzie, 2001; Kramer & Keller, 2008; Schroth & Dixon, 1996) have found that block scheduling has had a slight positive effect whereas other studies have reported either no effect (e.g., York, 1997) or a slight negative effect (e.g., Arnold, 2002). Differences in outcomes about the effects of block scheduling on student academic achievement are partially explained by variances in research purposes, practices, and foci. For example, studies that examined progress of students after they transitioned from traditional to block scheduling tend to produce more positive results—especially if the variables examined are course grades or teacher opinions and not achievement test scores. Moreover, some studies focus on achievement across multiple subject areas whereas others focus exclusively on one subject. Results of studies that have compared students in traditional scheduled and block-scheduled schools using achievement test scores as the criterion, however, have been mixed and inconclusive.

Though there are various forms of block scheduling, the most common and easily implemented is the 4 × 4 block based on four 90-minute periods per semester. Figure 5.2 is an illustration of this organizational format. To date, the trend toward adopting block scheduling in middle schools and high schools remains uncertain. Each year, some additional schools are adopting or experimenting with the plan but, at the same time, other schools that have used block scheduling have returned to traditional scheduling.

## ORGANIZING THE SCHOOL YEAR

The traditional school year calendar in most districts is approximately 180 days of instruction, now conducted between late August and early June. Originally the structure

*First Semester*

| Period | | Class | Begin | End |
|---|---|---|---|---|
| 1 | | 1 | 8:15 am | 9:45 am |
| 2 | | 2 | 9:55 am | 11:25 am |
| Lunch | (Group A) | | 11:30 am | 12:00 pm |
| | (Group B) | | 12:05 pm | 12:35 pm |
| 3 | | 3 | 12:45 pm | 1:15 pm |
| 4 | | 4 | 1:25 pm | 2:55 pm |

*Second Semester*

| Period | | Class | Begin | End |
|---|---|---|---|---|
| 1 | | 5 | 8:15 am | 9:45 am |
| 2 | | 6 | 9:55 am | 11:25 am |
| Lunch | (Group A) | | 11:30 am | 12:00 pm |
| | (Group B) | | 12:05 pm | 12:35 pm |
| 3 | | 7 | 12:45 pm | 1:15 pm |
| 4 | | 8 | 1:25 pm | 2:55 pm |

*Figure 5.2* Example of a 4 × 4 Block Schedule in a 450-Student High School.

of the school year was influenced most by an agrarian economy. School usually did not start until mid-September and concluded late May. Incrementally, the number of attendance days has increased; however, the summer vacation remains a staple. Academically, the effects of a protracted summer vacation on learning retention has remained a subject of debate and, fiscally, the fact that expensive school buildings are underutilized during the summer months is bothersome, especially when school officials seek to construct additional facilities. Growing interest in year-round calendars stems not only from these concerns, but also from pragmatic considerations such as inadequate space in existing schools. Two distinct approaches exist for year-round calendars: the single-track option and the multi-track. Both require school during the summer months, but they differ in purpose, attendance patterns, and facility utilization.

## Single-Track Year-Round Calendar

The single-track approach focuses on reducing the perceived negative effect of a 3-month summer vacation (i.e., a reduction of knowledge and skill retention). The most common type of single-track scheduling is the 45-15 plan (see Figure 5.3). Under this schedule, all students attend school for 9 consecutive weeks (45 attendance days) and then have 3 weeks of vacation. The school calendar spans 12 months and is basically divided into 4 blocks, each with 12 weeks. The remaining 4 weeks during the calendar year are used for a 2-week break in late December, a 1-week spring break, and miscellaneous holidays. Students attend 4 blocks of 45 days or 180 school days.

Though the single-track approach to year-round schooling is used more widely than the multi-track approach, it is used predominantly at the elementary school level and

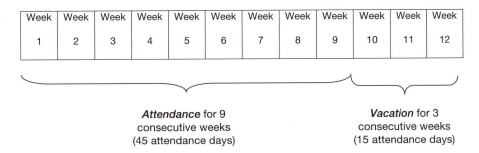

*Figure 5.3* A 12-Week Block in a Single-Track Schedule.

does not expand a school building's functional capacity (Kneese, 1996). All students are in the same track; that is, they all attend at the same time and all are on vacation at the same time. Both the traditional 9-month calendar and the year-round single-track calendar call for 36 weeks of attendance. The difference is that vacations in the latter are dispersed over four periods (or blocks), each lasting 3 weeks.

## Multi-Track Year-Round Calendar

The multi-track option is intended to increase the capacity of a school building by operating the facility for at least 48 weeks—12 more weeks than the traditional calendar. The plan uses 12-week blocks and four tracks (see Figure 5.4). At any given time over the 48 weeks, one-fourth of the students are on vacation. This iteration of a year-round calendar has been used at all levels of schooling, and it is almost always applied for the purpose of extending a school building's functional capacity by approximately 25 percent (Shields & Oberg, 2000). Thus, it usually has been adopted in districts experiencing rapid growth or districts in which taxpayers have been unwilling to fund construction to meet the needs for modest enrollment increases (Shields & LaRocque, 1996).

Experiences with multi-track calendars indicate that the expansion of functional capacity is often less than expected. This is because students on vacation continue to use space in the school; examples include maintaining a student locker and storing projects in laboratories (Kowalski, 2002). Transitioning from a traditional to a multi-track calendar is often complex and unpopular (Harp, 1995). The reasons for parental and student opposition have varied from personal philosophy to more practical concerns—such as being able to find childcare during periodic vacations (Shields & Oberg, 2000). Also, parents with several children enrolled in the district are likely to be opposed if their children have vacations at different times. The following are other concerns with the multi-track year-round calendar:

- Increased maintenance and equipment replacement costs are incurred because of expanded use (Chaika, 2007).
- Seasonal maintenance typically conducted between mid-June and mid-August must be done while school is in session (Kowalski, 2002).
- Administrator stress is more likely, due to the loss of a protracted vacation (Borba, 2000).

| Track | Week 1 | Week 2 | Week 3 | Week 4 | Week 5 | Week 6 | Week 7 | Week 8 | Week 9 | Week 10 | Week 11 | Week 12 |
|-------|--------|--------|--------|--------|--------|--------|--------|--------|--------|---------|---------|---------|
| 1 | A | A | A | A | A | A | A | A | A | V | V | V |
| 2 | A | A | A | A | A | A | V | V | V | A | A | A |
| 3 | A | A | A | V | V | V | A | A | A | A | A | A |
| 4 | V | V | V | A | A | A | A | A | A | A | A | A |

Legend: *A = attendance; V = vacation.*

*Figure 5.4* A 12-Week Block in a Multi-Track Schedule with Four Tracks.

- Increases in operating costs are incurred, due primarily to air conditioning during summer months (Agron, 1993).
- Many school employees, especially teachers, do not wish to work during the summer months (Shields & Oberg, 2000).
- Especially in secondary schools, problems in relation to co-curricular (e.g., band) and extra-curricular (e.g., athletics) activities; either students in the same activities cannot be placed in the same tracks or, if they are, the normal socialization patterns among students are disrupted (Sørensen, 1989).

## Effects of Year-Round Calendars on Academic Achievement

The underlying academic premise for year-round calendars is the prevention of an assumed regression of knowledge and skills during the summer months. This assumption has focused most directly on young children and it explains why the single-track approach has been applied most often in elementary schools. Interestingly, empirical data about summer reversions are not especially conclusive. In a major analysis of this topic, Alexander, Entwisle, and Olson (2001) reported that both upper socioeconomic status (SES) and lower SES students had comparable verbal and quantitative gains during the school year. During the summer months, however, learning gains for upper SES students increased but learning gains for low SES students were flat. This outcome suggests that absence from school during the summer months may widen already existing achievement among high and low SES students.

Overall, though, research on the effects of year-round schooling on student achievement provides limited insight into the academic efficacy of this organizational option. A notable study on this topic was conducted by McMillen (2001) in North Carolina. He found statistically significant interactions indicating that some students may benefit more from a year-round calendar. He cautioned, however that "these effects are probably too small to be educationally significant by most standards" (p. 73). He also advised that research on the student achievement has yet to discern whether any reported gains are due to increased instructional time or the distribution of instructional time.

# TRANSFORMING A SCHOOL INTO A LEARNING COMMUNITY

In his seminal book on the learning organization, *The Fifth Discipline*, Peter Senge (1990) advised that to be highly effective leaders had to replace change-resistant cultures with learning cultures. Unfortunately, terms such as "learning culture" and "learning organization" have often been defined in various ways. In addition, authors have often disagreed in setting qualification criteria for a learning organization. As examples, some believe that behavioral change is essential; others insist that new ways of thinking are sufficient. Some cite information processing as the medium for learning; others propose that it is shared insights. And some think that the process of organizational learning is common whereas others argue that flawed, self-serving interpretations are the norm (Garvin, 1993).

Several decades ago, Lezotte, Edmonds, and Brookover (n.d.) defined effective schools as institutions where all students learn. In their studies of such institutions, they found that the following characteristics recurred across these schools:

- Instructional leadership
- Clear and focused mission
- Safe and orderly environment
- Climate of high expectations
- Frequent monitoring of student progress
- Positive home–school relations
- Opportunity to learn and student time on task

Highly effective schools also provide nurturing environments for students and teachers by reconstructing traditional structure into relatively small subsystems "to increase personalization, relevance and rigor of coursework, and teacher collaboration" (David, 2008, p. 84). The intent is to convert schools into learning organizations, a state Garvin (1993) defined as being "skilled at creating, acquiring, and transferring knowledge, and at modifying its behavior to reflect new knowledge and insights" (p. 79). Properly arranged, schools can develop and capitalize on organizational competence—a quality that "is the sum of everything everybody knows and uses that leads to increased learning" (Sergiovanni, 2004, p. 48).

## Collaborative Cultures

To reiterate, a school's culture is grounded in shared assumptions about problem solving; given this, culture plays a pivotal role in determining if and how educators learn from their experiences. In traditional schools, independence and teacher isolation have been viewed favorably. Fullan (1999), however, argued that a collaborative culture is a more effective alternative and he identified its distinctive attributes:

- *Diversity is fostered in a context of trust building.* Teachers are encouraged to challenge highly complex problems by stating their views, especially when their viewpoints differ from those expressed by administrators and other teachers. But they are unlikely to do so unless they trust administrators and fellow teachers.

- *Anxiety is provoked and contained.* Administrators produce anxiety through dialogue in order to reduce comfort with current practices. However, they create safeguards to ensure that the anxiety generated is not counterproductive (i.e., excessive to the point that it discourages teachers from challenging complex problems).
- *Teachers and administrators engage in knowledge building.* They first share tacit knowledge (individual knowledge) and then convert it to explicit knowledge (shared knowledge). They also seek new knowledge both among themselves and from outside sources. They evolve to become a community of learners seeking pedagogical synergy by merging and expanding the school's (organizational) competence.
- *Connectedness and openness are combined.* The typical school is fragmented and inundated with unwanted and uncoordinated mandates. Concurrently, the principal encourages teachers to collaborate within the school and to become connected to the external environment in order to understand emerging needs and attitudes.
- *Spiritual, political, and intellectual issues are fused.* Moral purpose (the spiritual dimension), power (the political dimension), and ideas and best practices (the intellectual dimension) are melded to respond to realities of school climates.

## Schools as Learning Communities

Critics charge that most schools have failed to improve because they are not learning communities. After conducting two studies of public schools, one circa 1970 and the other in the early 1990s, Sarason (1996) concluded that most administrators and teachers had neither the knowledge nor the inclination to restructure schools. Even when educators appeared to have an open mind toward learning and pursuing change, reform often was pursued in superficial or inconsistent ways producing only temporary effects (Elmore, Peterson, & McCarthey, 1996). Partly because educators recognized they were supposed to engage in school reform, they often complied with mandates spitefully or otherwise created an illusion of change while remaining ensconced in the prevailing school culture. Thus, after pressures for change subsided, they reverted to their traditional practices (Fullan, 2001).

Past practices clearly demonstrate why meaningful reform requires cultural transformations—and embracing the concept of a learning community is probably the most essential change that must occur. In order to lead a school in this direction, you must first understand the nature of a learning organization. The concept was popularized by Senge (1990), who described it in relation to five core disciplines, a series of principles and practices that can be studied, mastered and integrated into an organization through its members:

- *Systems thinking.* The nature of schools as a social system was addressed earlier in this chapter. Systems thinking involves the application of systems theory to administrative practice. For example, principals understand subsystems integration and realize that problems and outcomes are an intricate mix of subsystem effects.
- *Personal mastery.* Learning in organizations occurs individually and collectively. Individual learning does not ensure organizational learning—but, without it, organizational learning cannot occur. To achieve personal mastery, persons must engage in continuous learning related to the organization's mission, vision, and development.

- *Mental models.* Mental models are assumptions, generalizations, and images of life, the world around us, and the organization in that world. The construction of these models begins at the individual level and requires a form of introspection called reflection, a process detailed by Schön (1987) and widely described in texts on teaching and school administration. Reflection is a process through which professionals use practice-based experiences to integrate theoretical and craft knowledge and to expand their personal knowledge base.
- *Building shared vision.* This process was discussed in chapter 3.
- *Team learning.* This discipline pertains to restructuring into small subsystems so that persons can align and develop their capacities to accurately define problems and forge effective solutions.

Though each of the disciplines is relevant to schools, there are other defining characteristics of a school as a learning community. The following are examples of pertinent attributes:

- *Change-supportive culture.* The principal and staff are guided by the assumption that the need for change is persistent, and they view innovation, critique, and quality to be essential for making successful adaptations to changing needs (Schwahn & Spady, 1998).
- *Communities of practice.* Teachers develop and principals honor formal and informal communities of practice—student-centered subsystems that encourage professionalism and mutual support among members (Sergiovanni, 2004).
- *Collegiality.* The principal and staff express mutual respect and support, share a common commitment to serve students and the broader community, and share responsibility for engaging in school improvement (Hall & Hord, 2001).
- *Collaboration.* The principal and staff cooperate rather than compete, especially when dealing with problems related to school effectiveness (Fullan, 1999).
- *Inquiry.* The principal and staff focus on lessons learned from effective and ineffective practice (Lashway, 1998). Individually and collectively they engage in a form of action research, and findings and conclusions are shared and critiqued in an environment of collegiality (DuFour & Eaker, 1998).
- *Adequate time for learning, collaboration, and inquiry.* The principal and staff are provided time to grow professionally and to engage in action research (Duke, 2004).
- *Best practices.* The principal and staff study best practices as defined in the professional knowledge base and, with appropriate adaptations, apply them to their practice (Duke, 2004; Hall & Hord, 2001).
- *Results orientation.* The principal and staff recognize that evaluation should focus on what is accomplished rather than on what is intended (DuFour & Eaker, 1998).
- *Relational communication.* The principal and staff exchange information openly, often, and in multiple directions. Communication is used to build and strengthen relationships, trust, and collaboration (Kowalski, 2005; Kowalski et al., 2007).

In summary, transforming a school into a learning community entails developing small synergistic subsystems that encourage (a) problems to be identified accurately, (b) individual learning to be melded into collective learning, and (c) new ideas to be forged, tried, and evaluated. Such restructuring will require educators in most schools to alter their values, beliefs, and assumptions—especially those pertaining to trust, collaboration, risk taking, and the potential for every student to succeed academically.

## Principal Responsibilities

Acting alone, a principal cannot build a professional learning community. Nevertheless, he or she usually is the single most important person determining if and how the goal will be pursued. In their analysis of schools, DuFour, DuFour, and Eaker (2008) assert that the principals must do three things. First, they must clearly understand and articulate that their role is to create conditions that help staff to capitalize on their collective capacity to ensure that all students learn. Second, they must share authority so that schools benefit from having multiple leaders. Third, they must "bring coherence to the complexities of schooling by aligning the structure and culture of the school with its core purposes" (p. 317).

In order to erect professional learning communities, a principal must have the requisite knowledge; that is, he or she must know the nature of this organizational structure and know how it can be established and sustained. Moreover, a principal must be committed to the concept philosophically; that is, he or she must value and believe in underlying objectives such as shared leadership, collegiality, trust, and experimentation. Finally, a principal must have the resources necessary to implement learning communities. This requirement necessitates economic and political support from school boards, superintendents, and other stakeholders.

## REFLECTIONS

In the vignette at the beginning of this chapter, a principal initiates a block scheduling program and, though he has the support of nearly all the faculty, parental opposition has placed him in a precarious position. His experience reminds us how difficult and risky it is to change traditional practices—and why principals have often been reluctant to be change agents.

Many low-performing schools, however, require bold leadership from principals willing to restructure or at least experiment with operational procedures that may make the institutions more effective. This chapter addressed several important dimensions of school organization, namely vertical and horizontal planning, the school day, the school year, and need to transform schools into learning communities. Although new approaches, such as interdisciplinary teams, block scheduling, and year-round school calendars, offer promise, their effects on student academic achievement have been inconsistent. Nevertheless, it is becoming increasingly clear that dividing a school into smaller instructional units and altering the school day so that teachers can work longer and more intensively with the same students are promising alternatives to the traditional delivery of instruction. The concept of learning communities is nested in these ideas and it provides a framework for organizing the delivery of instructional programs.

## Knowledge-Based Questions

1   Problems and outputs in social systems have multiple causes. In light of this fact, why is systems thinking relevant to improving the organization of instructional delivery in a school?

2   What are the advantages and disadvantages of having non-graded elementary schools?

3   What are the advantages and disadvantages of interdisciplinary teams in middle schools?

4   What is "looping"? Why is it considered a promising idea for improving instruction?

5   What are the differences between single-track and multi-track year-round school calendars?

6   What is organizational learning?

## Skill-Based Activities

1   If you were the principal in the vignette at the beginning of the chapter, identify what you would have done differently with respect to promoting block scheduling.

2   Assume you are the principal of a middle school employing 37 teachers. The school has been using a traditional eight-period day with departmentalized instruction. You want to move to interdisciplinary teams. Develop a recommendation for the superintendent identifying the reason for your recommendation and describing a typical team's membership.

3   Develop a plan to analyze a school's organization for instructional delivery.

4   Select a school and analyze its daily schedule. Identify strengths and weaknesses and share the outcomes with the class.

5   Identify how you could use the concept of a learning community to weigh options for organizing a school.

## CHAPTER 6

# Building and Maintaining Relationships

*Over the past few months, conflict between Principal Bart Jones and the faculty at Westside High School has intensified. When Mr. Jones arrived at the school just 18 months ago, the superintendent advised him many changes were needed to elevate the school's effectiveness. Describing why the previous principal had been asked to resign, the superintendent said, "Your predecessor was well-liked by the teachers, primarily because he let them do whatever they wanted to do. Some teachers, especially officers in the teachers' union, really were running the school." The superintendent added that Mr. Jones was selected for the position over 13 other applicants because he was known to be an effective manager and disciplinarian.*

*After arriving at Westside High School, Principal Jones made it clear that he would be in charge. He told employees he expected them to arrive at school on time and to perform all of their assigned duties diligently. He purposefully avoided social contact with teachers, fearing that personal relationships would make it difficult for him to evaluate employees objectively and to eliminate counterproductive behavior in the school.*

*At first, most employees were congenial but, after just 3 months, tensions in the school mounted. On two occasions, for example, the union president, an English teacher at Westside, asked if another teacher could cover her last period class, allowing her to attend a meeting outside the school. Though another teacher had volunteered to cover the class, and though the previous principal had consistently approved such requests, Principal Jones refused to do so. His decision infuriated the union president and she began to criticize him openly—in and outside the school.*

*Eventually, even small problems morphed into major disputes pitting the principal against teachers. At the urging of the union president, nearly 75 percent of the school's faculty signed a letter sent to the superintendent and school board stating Mr. Jones had destroyed morale in the school and requesting that his employment contract not be renewed. After Principal Jones turned to the superintendent for support, he was told that he should have been more diplomatic.*

## INTRODUCTION

Many variables contribute to or detract from school effectiveness including relationships inside the school and between school personnel and community stakeholders. Poor relationships, regardless of their cause, have a negative effect. In this chapter's vignette, for example, Bart Jones obviously inherited a difficult situation. Believing that the superintendent expected him to provide order and control immediately, he made it clear to teachers that he was in charge and they were his subordinates. Though his actions may appear to be appropriate in terms of eliminating rule violations, their longer-term effects on the school are likely to be negative.

The responsibility of providing leadership for school improvement can be overwhelming. Principals not only must challenge the status quo, they have to build trust, motivate teachers, and gain widespread support for necessary change (Leithwood & Jantzi, 2000). Though research provides little evidence of a direct effect of principal leadership on student learning, many studies have found that principals have a mediating effect on student learning (Barnett & McCormick, 2004). That is, principals influence conditions in a school that are associated with student learning—conditions such as setting clear and relevant learning goals (Waters, Marzano, & McNulty, 2004), establishing an environment of mutual trust and shared leadership (Wahlstrom & Seashore Louis, 2008), and revamping negative school cultures (Hallinger & Heck, 1998). A principal's ability to change a school's climate, however, is highly dependent on collaboration and support, qualities that are more probable in the context of positive relationships.

This chapter's content is divided into four parts. The first is devoted to explaining why relationships are relevant to school improvement—philosophically, educationally, and politically. The second section provides information describing the intricate connections among school public relations (PR), principal communication, and relationship building. Relationships with employees and students inside the school and with parents and the media outside the school are the third topic. The chapter concludes with suggestions for opening lines of communication with all stakeholders.

After reading this chapter, you should be able to demonstrate the ability to do the following correctly:

- Explain the philosophical, educational, and political reasons for having positive relationships
- Define school PR as a broad administrative process advantageous to school improvement
- Define the concept of relational communication and differentiate it from traditional communicative behavior
- Explain how relationships with stakeholders improve the probability of school improvement
- Identify positive and negative behaviors that influence principal relations with the media
- Define parental engagement and explain how it leads to positive relationships
- Identify guidelines for establishing school Web pages, preparing print materials, collecting public opinions, and conducting public forums

## IMPORTANCE OF RELATIONSHIPS AND STAKEHOLDER INVOLVEMENT

Principals are expected to identify relevant stakeholder groups and connect them to the school by establishing lines of communication. It is to be hoped that ongoing communication will evolve into positive relationships that prompt stakeholders to become more directly involved with education. Their engagement is relevant for philosophical, educational, and political reasons as illustrated in Figure 6.1.

### Philosophical Reasons

During the first half of the twentieth century, community members in most school districts could and often did impose their values and political dispositions on school policy decisions directly through a process known as democratic localism (Katz, 1971). After 1950, this form of citizen involvement started to be replaced by representative democracy, a form of government in which school officials (school board members and administrators) made decisions on behalf of local communities. Thus, citizen engagement in policy development became indirect and served as a complement or supplement and not a primary decision-making format (Pratchett, 1999). In a postindustrial America, democratic localism was considered impractical; though multiple reasons were used to defend this transition, three were especially prevalent:

- The growing complexity of public administration required technical, political, and administrative expertise most citizens did not have (Dahl, 1989).
- Most citizens could not or would not devote the time required to involve themselves directly in policy decisions (Roberts, 2004).
- The population in most school districts was no longer homogeneous. Often, residents held dissimilar and even competing values, and many preferred not to debate these differences publicly (Levin, 1999).

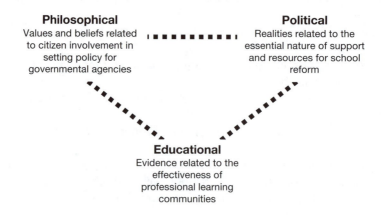

*Figure 6.1* Why Relationships are Critical to School Effectiveness.

Representative democracy assumes that school officials entrusted to make decisions on behalf of the public are (a) representative of the community's demographic profile and (b) committed to making impartial decisions in the best interests of the entire community (Meier, 1993). After 1980, however, mounting dissatisfaction with public schools implied that one or both assumptions were not being met in many school systems (Bauman, 1996; Lan, 1997). By the mid-1990s, efforts to achieve school improvement at the local level had again made democratic localism relevant. In the new political climate, relationships between school administrators and resident stakeholders have become increasingly essential. Philosophically, the importance of these associations is anchored in the following convictions:

- A democratic government is best served by a free two-way flow of ideas and accurate information so citizens and their government can make informed choices.
- A democratic government must report and be accountable to the citizens it serves.
- Citizens, as taxpayers, have a right to government information—but with some exceptions (exceptions to disclosing information may be predicated on laws and administrative judgments about balancing public interests with citizens' rights) (Baker, 1997, p. 456).

Based on these principles, citizens, including many who are dissatisfied with their local schools, believe they are entitled to influence important decisions by directly participating in school reform.

## Educational Reasons

From an education perspective, many principals believe that stakeholder relationships, especially with teachers and parents, are more important today than at any time in the past. This is true because authentic reform is unlikely unless teachers are motivated and given the authority to solve complex problems (Leithwood & Jantzi, 2000); and these conditions are less probable in schools where distrust is prevalent and teachers feel disempowered. Equally important, parental influence on academic success is an issue that should not be ignored. When principals and teachers encourage parents to help their children learn, and when they help parents by providing direction for involvement, they bridge learning that occurs in school and learning that occurs at home (Wherry, 2008).

In their investigation of social relationships pertinent to schools, Bryk and Schneider (2002) concluded that widespread trust had a positive effect on the day-to-day operations of schools. They also reported a direct relationship between the development of relational trust in a school community and long-term improvements in student achievement. Their findings support the growing belief that relationships built on mutual trust are an asset for principals and other leaders pursuing fundamental improvements in schools. According to Goldring and Hausman (2001), principals who reach out from the school to build or develop their respective communities through relationships erect "a new mental model of schooling" (p. 199).

## Political Reasons

Developing and implementing reforms locally is difficult because critical choices must be made at the point where societal rights intersect directly with individual rights (Levin, 1999). For example, some parents seek to control the experiences, influences, and values that get expressed to their children in school; concurrently, school and other governmental officials have had the responsibility of determining the experiences, influences, and values society wants reproduced through a common public school curriculum (Gutmann, 1987). In the context of pursuing reform at the district and school levels, citizens who feel that their individual rights are being ignored often pursue a confrontational approach to protect their interests (Björk & Gurley, 2005)—and the ensuing conflict almost always damages schools and administrators. Obviously, rekindling democratic localism is not easy, as the scope of potential conflict is widened, parameters of authority change, and decisions are less predictable (Zeichner, 1991). Moreover, power and authority need to be distributed in such a way as to encourage citizens to participate (Pateman, 1970). Nevertheless, emerging realities suggest that essential levels of school improvement will not occur without widespread stakeholder support.

Positive relationships make it more likely that stakeholders and school officials can collaborate by engaging in democratic discourse and shared decision making. For example, stakeholders in and outside the school collectively pursue a communicative strategy for school improvement; that is, they state and test their beliefs and priorities in a spirit of trust and collaboration (St. John & Daun-Barnett, 2008). Afforded this level of participation and respect, stakeholders are less likely to oppose change proposal (Bauman, 1996).

# SCHOOL PUBLIC RELATIONS, COMMUNICATION, AND RELATIONSHIP BUILDING

Prior to America becoming an information-based society, relatively little attention was given to school PR; and, when the topic was discussed, it often was referred to as *school–community relations*. Though branding the process as community relations was considered more politically acceptable, especially to those who conceptualized PR as simply self-promotion and propaganda (West, 1985), the label led administrators and others to overlook the critical nature of relationships inside the school. Arguably, relationships between principals and teachers and between school personnel and students are at least as important as those between school personnel and external stakeholders (Kowalski, 2008).

Prior to the information age, many principals acknowledged that relationships were important; but often a disjunction between this belief and actual behavior was apparent. Principals and district-level administrators often could and did insulate themselves from external interventions (i.e., interference caused by individuals and groups outside the school), believing that possible problems, such as excessive conflict, outweighed possible benefits, such as building goodwill (Hanson, 2003). Moreover, they often avoided developing collegial relationships with school employees, believing that doing so would compromise their managerial objectivity and legitimate authority (Hoy & Miskel, 2008).

Today, communities and school personnel are prone to be intolerant of principals who do not communicate effectively and who attempt to segregate themselves and schools from communities.

## Understanding School Public Relations

You can find myriad definitions of PR and school PR in the literature. Some are normative, prescribing standards for shaping public opinion and practitioner behavior. Others are descriptive, detailing what actually occurs in PR practice (Grunig & Hunt, 1984). Often normative and descriptive definitions are quite dissimilar, reflecting the fact that real practices are not congruent with ideal practices. In this book, school PR is defined normatively as:

> an evolving social science and leadership process utilizing multimedia approaches designed to build goodwill, enhance the public's attitude toward the value of education, augment interaction and two-way symmetrical communication between schools and their external communities, provide vital and useful information to the public and employees, improve decision making and problem solving, and facilitate school reform efforts. (Kowalski, 2008, p. 13)

Explanations for the key elements of this definition are provided in Table 6.1.

*Table 6.1* Explanations of the Normative Definition of School Public Relations

| Component | Meaning |
| --- | --- |
| Evolving social science and leadership process | School PR is both an evolving academic subject supported by research and theory and an evolving area of administrative practice informed by craft knowledge |
| Multi-media approaches | School PR entails using both print and electronic media |
| Build goodwill | The intent of school PR is to build positive relationships |
| Enhance the public's attitude toward the value of education | School PR seeks to inform the public of the essential nature of schooling, both as a foundational aspect of a democratic society and as an investment in human capital |
| Augment interaction and two-way symmetrical communication between schools and their external communities | School PR is intended (a) to expand interactions among persons and groups using two-way information exchanges, to benefit all parties, and (b) to build and maintain symbiotic relationships between schools and the communities they serve |
| Provide vital and useful information to the public and employees | Information generated through school PR is intended to benefit both internal and external stakeholders |
| Improve decision making and problem solving | Data collected and stored through school PR are used by administrators and teachers to make effective decisions that contribute to solving the myriad problems schools face |
| Facilitate school reform efforts | By providing information and goodwill, school PR makes vital contributions to school improvement, especially when reform is being pursued locally |

Defined accurately, school PR is broader than community relations. Most notably, the process includes internal operations, such as communication with school employees and activities such as exchanging, collecting, and storing information (Kowalski, 2008). In this more expansive conceptualization, a school PR program serves multiple purposes—some of which are relevant to school improvement. The following examples demonstrate the breadth of school PR goals:

- Improving education quality by helping to determine real needs and valid public opinions (Armistead, 2000)
- Ensuring open political dialogue among stakeholders seeking to have input into school operations and improvement (Baker, 1997)
- Allowing divergent opinions to be expressed and evaluated (Martinson, 1999)
- Enhancing a school's image by accurately and continuously communicating with stakeholders (Pfeiffer & Dunlap, 1988)
- Engaging in educational marketing by "developing or refining specific school programs in response to the needs and desires of specific target-markets" (Hanson, 2003, p. 235)
- Establishing goodwill and a sense of ownership among stakeholders (Pawlas, 2005)
- Collecting data that inform school-improvement decisions (Kowalski, 2008)
- Building economic and political support for school improvement (Kowalski, Petersen, & Fusarelli, 2007)

## Communicative Behavior and Relationships

School PR is all about relationships—among educators, between schools and other institutions, and between educators and the publics they serve. Relationships are a measure of participant perceptions or a function of those perceptions (Broom, Casey, & Ritchey, 2000). As an example, a principal may view her relationship with teachers positively based on the manner in which she treats teachers and they treat her. Perceptions, however, are not always accurate. Principals who do not relate well to others may fail to recognize this shortcoming—or, if they do recognize the problem, they may fail to objectively assess the underlying reasons for the condition. Regardless of whether a principal's relationships are objective or subjective realities, they constitute behavioral contexts that determine how principals act toward other people and how people act toward them (Kowalski et al., 2007). Equally important, the associations influence a principal's understanding of other persons, especially in terms of predicting how they will behave (Surra & Ridley, 1991).

Positive relationships are erected on four pillars of mutuality: control (power sharing), trust, commitment, and satisfaction (Grunig & Huang, 2000). Communicative behavior affects each of them (see Figure 6.2). That is, regardless of whether relationships are positive or negative, interpersonal or role specific, they are "bestowed, sustained, and transformed through communicative behavior" (Millar & Rogers, 1976, p. 87).

Traditionally, managers communicated in ways that prevented or hindered positive relationships. Specifically, they controlled information, discouraged subordinates from initiating conversations with them (Hanson, 2003), exhibited a disregard for employee interests, and disseminated information in ways that emphasized their

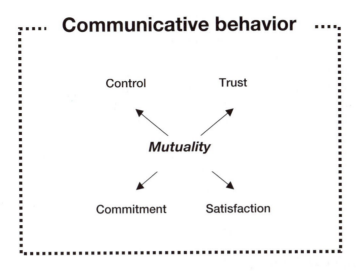

*Figure 6.2*  Principal's Communicative Behavior and the Pillars of Positive Relationships.

# Relational communication

| *Attribute* | | *Effect* |
|---|---|---|
| *Interpersonal* | ⇨ | *Communication is viewed as being person related rather than role related* |
| *Multidirectional* | ⇨ | *Communication flows in multiple directions* |
| *Mutual influence* | ⇨ | *Persons communicate in ways that neutralize roles, rank, and status* |
| *Symmetrical* | ⇨ | *Communication is intended to benefit all communicants* |
| *Objective* | ⇨ | *Communication is used to build positive relationships* |

*Figure 6.3*  Attributes and Effects of Relational Communication.

superior organizational role (Grunig, 1989). A new normative standard, called *relational communication*, emerged in conjunction with the development of an information-based society. It is characterized by interpersonal and symmetrical information exchanges (see Figure 6.3). Being interpersonal, relational communication prescribes multidirectional exchanges (top-down, horizontal, and bottom-up) and personal behavior that allows communicants to influence one another's behavior over and above their organizational role, rank, and status (Burgoon & Hale, 1984). Being symmetrical, relational communication prescribes information exchanges intended to benefit all communicants (Grunig, 1989). Moreover, the process directs persons to focus on perceptions, especially assessments of personal behavior (Littlejohn, 1992); for example, a principal should attempt to determine how his or her actions are interpreted and judged. Lastly, the value of relational communication extends beyond individuals; the ultimate goal is to develop and maintain positive relationships between an organization and the organization's stakeholder publics (Bruning & Ledingham, 2000).

By engaging in relational communication, principals are more likely to identify and address unmet needs (Conrad, 1994); and schools that successfully address unmet needs are more likely to be viewed as community assets rather than community liabilities (Kowalski, 2005). Table 6.2 provides a profile of a principal's motives and behavior using relational communication.

## FOCUSED RELATIONSHIPS

Though principals benefit from positive relationships with all stakeholders, their associations with teachers and students in the school and with parents and the media outside schools are especially meaningful. In large measure, these associations either enhance or hinder efforts to build professional learning communities and to otherwise transform schools into more effective social institutions.

### Internal Relations

As noted in the introduction to this chapter, principal–employee relationships have both direct and indirect effects on school climate and student learning. As examples, these

*Table 6.2* Characteristics of a Principal Engaging in Relational Communication

| Characteristic | Principal's intent and behavior |
| --- | --- |
| Multidirectional exchanges | In an effort to improve the quantity and quality of information obtained and made available to employees and other stakeholders, the principal encourages and engages in information exchanges that are top-down, lateral, and bottom-up |
| Relationship building | In an effort to build and maintain personal relationships and relationships between the school and community, the principal consistently views communication as a means for strengthening associations |
| Power and dominance | In an effort to minimize the effects of authority and power in relationships, the principal communicates in ways that do not threaten or intimidate others |
| Symmetry | In an effort to build and maintain trust and confidence, the principal seeks to ensure that all parties benefit from communication |
| Constructive exchanges | In an effort to identify and address unmet school and community needs, the principal engages in and encourages open and continuous communication, using information to make important decisions and to identify and solve problems |

associations directly influence how individuals treat each other and how they address problems of practice (Hanson, 2003; Hoy & Miskel, 2008). Indirectly, internal relations with staff have been found to influence mediating conditions that affect student learning (Hausman & Goldring, 2001; Marzano, Waters, & McNulty, 2005; Wahlstrom & Seashore Louis, 2008).

Understandably, the vast majority of research pertaining to internal relations has focused on teachers. In addition to relational communication, three other factors have been especially influential in shaping positive relationships between principals and teachers (see Figure 6.4):

- *Credibility*. This variable involves the extent to which teachers and other staff view the principal as a credible source of information. As such, credibility has often been associated with expert power—the ability to influence others by possessing needed knowledge and skills (Martin, 1978). Staff members are more prone to forge positive relationships with principals who provide them with formative counsel and direction.
- *Trust*. This variable involves having confidence that principals treat employees fairly, justly, ethically, and respectfully. Studies of trust in schools (e.g., Bryk & Schneider, 2002; Hoy & Sweetland, 2001) suggest that trust is commonly associated with leadership style. For instance, principals who behave democratically and transformatively usually enjoy higher degrees of trust (Tschannen-Moran, 2004).
- *Shared leadership*. This variable involves employee empowerment. Principals who share power by involving employees in key decisions and providing reasonable levels of autonomy to other professionals in the school are more likely to have positive relationships with staff (Johnson & Venable, 1986; Wahlstrom & Seashore Louis, 2008).

Despite the obvious importance of relations between principals and students, surprisingly little research has been conducted on this topic. Nevertheless, two factors appear to enhance positive associations: they are being student-centered and promoting student engagement. A student-centered principal purposefully makes connections with students, especially by maintaining high visibility. He or she intentionally and continuously interacts with students during the school day and at school functions (Waters et al., 2004). Promoting student engagement refers to making students feel that they are important and an integral part of the school; for example, a principal takes interest in them and seeks their opinions (Cook-Sather, 2007).

Too often, student contact with principals is initiated by problems. If student misconduct or academic difficulties are the only reasons why students interact with the principal, establishing a relationship of mutual trust becomes extremely difficult. Indirectly, principal relations with students are affected by the quality of teacher–student relations in the school. If students distrust and dislike teachers, they are apt to have the same feelings about principals and assistant principals. Last, positive relations with students are more likely when schools are professional learning communities. In this climate, educators care deeply about every student; they give students direction and ensure learning opportunities to maximize every student's potential (Hord, 1997).

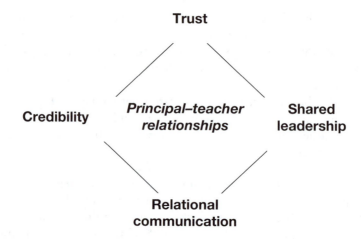

*Figure 6.4* Influential Attributes of Positive Principal–Teacher Relationships.

## Parental Relations

Parents actively involved with the schools usually develop more positive attitudes about themselves, schools, teachers, and administrators (Smrekar & Cohen-Vogel, 2001). Clearly then, parental engagement is a high priority that allows principals to forge relationships resulting in "an on-going, developmental process of mutual or reciprocating empowerment" (Shepard, Trimberger, McClintock, & Lecklider, 1999, p. 34). Engagement, however, requires more than getting parents to visit schools periodically (Wadsworth 1997) or even getting them to spend a few hours per month helping with homework (Herman, 1998). Disconnected sporadic activities do not provide sufficient engagement that nurtures positive relationships (Coleman & Churchill, 1997).

Auditing and planning are two actions principals can take to enhance parental relations. With respect to the former, quantitative and qualitative data regarding parental involvement should be collected and analyzed. This information should include (a) the types of activities in which parents are involved, (b) the extent to which they are involved in them, and (c) their opinions about their involvement (e.g., how they were treated by school employees). Also, an effort should be made to determine why and by whom the activities were initiated (Soholt, 1998). Equally important, principals should identify families that have not interacted with the school and determine the reasons for their inactivity (Kowalski et al., 2007). Next, a plan to address identified deficiencies should be developed. The document should include achievable goals and strategies developed collaboratively with staff members. As part of the planning process, the principal should identify necessary resources and alternatives for obtaining them (L. J. White, 1998).

Despite the elevated importance of education in an information-based society and global economy, parental engagement, even at the basic level of school visits, has declined (Solo, 1997). In addition, increased demographic and political diversity in districts and schools made many parents reluctant to get involved with public education (Wherry, 2008). For example, parents may fear that engagement will cause conflict with educators and with other parents whose values and beliefs are dissimilar to theirs.

## Media Relations

School administrators generally have been displeased with the quality of press coverage they and schools have received (Batory, 1999). Given their dissatisfaction, many of them have come to see journalists as adversaries—persons who should be avoided or at least manipulated (Borja, 2004). Conversely, many reporters have developed negative impressions of school administrators as bureaucrats who exaggerate positive information and conceal negative information (Spicer, 1997). These hostilities have assumed added importance as a result of public education's image being tarnished by more than two decades of intense criticism.

Despite what novice principals may be told by veteran administrators, working effectively with the media, even when it is highly difficult to do so, is an essential leadership responsibility. In contemporary society, the public expects government officials, including principals, to communicate openly, honestly, and frequently—and much of their communication occurs through media outlets. Thus, prudent principals adhere to guidelines for building positive media relations. They are presented here as positives and negatives—that is, as things principals should and should not do. The following are the positive actions:

- *Having a media relations plan.* Media relations plans ideally are developed at the district level and augmented at the school level. In smaller districts, though, no plan may exist. If this is the case, you should attempt to develop a school plan and gain the superintendent's approval before adopting it. Before developing a plan, you should learn the current status of relationships between the media and schools to determine if the overall objective is to sustain or improve relations (J. White, 1998). The plan should be designed to provide guidance for all school employees. Specifically, it should detail why communication with reporters occurs, identify responsibilities for dealing with reporters, set goals for media relations, and provide strategies for goal attainment (Gonring, 1997).
- *Taking the initiative to meet reporters.* A new principal unfamiliar with the local community should identify journalists assigned to cover schools. These persons should be invited to the school so the principal can meet them even before the school year begins. If a principal waits for the reporters to contact him or her, the first meeting is likely to be an interview regarding negative news or a presumed problem (Sielke, 2000).
- *Understanding what journalists are expected to do.* Poor relationships between principals and reporters often stem from a lack of mutual understanding about job responsibilities. Both parties should be aware and respectful of job responsibilities (Raisman, 2000). Most notably, principals should always remind themselves that reporters are not school employees (Horowitz, 1996).
- *Honoring deadlines.* Reporters commonly have deadlines; thus, principals should respond to reporter questions or data requests within the timeframe specified. If this is not done, the reporter is likely to move forward without the principal's input, creating the possibility of a one-sided column or report (Frohlichstein, 1993). If it is impossible to comply with the deadline, this fact should be explained to the reporter.

- *Staying on course.* Principals should remain focused on the topic being discussed with reporters (Brunner & Lewis, 2006). Drifting into other topics often makes the reporter's assignment more difficult and makes it less likely that the principal's comments are interpreted correctly.
- *Being helpful.* Reporters assigned to cover schools are often relatively inexperienced journalists who know little about education and even less about school governance. When possible, principals should identify emerging issues, connect the issues to their schools, and identify possible information sources regarding the issues (Kidwai, 2008; Rhoades & Rhoades, 1991).
- *Dealing with negative news.* When a problem or piece of negative news surfaces, reporters are almost certain to call the principal. If he or she knows the matter to be untrue, the relevant evidence or explanation should be provided to the reporter. If the principal is unable to determine authenticity of the negative news, he or she should indicate that the matter will be investigated and information provided to the reporter as soon as it is available. If the matter proves to be true, the principal should acknowledge that fact and communicate a plan that has been developed to deal with the situation (Kowalski, 2008).
- *Seeking positive publicity.* Principals should seek positive media coverage for their schools. The likelihood of getting a positive story told becomes greater when the proposed topic is timely; that is, it is relevant to current news or seasonal events (Parker, 1991). As an example, a column describing how high school students conducted a food drive for needy individuals is more likely to be printed during a holiday season (e.g., Thanksgiving or Christmas).
- *Correcting the record.* When errors occur in media reports, administrators should always attempt to correct the record (Ordovensky & Marx, 1993). This includes correcting errors that are favorable to the school (e.g., an error that inflates the percentage of a high school's graduates enrolling in college).

The following are things principals should avoid doing when dealing with media:

- *Being untruthful.* Good reporters usually discover the truth. If they learn that a principal lied, they almost certainly will report that fact—and they are unlikely to trust the administrator in the future. As noted previously, loss of trust damages relationships (Howard & Mathews, 2000).
- *Refusing to comment.* When confronted with unpleasant questions, public officials have been prone to answer, "No comment." Though this response may appear rational and safe, it actually is a very poor response. The public is likely to interpret a refusal to comment as evasive behavior indicative of a person who has something to conceal (Million, 2000).
- *Speaking off the record to a reporter.* Principals may be tempted to speak to reporters under the guise of confidentiality. In fact, one can never be sure that what is said or written to a reporter will not be made public (Howard & Mathews, 2000).
- *Being manipulative.* Often reporters assigned to cover schools are relatively inexperienced journalists, and principals may conclude that they can be manipulated. For example, a principal may pretend to like a reporter in an effort to influence what will appear in the media. Besides being unethical, such behavior is destructive to positive relationships.

In summary, mutually rewarding relationships between principals and journalists do not evolve naturally. Rather, they must be cultivated by establishing mutual trust, respect, and benefits (Kidwai, 2008). The guidelines provided here constitute a framework for achieving that objective.

## COMMUNICATING WITH STAKEHOLDERS

Because communication is at the heart of relationship building, principals need to exchange information openly and consistently with internal and external stakeholder groups. Though modern technologies broaden oppportunities for this communicative behavior, they also can depersonalize relationships. For this reason, principals should consider multiple ways of exchanging information. The purpose here is to provide brief descriptions of several options that principals frequently deploy.

### School Web Pages

If you randomly examined school Web pages, you probably would discover that they differ markedly in quality and purpose. Poorly constructed sites usually are uninviting, intended to disseminate selective information, not user-friendly, and void of feedback capacity, including basic information one would need to contact the principal or other school officials. Such Web pages are actually counterproductive, because, like other communication channels, they influence stakeholder perceptions of the school and possibly of the principal.

Though principals rarely construct school Web pages, they are responsible for seeing that the product is functional and an asset rather than a liability. Both design and content are important in this regard. Kowalski and associates (2007) offer the following guidelines for this responsibility:

- Design the site so that it can be updated frequently (at least weekly if not daily)
- Provide essential information that defines the school (e.g., mission, vision, and philosophy statements)
- Provide contact information so that users know how they can communicate with school personnel
- Provide pertinent information (e.g., school calendars, lunch menus, and announcements) that is likely to attract parents, students, and other stakeholders to the Web site
- Provide updated and active links that allow site visitors to obtain more detailed information (e.g., links to the district's Web site and the state department of education's Web site)
- Include school performance information (e.g., assessment data and state report cards)
- Feature teachers, staff, and students as often as possible
- Provide a navigation system that allows users to move through the site easily and without confusion
- Make sure all information provided is correct

- Provide a feedback mechanism (e.g., electronic bulletin board) that permits site visitors to exchange information and ask questions
- Establish and enforce relevant rules for posting material on the Web site

## Print Materials

School newsletters, brochures, student handbooks, policy manuals, and promotional material (e.g., for a tax referendum) exemplify products that remain relevant. If constructed professionally, such documents enhance the credibility of school officials and provide a relatively convenient way to reach multiple stakeholders. When preparing print materials, Hyde (2004) advises principals to answer the following key questions: *What* do you want the printed materials to accomplish? *What* are your objectives and goals with this brochure, report, bulletin, or newsletter? *Who* are included in the target audiences? *How* must you communicate to deliver the intended messages to the targeted audiences?

Only after answering these queries should the materials be developed. Ferrari (2005) offers these suggestions to make the final products look professional:

- Keep the look clean and simple; don't overload the reader visually
- Avoid too much type; pages filled with writing are not appealing
- Use headers and subheadings to lead the reader
- Make sure words are spelled correctly
- Avoid jargon or terms that some readers will not comprehend
- Do not use every inch of paper otherwise the product will have a cluttered appearance
- Include captions for photographs
- Use charts and graphs rather than tables; most readers respond more favorably to items that are visually appealing

Though feedback capability is less common in printed materials, principals should at least indicate how readers can contact school officials if they have questions, concerns, or comments about the publication (Kowalski, 2008).

## Focus Groups and Opinion Polls

Focus groups and polling can be deployed by principals to ascertain stakeholder attitudes or opinions. Each option has advantages and disadvantages. Polling is typically conducted through written (mail or internet) or telephone surveys. The process allows a principal to get a broad perspective of opinions from large groups rather quickly. Disadvantages depend on the format used. As examples, mail surveys are expensive; telephone surveys anger respondents who do not wish to be bothered; internet surveys are perceived as lacking confidentiality. Overall, polling frequently produces low return rates. Focus groups, typically consisting of 12 to 15 randomly selected stakeholders, entail face-to-face discussions. The primary advantage is that qualitative information (e.g., explanations of why stakeholders express certain opinions) can be obtained. Possible disadvantages include misinterpretations, respondent reluctance to be candid, and relying on information obtained from relatively few stakeholders (Kowalski et al., 2007).

In addition to securing data that can inform administrative decisions, ascertaining stakeholder opinions can confirm or refute assumptions held by school staff (Cambron-McCabe, Cunningham, Harvey, & Koff, 2005). For example, the staff at a middle school may be surprised to learn that many parents are dissatisfied with the school's approach to block scheduling. In addition, stakeholders often feel good about being given input opportunities (Walker, 1987).

## Public Forums

Public forums are one of the most common approaches to communicating with the public. Most forums initiated by school officials are really limited public forums; that is, they are conducted with rules (e.g., determining who may speak, how much time is granted to a speaker). Truly open forums are conducted without restrictions. Limited public forums are usually conducted for a specific purpose (e.g., to gain opinions about adopting block scheduling), but some principals schedule them periodically without a topic in mind.

In addition to ensuring that a forum will be conducted properly, principals benefit from following basic guidelines. The following have been suggested by Cambron-McCabe and associates (2005):

- The administrator should welcome attendees and specify purpose and rules.
- Effort should be made to attract persons who do not usually attend school board meetings or other school functions. These individuals may provide viewpoints that school officials do not normally hear.
- Educators should not dominate the discourse in these sessions. Their primary role should be to facilitate the process and answer questions.
- Provide a social dimension, such as refreshments.
- Focus on one or a few select topics. Otherwise, much of the time may be spent discussing personal issues that may not be relevant to most attendees.
- If the forum is held to discuss a controversial issue, it is best to select a neutral site and to have a person considered to be neutral serve as the moderator.
- Attendees should have the option of extending their remarks in a letter to school officials, especially if time limits are placed on speakers.

## REFLECTIONS

A principal's role in building stakeholder relationships is probably the least considered leadership responsibility in schools. The need for positive associations emanates from democratic values, education research, and political realities. In seeking to forge symbiotic relationships with school employees, students, parents, and other stakeholders, principals need to understand modern interpretations of public relations and the concept of relational communication. Equally importantly, they must develop dispositions that motivate them to apply this knowledge in shaping and pursuing school-improvement initiatives.

Special attention was given to relationships with school employees, students, parents, and media. These groups usually are most directly involved in school reform and their feelings toward a principal often determine whether they accept him or her as a legitimate leader.

As you reflect on this chapter's content, consider how you would apply what you have learned to your practice as a principal. For example, to what extent do the key points presented here reinforce or refute your values, beliefs, and communicative behavior? Also consider the content in relation to principals you have observed. To what extent have they established positive relations with stakeholders? To what extent do they open lines of communication in and out of the school?

### Knowledge-Based Questions

1   Why have relationships with a school generally and with a principal specifically become more important over the past three decades?
2   Why should a principal engage in school public relations?
3   What is relational communication? How does it differ from traditional communicative behavior?
4   Why is parental engagement considered beneficial for schools?
5   Why is stakeholder involvement in school improvement considered to be politically beneficial?
6   What factors enhance positive principal–teacher relationships?
7   What is democratic localism? Why has it resurfaced as a relevant topic for school administrators?

## Skill-Based Activities

1   Detail a plan you would use to determine the extent to which parents were engaged with the school.

2   Visit three school Web sites and evaluate them from the perspective of a parent.

3   Identify actions principals could take to improve relations with teachers.

4   Evaluate the situation faced by Principal Jones in the vignette at the beginning of this chapter. If you had inherited the situation he did, what would you have done differently?

5   Assume you are an elementary school principal and you are scheduling a public forum regarding the possibility of the school board redrawing attendance boundaries for the district's schools. Develop an agenda and rules for the forum and indicate where you would conduct it.

# PART III

# Managerial Responsibilities

## CHAPTER 7

# Managing Material Resources

Sharon Carter's appointment as principal of Eastside Elementary School neither surprised nor disappointed the school's employees. She had been teaching third grade at the school for 13 years and was the most respected teacher on staff. Enrolling approximately 350 students, Eastside is located in an established neighborhood, and the two-story facility, though 47 years old, remains aesthetically pleasing. Anticipating that the long-term principal, John Asher, would retire, Sharon's colleagues had urged her to pursue the position.

Having an opportunity to assist teachers through instructional supervision was Mrs. Carter's primary motive for becoming an administrator. During her tenure at Eastside, she had mentored three novice teachers, and each protégé remained a productive member of the school's faculty. Seeing her recommendations influencing the professional growth of young teachers was exhilarating and intrinsically rewarding. She saw herself as having a special talent for guiding teachers to collaborate and elevate their performance in the classroom.

Just 17 days into the school year, Mrs. Carter encountered her first unexpected mini-crisis. The school's custodian resigned. He had been at the school longer than the principal and his departure was a shock. The district's director of facilities assigned a temporary custodian and told the principal she should begin a search for a permanent replacement. Mrs. Carter knew little about custodial services and even less about the local labor market. She requested that the director of facilities conduct the search but, under district policy, the responsibility belonged to her. The task became time-consuming and it took her nearly 2 months to find an acceptable applicant.

Her next surprise occurred in late November when the superintendent informed her that the school would need to be renovated. A recent evaluation of the facility by an architectural firm indicated that the building required extensive work. Because the length of construction would be 7–9 months, Mrs. Carter and the architects had to devise a plan allowing the construction to be done in phases. At any given time, approximately 15 percent of the facility would not be available for use. Over the next 4 months, Principal Carter sat through *what seemed like a hundred meetings discussing issues she knew little about. At the same time, she was becoming increasingly disappointed because she was unable to work with teachers as intended. Frustrated, she asked the superintendent if he could appoint a district-level administrator to work with architects so that she could again devote her time to "normal" responsibilities. The superintendent said, "As principal, you must be personally involved. Problems will occur during construction; they are inevitable. If you do not know the plan, you will be at a real disadvantage. Besides, after the construction is completed, you will need to make important decisions about reoccupying the entire facility."*

*Mrs. Carter left the superintendent's office somewhat depressed. Hearing that she would have to devote even more time to the facility project was not what she hoped to hear.*

## INTRODUCTION

Novice principals often believe that they can devote much of their time to preferred responsibilities—that is, to assignments they enjoy and feel confident doing. In the case of Principal Carter, her intentions and ability with respect to instructional supervision are admirable. Her assumptions about her position, however, are unrealistic. Few superintendents allow principals to self-determine what they will and will not do. Rather, novice principals are commonly expected to learn on the job to augment the knowledge and skills they initially bring to the position.

This chapter is the first to address traditional managerial responsibilities. Despite the emphasis placed on teaching and learning in the literature, experienced principals know that they will not survive long if they mismanage fiscal resources—and this includes caring for a multi-million dollar school building. Principals are expected to begin practice with basic managerial knowledge and skills and to expand their expertise through experiential learning and continuing education.

The primary purposes of this chapter are to examine fiscal and facility management. After reading the chapter, you should be able to demonstrate the ability to do the following tasks correctly:

- Define the three basic elements of fiscal management: budgeting, accounting, and auditing
- Identify a principal's responsibilities for managing school-based funds (e.g., extracurricular accounts)
- Describe a principal's role in facility utilization planning and evaluation
- Explain the advantages and disadvantages of principals being actively involved in facility planning and construction projects
- Describe a principal's managerial responsibilities for facility maintenance

## MANAGING FISCAL RESOURCES

The extent to which principals are responsible for and involved in fiscal management varies considerably. Thus, generalizations about this topic are precarious. Even so, you should understand that all principals need basic knowledge and skills in this area. The following factors exemplify reasons underlying variability for this responsibility.

- *District centralization.* Some school systems are highly centralized; therefore, fiscal management is concentrated at the top of the school system (e.g., the superintendent or designee tightly controls operations). The perceived advantage of this organizational design is uniformity for district operations and the perceived advantage for principals is freeing them to address school-specific responsibilities. The perceived disadvantage of centralization is that principals end up having little or no control over money. As a result, their authority and power are usually diminished. The negative effects of centralization increased the popularity of site-based management over the past 30 years. This iteration of decentralized authority often gave principals substantial autonomy over the allocation and management of fiscal resources (Kedro, 2003).
- *School size.* Principals in smaller schools may have less responsibility for fiscal management than do principals in larger schools, especially if the schools operate several school-based accounts (e.g., textbook rental fund, cafeteria fund). In addition, overall budget allocations are less for smaller schools.
- *School district policy.* State laws and school board policy also determine the extent to which principals are accountable for managing money. Statutes, however, apply to all principals in a given state whereas district policies usually vary across districts in a state.
- *School administrative staff.* Principals aided by assistant principals or school-based bookkeepers may be able to relegate fiscal responsibilities.
- *District administrative staff.* Small districts (i.e., those with fewer than 1,500 students) remain the norm in the United States. Many of them do not employ business managers; as a result, superintendents assume most of the responsibility for fiscal management. In these situations, principals are apt to have fiscal management responsibilities that otherwise would be carried out by district-level personnel (Kowalski, 2006).

To some, fiscal management entails routine, mundane tasks that should be assigned to clerks, allowing principals to devote their time to curriculum and instruction. In reality, however, many stakeholders, including school board members, view the situation differently. Business operations in public schools are closely scrutinized by state government and, when management deficiencies are identified (e.g., via state audits), they are made public and reported in the media (King, Swanson, & Sweetland, 2003). In the aftermath, the superintendent and school board are reminded that all administrators have a fiduciary responsibility for public funds.

## Understanding Budgeting and Budgets

Even when principals have no direct role in developing a district budget, they are affected by it. Moreover, school boards, through the superintendent, may require individual schools to have budgets (e.g., if the district is highly decentralized and using site-based management). Properly developed, annual budgets provide a planning resource, a document that communicates educational intentions to the broader community, a legal justification for expending public dollars, a control mechanism for revenue and expenditure decisions, and a guide for evaluating fiscal performance (Hartman, 1988). Ideally, therefore, a school district's budget is developed from three plans as shown in Figure 7.1: an education plan, a revenue plan, and an expenditure plan (Ray, Candoli, & Hack, 2005). Not uncommonly, education plans are ignored; yet education planning is the area where principals could have considerable influence. An education plan should specify needs, goals, and programs intended to meet needs and goals; and, because it provides a rationale for allocating resources, it should be developed prior to the revenue or expenditure plans (Brimley & Garfield, 2008).

A revenue plan details the origin and amount of anticipated funds flowing into the district during the fiscal year. Most school districts operate on a fiscal year calendar that begins on July 1 and ends on June 30. This calendar permits one budget to cover a school year. For public schools, the primary sources of revenue are state support, local property and income taxes, federal support, and grants; and, because principals are often asked questions about school finance, they should have a basic understanding of these revenue sources (Sharp, 1994). In private schools, the primary revenue source is typically student tuition. An expenditure plan details the amount of revenue the district intends to spend during the fiscal year. Expenditures are detailed by accounts (categories such as personnel costs, utilities, and so forth).

According to Ray and associates (2005), two problems are relatively common with district budgets: they are mechanical documents, meaning that they may comply with state law but are void of educational planning; or they are administration-dominated and highly centralized documents, meaning that principals, teachers, and other stakeholders did not have input for their development. Principals need to recognize both the economic and political aspects of budgeting. Economically, the end product is expected to provide an adequate and reasonably equal distribution of resources and a framework for fiscal efficiency (King et al., 2003). Politically, the end product is affected by competition for scarce resources—meaning that principals often are expected to identify school needs and to lobby for fiscal resources to meet them (Vann, 1995).

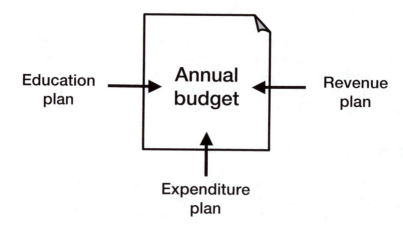

*Figure 7.1* Inputs for a District or School Annual Budget.

## Accounting and Auditing

Accounting and auditing are intended to produce efficiency and effectiveness in fiscal operations. Accounting systems protect against carelessness, inappropriate expenditures, theft, embezzlement, or malfeasance on the part of administrators. They also provide (a) a systematic process for interfacing fiscal expenditures with educational goal attainment, (b) a process for meeting requirements established by local and state governmental units, and (c) accountability data for stakeholders (Ray et al., 2005).

Accounting procedures per se should enhance administrative decision making. A principal, for example, can determine how much remains in a given fund before giving his or her approval for a requested expenditure. If properly construed, a district or school accounting system should ensure that (a) appropriate records are maintained and protected against loss and damage, (b) cash receipts are properly handled, (c) safety practices are used for check writing and recording financial transactions, and (d) two or more persons share responsibility for dispersing funds (Drake & Roe, 1994).

Auditing is an extension of accounting intended to verify the accuracy and completeness of financial transactions as they relate to the general budget and specific accounts (Ray et al., 2005). Audits may be conducted internally (e.g., by a school district official) or externally (e.g., by state-appointed auditors or by independent third parties). States typically require year-end, external audits to (a) ensure that expenditures were approved properly by district officials, (b) verify revenue receipts, (c) verify transactions through requisitions, purchase orders, vouchers, and canceled checks, (d) verify the accuracy of journal and ledger entries, and (e) verify the accuracy of bank statements, accounts, and investments (Brimley & Garfield, 2008).

## Purchasing

Principals are continuously involved with purchasing materials and equipment. In public schools, expenditures are controlled by federal and state laws, governmental regulations, and local district policies (Kowalski, 2006). School district policy and rules should provide procedures for requesting, approving, and purchasing items. Most often a principal or his designee is required to approve or deny a purchase order. As a principal, your decision may connote the appropriateness of the item being purchased, acknowledgement that sufficient funds for the purchase are available, or both. Most often, principals are responsible for determining appropriateness and a district-level administrator (superintendent or business manager) is responsible for determining the availability of adequate funds.

## School-Controlled Funds

Depending on state laws, public schools are allowed to have independent accounts under the jurisdiction of principals and private schools always have their own accounts. The most common accounts are for extracurricular activities (e.g., revenue and expenditures for athletic programs), textbook rental funds, and lunch program funds. If they exist, principals have a fiduciary responsibility for managing them. Therefore, you should be familiar with relevant state statutes and district policy.

The number of school-controlled accounts has grown over time, in part because principals have been urged to secure non-traditional funding sources to offset inadequate public funding. The following exemplify such efforts.

- *School foundations*. District and school foundations are not-for-profit, tax-exempt community-based corporations functioning as third parties that generate revenues primarily from private gifts, businesses, and other foundations. In 2006, $41 billion was donated to education in this country, making schools the second largest recipient category (behind religion) of philanthropic donations (National School Foundation Association, n.d.). Increasingly, public elementary and secondary school principals have tried to capture some of this revenue, much of which has been given to colleges and universities and private elementary and secondary schools in the past. If school foundations are established, principals typically play an active role in their governance; for example, they serve as a member of the foundation's governing board. Though foundations have positive attributes (e.g., funds for special projects, monetary teacher awards, student scholarships), they also can generate problems. In districts with a relatively large number of schools, officials need to ensure that foundations do not create or exacerbate inequalities among schools. In Portland, Oregon, for example, one-third of revenue raised by the district's thirty-one school foundations must be transferred to an equity fund that is administered by district officials (Portland Schools Foundation, n.d.). Based on the premise that schools do not have equal opportunities to raise private revenues, this policy is intended to prevent some schools from using foundations to gain a substantial fiscal advantage. Foundations also can generate managerial concerns (e.g., they require attention from principals), legal concerns (e.g., the funds must be controlled and audited properly), and political concerns (e.g., distinctions of authority between a school foundation and school district may be ambiguous or disputed).
- *Solicitation of goods, services, and money*. Principals frequently seek direct and indirect donations for schools. The most prevalent activity in this respect is the development of school partnerships. Typically, these associations are forged to provide added human or material resources; however, the donations are not typically ongoing contributions. Partnerships too can be time-consuming and a source of conflict. Moreover, principals are accountable for using the assets generated by these associations in accordance with state laws and district policy (Addonizio, 2000).
- *Enterprise activities*. Some school officials have leased empty school buildings or unused space in school buildings as a means for generating revenue (Addonizio, 2000). Leasing space within a school is an issue principals should examine carefully, because doing so inevitably has consequences for routine operations. Another enterprise activity growing in popularity is facility user fees. This involves a charge for using the school, typically outside the school day, for meetings or activities (e.g., a recreational basketball league). All school districts should have a policy addressing facility use; if a district does not, principals should recommend that a policy be adopted. Otherwise, principals are placed in the precarious position of deciding who is allowed to use a school, the conditions under which a school may be used,

and whether a fee should be charged. In most instances, use of school buildings by outside groups adds cost to facility operations; custodial services, utilities, and insurance are examples (Kowalski, 2002).

• *Vending contracts.* Exclusive vending rights contracts have become the most controversial effort to raise additional school revenues. In these arrangements, a principal agrees to sell or promote only certain products in a school in return for a fee, a share of revenues, or gifts (e.g., athletic score boards). Many high schools now have such agreements giving soft drink companies exclusive distribution and advertising rights. According to White (1999), these agreements are controversial because they may be judged to be disadvantageous for students (e.g., they expose them to poor nutritional products), problematic for administrators (e.g., principals often must spend considerable time managing the agreements), and unfair for vendors who do not have such a contract.

The management of school-based funds has several dimensions. As examples, principals must ensure that revenue is recorded properly, that accounting procedures are in place, that funds are invested when permissible and prudent, that expenditures are made properly, and that the accounts are audited as prescribed by state statutes and district policy.

Raising and expending alternative funds for schools is a two-edged sword, especially in the realm of public schools. On the one hand, principals are strongly encouraged to secure additional school resources but, on the other hand, making schools reliant on alternative funding can be precarious. As examples, revenue streams for alternative funding are usually unpredictable and inconsistent; alternative sources of revenue require principals to spend more time on fiscal management, often at the expense of providing instructional leadership; and alternative funding can contribute to public convictions that schools really can do more without receiving additional public funding—a belief that may affect state funding legislation and the passage of school district tax referenda (Kowalski, 2006).

## MANAGING SCHOOL BUILDINGS

Indifference toward school facilities was made apparent by a national study conducted in the late 1980s. Reporting the findings, Lewis (1989) highlighted the fact that at least 25 percent of the nation's school buildings were in poor physical condition and they provided inappropriate learning environments. By the mid-1990s, updates indicated that the percentage of inadequate school buildings had increased to about 35 percent (General Accounting Office, 1996). Poor facility conditions were compounded by two other problems. First, many schools could not accommodate the rapid expansion of technology (e.g., classrooms were too small to permit the inclusion of computers and space was unavailable to develop computer laboratories); second, many schools lacked design flexibility and adaptability, thus making it difficult or impossible for principals to adjust to evolving curricular and instructional needs (Kowalski, 1995).

The topics of school facility planning, development, and management are broad and addressing them in depth here is not practical. Nevertheless, principals should have a fundamental understanding of these responsibilities. Why? When stakeholders are dissatisfied with school facilities, they usually voice their concerns, at least initially, to principals. Moreover, principals play an important role in identifying and ameliorating facility problems. Last, principals almost always have a responsibility to ensure that school buildings are used and maintained properly. Accordingly, principals should at the least know (a) how school construction is funded in their respective states, (b) the elements of district and school planning, (c) a principal's role in a facility project, and (d) a principal's responsibility for facility maintenance (see Figure 7.2).

## Funding School Construction

State statutes covering school facility construction remain highly dissimilar. They range from states providing 100 percent of construction funds to states providing no fiscal support for construction. Historically, the local property tax has been the primary revenue source for building or renovating schools. In the spirit of liberty, local taxpayers often were able to determine if construction would occur and the amount of money that would be made available for construction. They did this either through state-mandated referenda (bond elections) or through exerting political influence on school board members (King et al., 2003). Taxpayer refusal to support school construction totally or adequately explains why many school buildings in this country became old, ineffective, and even unsafe (Thompson, Wood, & Honeyman, 1994). Moreover, it explains why the quantity and quality of school facilities among states and among districts in a given state may be blatantly unequal (Kowalski & Schmielau, 2001).

Over the past 50 years, there has been a discernible shift toward greater state funding for school construction. According to McKinley and Phillis (2008) the trend has been affected most directly by lawsuits challenging state funding formulas on the basis of either equity (having reasonably equal facilities across a state) or adequacy (having acceptable facilities across a state). As has been less recognized, the trend has been influenced by the growing realization that school facilities have become a relevant school reform issue (Augenblick & Silverstein, 2002). Most stakeholders, however, remain unaware of past or current statutes for construction. Recognizing this fact, prudent principals

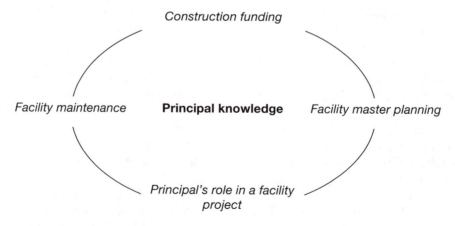

*Figure 7.2* What Principals Should Know about Facility Planning and Maintenance.

learn the funding laws in their state and they subsequently educate their staff and other stakeholders.

## General Facility Planning

School facility planning entails developing a long-range plan for improving or replacing school buildings. The process is concurrently an educational, philosophical, economic, and political issue (see Figure 7.3). From an education perspective, planning should be anchored in a realistic mission and shared vision delineating what is to be accomplished and how it is intended to be accomplished (Smith, 2003). From a philosophical perspective, it should take into account values shared by local stakeholders (Castaldi, 1994). From an economic perspective, it should take into account projected costs and sources of revenue, and be feasible (Kowalski, 2002). And from a political perspective, it should address stakeholder participation and support (Erwood & Frum, 1996).

Ideally, a district's facility plan should include subplans for each school. Accordingly, principal involvement in facility planning is considered essential. A principal should contribute to facility planning in four important ways:

- Providing and explaining a school's mission, shared vision, and strategic plan for achieving the vision
- Collaborating with school staff and other stakeholders to develop or update a school-specific facility plan
- Identifying key stakeholders who should be involved in developing the district facility plan
- Keeping school employees and other relevant stakeholders informed about the school's and district's facility plans

In the absence of adequate planning, school officials often err by treating facility projects as independent events. For example, replacing an existing high school without

*Figure 7.3* Issues Affecting School Facility Planning.

considering the needs of other district schools and without considering how the cost of that project may prevent timely construction at other sites can be a serious mistake. School construction almost always expends both fiscal (available and future revenues) and political (e.g., taxpayer goodwill and support) capital. As discussed previously in relation to systems theory, a facility project has implications for all the district's schools. Therefore, planning should take into account that decisions for individual projects should be made from a systems perspective (Smith, 2003).

## Principal's Role in a Facility Project

Once a decision is made to renovate, expand, or replace an existing school, the principal is apt to become highly involved in the project. Ideally, that involvement begins in the earliest stages so that the principal, representing the school's staff and other stakeholders, can influence design decisions. During construction, "a principal should have access to every detail of the building to ensure improved operations once the school is opened" (Tanner & Lackney, 2006, p. 206). Thus, throughout the planning and construction phases, a principal is likely to attend myriad meetings, be required to spend time reading pertinent documents, and attend several relevant public hearings.

Though architects design school buildings, they are expected to follow the rule that "form follows function." That is, they will design a school building that accommodates intended educational and extracurricular programming. To ensure that this occurs, principals should insist that educational specifications are developed prior to the design phase. Also referred to as program specifications, these standards are qualitative and quantitative statements detailing the programs and activities that will occur in the facility and data regarding the number, type, size, layout, association, location, and content of spaces (Kowalski, 2002). Thus, educational specifications provide design architects with information about how the building will be used but they do not dictate design decisions (Affleck & Fuller, 1988). The principal's responsibility in relation to this document includes ensuring that (a) an educational program is in place prior to the development of specifications, (b) faculty and other school employees have an opportunity for input, and (c) specifications are neither excessive nor inaccurate.

Planning for a specific project can be an exclusive or inclusive process. In the former, decisions about the project are made by relatively few individuals (e.g., superintendent, architect, and school board members) with no input from school employees or community stakeholders. This approach is typically ineffective both because important issues such as community values, education priorities are not integrated and because it fails to build stakeholder support for the project. Inclusive planning, by comparison, involves representatives of multiple stakeholder groups as well as the architect and key district officials (Kowalski, 2002). Though inclusive planning is clearly more effective and philosophically acceptable, it is far from perfect. Most notably, teachers and community representatives are prone to draw up wish lists that inject politics and subjectivity (Hunter, 2004). Ideally, principals are present to distinguish between questionable preferences and real needs. Specifically, they should provide benchmarks, ensuring that the school will serve its intended purposes, and guidance, ensuring that conflict between school staff and other parties does not become destructive.

## Maintaining School Facilities

School buildings began to deteriorate the day they open; and, regardless of construction quality, poor maintenance accelerates deterioration (Chan & Richardson, 2005). Maintenance is generally defined as those actions intended to keep a building in relatively good condition and functioning properly, and the process consists of general maintenance services, typically provided by district-level employees or contractors, and custodial services, provided by school-level employees or private contractors.

Some school systems opt to outsource (i.e., engage in contracts with private companies) general maintenance, custodial services, or both. Advocates for this alternative (e.g., Lieberman, 1986) contend that it is more economical than the traditional option of hiring employees, primarily because school boards evade union contracts and administrators evade hiring, supervising, and evaluating maintenance personnel. Private contracting, however, can produce problems. For example, principals may not be able to discipline or dismiss custodians; and, if the private contractor's employees strike, school officials will have a major predicament (Kowalski, 2002).

Most schools are staffed by custodians who are district employees, assigned full time to one school, and supervised by a building principal. Generally, they have these primary duties:

- Protecting the facility and its equipment
- Maintaining a healthful and safe environment
- Keeping the building functional for instructional purposes
- Ensuring that public perceptions of the building are positive
- Maintaining a clean environment (Jordan, McKeown, Salmon, & Webb, 1985)

A list of typical custodial services is provided in Table 7.1. In some smaller school districts, custodians also may be assigned to do light maintenance work such as minor electrical repairs, minor carpentry tasks, light painting, minor plumbing repairs, and replacing

*Table 7.1* Typical Custodial Responsibilities

| Duty | Examples |
| --- | --- |
| Clean floor surfaces | Sweeping, waxing, and buffing |
| Removing trash | Emptying waste baskets and other receptacles |
| Cleaning wall surfaces | Washing windows and mirrors |
| Sanitizing areas | Mopping up spills and cleaning up blood |
| Monitoring equipment | Checking to see that mechanical systems are functioning properly and reporting them to maintenance if not |
| Keeping fixtures operational | Filling soap dispensers, replacing toilet paper, and cleaning sink drains |
| Regulating climate control | Setting thermostats and ventilation fans |
| Maintaining the school site | Mowing lawns and sweeping sidewalks |
| Inventory | Monitoring custodial supplies and equipment |
| Building security | Locking doors and checking alarm systems |

broken windows. Divisions of labor between maintenance and custodial staff depend on management philosophy, staffing patterns, policy, and possibly union master contracts.

Other than outsourcing, the employment and direct supervision of custodial staff is done in one of three ways:

- The responsibilities are assigned to a district-level administrator (e.g., facilities director)
- The responsibilities are shared by a district-level administrator and a principal (e.g., they collaborate to hire and evaluate custodial personnel)
- The responsibilities are assigned to a principal

Especially when the third alternative is applied, a principal should know how many custodians are needed. This figure can be determined in three ways:

- The traditional guideline is based on school size; it recommends that one custodian be employed for every 15,000 square feet of space, 11 classrooms, 8 teachers, and 250 pupils (Greenhalgh, 1978).
- A second guideline is based on time needed. It uses the following formula: (time needed per square foot) × (number of square feet) × (frequency). The product (hours needed) is then divided by the hours in a working day to determine the number of employees needed (Milshtein, 1998).
- The third guideline uses traditional quantitative data as in the first two guidelines but infuses qualitative data such as the building's age, quality of original construction, equipment condition, division of labor between district maintenance staff and school custodians, site development and size, frequency of building use outside the normal school day, and the extent to which technology is used to automate mechanical systems (Rondeau, 1989).

Evaluating custodian job performance is important; if the principal does not do this directly, he or she should have input into the process. As with all employees, annual evaluations should be both formative and summative; that is, they are intended to improve a custodian's work and to determine if a custodian should be retained.

## REFLECTIONS

Both managing money and managing school buildings remain primary responsibilities for principals. The extent to which you may have to engage in these two duties, however, will depend greatly on the nature of the district and school in which you are employed. If you are in a smaller district or in a school without an assistant principal, you may have to spend considerable time fulfilling these duties. Regardless of how much time you must devote to fiscal management and facility management, however, you need to have a basic understanding of both.

Contemporary principals increasingly are being pressured to compensate for inadequate funding. As discussed here, school foundations, grants, partnerships, and exclusive vending contracts exemplify efforts to respond to this need—and they exemplify added responsibilities being assumed by principals. At the same time, principals are required to oversee the operation of a multi-million-dollar facility; and occasionally they must devote a considerable amount of time to being part of a planning team for a construction project.

## Knowledge-Based Questions

1   District and school budgets serve multiple purposes. What are they?
2   What should be the basis for a district or school budget?
3   What is the difference between accounting and auditing?
4   What are the primary revenue sources for public schools?
5   What are the advantages and disadvantages of exclusive vending contracts?
6   What is the purpose of having a district facility master plan?
7   What role should a principal play in planning for the renovation, expansion, or replacement of the school to which he or she is assigned?

## Skill-Based Activities

1   Assume you are a high school principal and the school to which you are assigned has an extracurricular account. Establish rules and regulations governing the operation of this account.
2   Assume you are an elementary school principal and you intend to establish a school foundation. To do so, however, you must gain the approval of the superintendent and school board. Develop a recommendation to send to the superintendent that details (a) the purpose of the foundation, (b) the intended governance structure, and (c) intended fiscal controls.
3   Assume you have just been appointed principal of a middle school. Your assistant principal tells you that the school does not have sufficient custodial services. Detail how you would address this matter.
4   As a principal, identify ways you would use the district's annual budget as a data resource to inform your decisions.

## CHAPTER 8

# Managing Human Resources

*Most Saturday mornings in early April, Bob Marsh would be on the golf course. But today he was sitting in his office at Blue Ridge High School. He became principal of the school less than 2 years ago; and, up until a few weeks ago, his first principalship had been a pleasant experience. As he stared out of his office window, he wondered how things could have changed so abruptly.*

*Blue Ridge High School is relatively small—fewer than 300 students are enrolled in four grade levels. Principal Marsh was employed at the school after serving 2 years as an assistant principal in a middle school in another district. The problem he now faced involved the evaluation of a veteran mathematics teacher, Mrs. Relles. In accordance with district policy, he had observed her in the classroom on two occasions during the first semester and a third time in early February. In accordance with provisions in the master contract with the teachers' union, principals are required to inform teachers at least 48 hours in advance that they will be conducting a classroom observation. In addition, they are required to share the results of observations and to have a personal meeting with each teacher during March to discuss annual performance evaluations.*

*On the date and at the time that Principal Marsh had informed Mrs. Relles he would be conducting a third evaluation, he had to attend to a disruptive student who had gotten into an altercation with a teacher. In the heat of the moment, he neglected to inform Mrs. Relles that he would have to reschedule the observation. The next day, he entered her classroom just prior to the first period and explained what had occurred. He then asked if he could conduct the observation during the first period since he was already in her classroom. Her reply was, "Whatever." Inferring that she was agreeable, he remained and observed the class. His report of the observation was mostly positive, but he commented that she did not appear to be as well prepared as she was during the first two observations.*

*After Mrs. Relles received a copy of the observation report, she met with Mr. Marsh. Visibly angry, she made three points. First, she expressed doubt that Mr. Marsh, a former physical education teacher, was competent to judge her teaching. Second, she described his behavior in not informing her immediately that he would not be conducting the third observation as scheduled as "inconsiderate." Third, she charged that he had violated a provision in the master contract by not giving her at least a 48 hour notice prior to the third observation.*

*Principal Marsh was stunned. This was the first instance in which he had experienced conflict with her. He responded to each of her points, but she remained upset. He then told her she should expect a positive annual evaluation since collectively the observation reports were far more positive than negative. She then thanked him for agreeing to meet with her and left the office. A week later, he received notice that Mrs. Relles had filed a grievance in relation to the third observation. In doing so, she charged that the scheduled observation was cancelled without notice and that the principal conducted an evaluation the following day without following the notice procedure in the master contract.*

*So instead of playing golf today, Principal Marsh is stuck in his office drafting a response to the grievance as ordered by the superintendent. Though he knew there would be unpleasant moments as a principal, he was surprised by how unexpectedly and quickly this one had evolved.*

## INTRODUCTION

Human resources may be defined as all the people who have the capacity to influence a school. In this chapter, however, only primary issues pertaining to employees are addressed (student-related issues are examined in the next chapter). Human resources administration (HRA) involves a range of personnel management functions such as securing, evaluating, and developing teachers and other staff members. Some authors (e.g., Norton, 2008) posit that HRA even extends to fostering an organizational climate in which the benefits of resources can be applied effectively to meet a school's goals. Delineating precise boundaries for human resources management, however, is difficult because some relevant aspects (e.g., performance evaluation and staff development) require both leadership and management decisions.

As the vignette involving Principal Marsh demonstrates, conflict with employees can develop without notice; and, if it is not managed effectively, it has a deleterious effect on the school—and possibly the principal. In this chapter, four dimensions of HRA for employees are addressed:

- Staffing schools
- Staff development
- Evaluating employee performance
- Diagnosing and managing conflict

The chapter's purpose is to provide principal guidelines for these functions. As with all aspects of administration, district and school size are factors affecting the extent to which specific HRA duties are carried out by principals directly, assumed by district-level administrators, or relegated partially or entirely to assistant principals, department chairs, or grade-level supervisors. After reading this chapter, you should be able to demonstrate the ability to do the following correctly:

- Identify effective measures for recruiting and selecting school employees
- Outline an orientation program for new employees
- Identify principles of effective staff development
- Differentiate between assessment and evaluation
- Differentiate between summative and formative evaluation
- Identify guidelines for involuntary employee dismissals
- Identify types of conflict occurring in schools
- Identify conflict management techniques, their advantages, and disadvantages

## STAFFING A SCHOOL

In the past, disjunctions between what principals knew to be important employment criteria and actual employment activities were relatively common (Place & Kowalski, 1993). As an example, prior to the 1960s, administrators based employment decisions on interviews—a practice that made employment an event rather than a process (Young & Prince, 1999). This myopic perspective changed gradually after research produced two highly relevant findings: a significant relationship between interview assessments and subsequent job performance had not been established (Wagner, 1949) and employment decisions based on interview assessments often differed from employment decisions based on paper credential assessments (Gorman, Clover, & Doherty, 1978). This expanded knowledge prompted scholars in school administration to reconceptualize employment as a process—that is, as a function with several relevant and interrelated functions (Young, 2008). These functions are addressed here in four categories: essential principal knowledge, recruitment, selection, and orientation (see Figure 8.1).

### Essential Principal Knowledge

Because employment procedures across districts vary considerably, a principal should have a clear understanding of policy and practices used and of his or her specific role

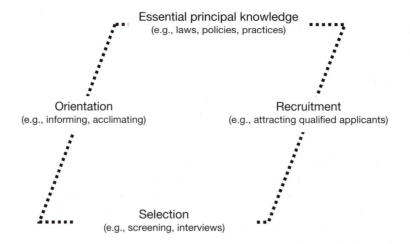

*Figure 8.1* School Staffing Functions.

and responsibilities in hiring personnel. Though employment may be highly centralized (carried out exclusively by the superintendent or other district-level administrators) or highly decentralized (carried out exclusively by a principal), the most common approach found in school systems is a combination of centralization and decentralization. That is, a principal collaborates with one or more district-level administrators in the process.

Employing teachers and other staff is a potential minefield for principals ignorant of the law. Most notably, federal antidiscrimination laws make it illegal to discriminate on the basis of certain class membership (e.g., race) unless class membership is shown to be a bona fide occupational qualification—for example, stipulating that applicants must be Catholic to teach religion in a Catholic high school. Both Title VII of the Civil Rights Act and the Age Discrimination in Employment Act are relevant to employing school personnel; and principals should have a basic understanding of these laws. In addition, they should seek counsel from the superintendent, the director of personnel (if one is employed by the district), or the school district's attorney when in doubt about the applicability of laws to their recruitment and selection activities.

## Recruitment

Recruitment involves identifying viable applicants for a school's vacancies and motivating them to seek employment in the school (Young, 2008). The intended outcomes are (a) generating multiple applications, (b) generating applications from highly qualified persons, and (c) facilitating a fair and equitable selection process.

The importance of this operational function is greatest under three conditions:

- When there is significant competition among employers as exhibited by small or unacceptable applicant pools
- When a school is required legally to address underutilization problems (e.g., hiring more persons of color)
- When you intend to employ the most outstanding persons available

Three types of recruitment activities can occur, although this fact often is unrecognized by administrators. General recruitment is used to fill vacancies for which neither problems nor special considerations are an issue. Targeted recruitment is required when an employer needs to address underutilization or underrepresentation issues (e.g., gender or ethnicity). And expedited recruitment is used when an employer expects that securing qualified applicants will be difficult (e.g., recruiting teachers with specializations that have a high demand and low supply).

The extent to which a school district engages in recruitment varies considerably. Factors such as financial resources, philosophy toward employment activities, local labor pools, and prevailing employee profiles usually are relevant factors. Overall, employment recruitment typically involves several stages.

- *Verifying a vacancy.* Before moving forward with an applicant search, principals must verify that a vacancy exists and that approval has been granted to move forward to fill it. There are occasions when positions are either eliminated or not filled for a period of time (e.g., on account of budget constraints).

- *Developing job specification.* After a vacancy is validated, specifications for the position in question need to be developed. This includes a description of role and responsibilities and a listing of required and desired qualifications. It may also include other pertinent information such as the salary range and employment contract specifications.
- *Reaching qualified candidates.* Typically, employees are recruited externally and internally. Job vacancies and pertinent information for filing an application should be posted in a variety of outlets to maximize the probability that highly qualified individuals will be reached. School Web pages have become a useful outlet for vacancy notices; and often school districts have brochures or video tapes providing information about the community, district, and specific schools.
- *Communicating with prospective applicants.* Often, potential applicants have questions or they seek additional information. It is helpful to have a process in place allowing them to communicate with a school official on these matters (e.g., principal, director of personnel, or superintendent). Vacancy announcements should include a specific contact person and contact information (Winter, 2006).

Given the potential for legal problems associated with employment, principals need to be aware of laws and school board policy that affect recruitment. School districts may have employment restrictions. Examples include a nepotism policy and a employee residence policy (requiring employees to reside in the school district).

Young (2008) recommends that a job analysis should have been completed prior to commencing recruitment for a given position. This process should yield essential information about position requirements (i.e., tasks and responsibilities inherent in the position) and applicant requirements in relation to minimum and desired qualifications. In addition, Young posits that job descriptions should have been developed and made available to guide employment activities. He recommends the following components for these descriptions:

- Job title
- Position summary
- Job duties
- Minimum requirements
- Reporting relationships (e.g., to whom does the person in the position report?)
- Closure clause (a disclaimer indicating the content of the job description is not all inclusive)
- Running dates (a list of dates indicating when the job description was developed and modified)

## Selection

Screening is a process in which school officials evaluate written materials submitted by applicants. Such materials commonly include a completed application form, academic transcripts, verification of previous employment, and references. The intent is to rank the applicants and to determine which of them will be invited to have an interview.

If principals are responsible for screening application files, they should carry out the following procedures or ensure that they have been addressed by other administrators.

- *Evaluating qualifications.* The objective is to determine if an applicant meets minimum qualifications (e.g., licensing, degrees, and experience) and the extent to which she or he exceeds them.
- *Examining for discrepancies.* The objective is to determine if discrepancies exist in an applicant's materials. For example, an applicant may claim to have been employed in two different districts at the same time. If discrepancies are discovered, they should be investigated.
- *Checking references.* The objective is to obtain accurate information about the applicant's qualifications and previous job performance. Reference letters are either personal or professional. The former, written by persons who know the applicant on a personal basis, address issues such as personality, honesty, and work ethic; and the latter, written by professors or practitioners in the profession, address job competencies (Young, 2008).

The value of employment interviews depends on the manner in which they are conducted. They can be unstructured (i.e., the interviewers have not predetermined which questions will be asked) or structured (i.e., questions are predetermined and asked in the same manner to all interviewees). Structured interviews are preferable because they lend themselves to objective evaluations. Several other guidelines are helpful, especially for principals who have limited experience interviewing job applicants.

- *Try to involve at least several other school employees.* Having more than one interviewer is beneficial because multiple perspectives are provided, making it less likely that a principal's personal dispositions will be the sole determinant. This is a critical consideration because research demonstrates that a principal's work values affect teacher selection decisions (e.g., Winter, Newton, & Kilpatrick, 1998). Involving several teachers in job interviews for teaching vacancies may prevent selection decisions from being based on negative values.
- *Know which questions you cannot ask.* All persons involved in interviewing should know the nature of questions that can and cannot be asked. Ideally, this issue has been addressed in district policy or in manuals provided to administrators. As examples, a principal cannot legally ask about an applicant's marital status, religion, or disabilities (Clark, 1998).
- *Refrain from making premature judgments.* Interviewers often make quick judgments based on an applicant's appearance or demeanor. Though such factors are important, they should be considered in light of a person's overall qualities and qualifications.
- *Use an assessment instrument.* A standard instrument should be used to evaluate interviewees. In structured interviews, such an instrument allows a principal to compare interviewee responses to the same questions.

In weighing the merits of applicants for faculty positions, administrators should (a) rely on predictors of teaching performance, (b) consider the tasks a newly hired teacher will have to perform, and (c) consider the environment in which he or she must perform these tasks (Winter, 1995). When these considerations are integrated into the employment process, employers are more likely to require applicants to demonstrate competencies. This can be done through simulations, written tests (e.g., writing skills), developing sample lesson plans, or having to teach a class as part of the selection process.

Last, a principal needs to know what his or her role is in the employment process. As examples, some principals merely determine if candidates are acceptable; some are required to recommend two or more candidates; and some are required to recommend just one candidate. Almost always, the superintendent reserves the right to determine who will be recommended to the school board for employment (Kowalski, 2006).

## Orientation

Principals commonly have a responsibility to provide orientation sessions for new employees. Some new employees require more information than others; for example, novice teachers typically require the most information and teachers transferring to the school from within the district typically require the least amount of information.

In most districts, orientation occurs in two stages: orientation to the school district provided for employees new to the school system and orientation to the school provided for employees new to the school. In planning school-level orientation programs, a principal should address the following tasks:

- Determine what is to be accomplished
- Determine when and where the session will be conducted
- Determine the session's length and time allocations for planned activities
- Determine the materials that need to be distributed
- Provide a communication component allowing participants to introduce themselves, ask questions, make comments, and request additional information
- Provide a formative evaluation component that provides feedback for future orientation sessions

## STAFF DEVELOPMENT

Staff development or in-service programs have been a preferred course of action for improving employee performance and schools generally. As an example, districts and schools provide workshops and other programs intended to introduce new ideas, curricula, or instructional approaches. But the value of staff development continues to be questioned. Most scholars who have examined this issue conclude that it has been largely ineffective. Fullan (2007), for example, contends that traditional staff development has been little more than a few half-days of disconnected presentations provided annually. Teachers usually have been passive participants—listening but never doing. Cole (2004) goes further, arguing that the process actually has deterred change by diverting attention away from real problems and solutions.

Forward-thinking principals now envision staff development differently. They see it as an integral part of school improvement. In their mind, the process must be long-term, coordinated, and erected around specific goals relevant to achieving the school's shared vision. In order to meet these benchmarks, the following principles must be honored:

- Needs must be validated (Hirsh, 2009). Needs evolve from periodic assessments of goals embedded in a strategic plan.
- Activities should be based on principles of adult learning (Lieberman & Miller, 1991).
- Principals must create opportunities for teachers to engage in continuous and sustained learning (Elmore, 2004). These opportunities include observing and collaborating with other teachers to address real problems of practice.
- Learning must be continuous. Staff development is not a periodic event; it is an ongoing program that gets woven into the daily practice of teachers (Fullan, 2007).
- Activities need to be grounded in knowledge about effective teaching, effective schools, and institutional change (Loucks-Horsley & Stiegelbauer, 1991).
- Set goals and secure necessary resources (Little, 1993). The effectiveness of staff development cannot be determined in the absence of clearly defined goals and adequate resources.
- Culture matters with respect to school outcomes (Sarason, 1996). When staff development contradicts school culture, new ideas and methods are eventually discarded, regardless of initial enthusiasm, because they are incongruent with shared values.

## EVALUATING EMPLOYEE PERFORMANCE

For most principals, evaluating employee performance is a demanding, time-consuming, and essential responsibility. The manner in which the process is carried out can have multiple legal, professional, and personal consequences. In large measure, the precarious nature of this assignment stems from past practices indicating that, despite the importance of evaluation, it often was ignored or conducted ineffectively. In his analysis of the literature, Peterson (2000) concluded that teacher evaluations generally were neither valid nor instrumental in improving employee performance. Poor evaluative practices are unacceptable, and especially detrimental in low-performing districts and schools.

As with most specific responsibilities discussed in this book, performance evaluation is a broad task that prospective principals commonly study in greater detail in a separate course on human resources management. The intent here is to outline the responsibility in the context of contemporary practice.

### Why Employees are Evaluated

Across organizations, employees are commonly evaluated for one or more of the following reasons: (a) to determine employment continuation, (b) to foster personal development, and (c) to determine compensation (Young, 2008). In schools, however, compensation is almost always determined by a pay scale and not a merit system; thus, salary increases are predetermined and ensured by re-employment. Assessments and judgments conducted to determine employment continuation are referred to as *summative evaluations*. Basically, the outcome of a summative evaluation is a determination that an employee has or has not performed at an acceptable level (Manatt, 1988). If an employee's performance is deemed acceptable, he or she is recommended for re-employment; if performance is

deemed unacceptable, he or she is either recommended to be placed on probation or terminated.

Today, officials in many school systems also espouse the view that performance evaluation is conducted to foster personal development. Assessments and judgments conducted for this purpose are referred to as *formative evaluations*. The intent is to provide an employee with ongoing suggestions for improving his or her performance based on analysis of past performance (Gullatt & Ballard, 1998). Figure 8.2 provides a comparison of summative and formative performance evaluation.

## Basic Considerations

The responsibility for evaluating employee performance in schools is relegated to principals; typically they spend considerable time over the school term addressing this assignment. In larger schools, principals may share the task with assistant principals or possibly department chairs. Today, it is standard for school systems to have a uniform performance evaluation program (including assessment instruments) that must be applied in accordance with laws and policy.

Regardless of the evaluation program being applied, principals need to know the difference between assessment and evaluation. The former defines a measure, typically of performance (e.g., how often a teacher praises students during class). Evaluation is a judgment regarding an assessment (e.g., whether measured performance is effective). In order to conduct effective evaluation, a principal needs to possess knowledge and skills essential to making correct judgments about performance assessments.

Explaining the complexity of teacher evaluation, Medley, Coker, and Soar (1984) emphasize two other key points highly relevant for principals. First, there is a fundamental difference between evaluating competence and evaluating performance. The former is a repertoire of teacher competencies (e.g., knowledge, skills, or dispositions); the latter is a judgment of actual behavior. Though competence enhances performance, it does not

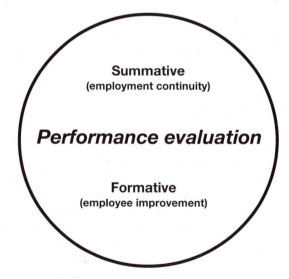

*Figure 8.2* Purposes for Performance Evaluations.

ensure an acceptable level of performance. Second, there is a fundamental difference between evaluating performance and effectiveness. Whereas the former is based on a teacher's behavior, the latter is commonly based on student outcomes (e.g., test scores). In recent years, some would-be reformers have suggested that teachers should be evaluated on the basis of their student achievement test scores. Medley and his associates make clear that such a practice can be precarious because

> the number and the potency of contextual factors not under the teacher's control that affect pupil learning outcomes are both so great that valid measures of effectiveness of individual teachers are extremely difficult and costly to obtain from pupil outcome data. (p. 22)

Recognizing distinctions between teacher performance and teacher effectiveness, policymakers in a growing number of states have advocated the use of value-added assessments[9] to evaluate school effectiveness. Though teacher evaluation remains focused on individual performance, researchers (e.g., Kimball & Milanowski, 2009) recognize the need to reconcile differences between performance evaluations and student outcomes—even when the latter are determined through value-added assessments.

## Critical Facets

Before conducting performance evaluations, principals should carefully analyze relevant laws, district policy, and the district's evaluation program. Specifically, the principal should be knowledgeable of the following facets of this responsibility:

- *Definition.* How is evaluation defined? Is evaluation defined uniformly across employee groups (e.g., teachers, custodians, and clerical staff)?
- *Purpose.* What purposes are served by the process?
- *Responsibility.* Who must conduct the evaluations? Who may participate in the process?
- *Frequency.* How often must evaluations be conducted?
- *Instrumentation.* What instruments must or may be used to conduct assessments?
- *Location.* Where are assessments conducted?
- *Communication.* What forms of communication are required (e.g., conferences, feedback, final reports)?
- *Employee rights.* What rights (e.g., being notified of an impending classroom observation or being able to rebut the outcome of an observation) do employees have under either law or policy (including provisions in master contracts)?
- *Employee recourse.* What may employees do if they disagree with the summative evaluation?
- *Process.* What records must be maintained? How, when, and to whom does the principal transmit the summative evaluation?

Though evaluation systems vary markedly in quality and complexity, the following guidelines provide insights into effective practices:

- *Provide both summative and formative evaluation.* A structured employee growth component is beneficial to both the school and the employee (Edwards, 1995).
- *Rely on multiple data sources.* Evaluations based on multiple data sources—for example, integrating peer assessments and self-assessment with principal assessment—are more likely to be accurate than those based on a single type of assessment (Peterson, 2004). Two sources of evidence being used more frequently are portfolios and work diaries. In both, employees accumulate evidence pertinent to their performance.
- *Use input from multiple assessors.* Traditionally, a principal has been the only person assessing teacher performance. Inputs from peer teachers, parents, and possibly other administrators enhance evaluative decisions (Manatt & Kemis, 1997).
- *Define and agree upon performance targets.* Employees should know and accept the parameters of acceptable performance (VanScriver, 1999).
- *Use rating scales that discriminate sufficiently.* Having just two anchor points (acceptable and unacceptable) provides very limited information for making judgments. Research indicates that effective rating scales have at least five anchor points (Young, 2008)—for example, *poor, below average, average, above average,* and *excellent.*
- *Be objective and honest.* Accurate assessments, regardless of the quality of an evaluation program, require principals to control subjectivity (e.g., friendships, bias, and emotion) and report outcomes truthfully (Schwartz, 1997).

## Terminating Employees

Involuntary dismissal of an employee can be one of the most unpleasant tasks performed by a principal. State tenure laws and due process guarantees make teacher dismissal an especially intricate task that can linger in the courts for 2 or more years. Knowing this, principals often have been reluctant to recommend dismissal, especially when it is known that the employee will contest the matter legally (Jones, 1997). Yet a principal has a professional responsibility to protect student interests, and this includes dismissing incompetent or otherwise unacceptable teachers who have not responded to appropriate interventions.

Aside from voluntary terminations (e.g., resignations or retirements), employees may be dismissed for financial reasons (e.g., reductions in force), performance reasons (e.g., incompetence), or other reasons identified by state statute (e.g., immoral behavior even when it occurs away from school). The following guidelines provide a framework for recommending an involuntary dismissal other than for financial reasons:

- *Know the relevant statutes.* Both federal and state laws may pertain to dismissal cases. Examples of the former are discrimination laws; examples of the latter are statutes covering non-tenured teachers, tenured teachers, and other school employees.
- *Know district policy.* Though district policy must comply with federal and state statutes, it may include additional provisions and specific procedures.
- *Know due process rights.* Employees have due process guarantees and a solid case for dismissal can be derailed by procedural errors.
- *Verify compliance with proper procedures.* Principals should accumulate evidence verifying that they have followed legal and policy requirements related to dismissal.

- *Identify and verify interventions.* Principals are expected to help employees improve. Thus, it is important to provide evidence that this responsibility was met and evidence that the employee could not or would not respond to the interventions adequately.
- *Identify and verify evidence supporting the reason for dismissal.* In anticipation of appeals and litigation, principals need to accumulate evidence that substantiates the cause for recommended dismissal. In such matters, facts rather than opinions matter.
- *Collaborate with the superintendent and school attorney.* Seek the counsel and cooperation of the superintendent and the attorney representing the district and school.

## DIAGNOSING AND MANAGING CONFLICT

Conflict is inevitable in all organizations including schools; however, contrary to popular opinion, it is not always counterproductive. Principals, and especially those seeking to improve school climate, need to recognize this fact. In professional learning communities, for example, disagreements among trusting colleagues are considered normal (Fullan, Bertani, & Quinn, 2005). Thus, the challenge for principals is not to avoid or eliminate conflict; it is to manage conflict productively when it occurs.

### Understanding Conflict and Its Causes

In simple terms, conflict involves two or more competing interests of individuals and groups. These interests are recognized, and each party believes that the opposing party will thwart or already has thwarted its interests. Equally notably, tensions underlying conflict evolve out of relationships and reflect past interactions and the context in which they occurred (Rahim, 2001). For example, conflict may emerge between a group of teachers promoting block scheduling and a group opposing it.

Conflict in organizations is often categorized based on the types of disputes that occur. Harvey and Drolet (1994), for instance, use the following typology:

- *Value disputes.* Often individuals and groups hold dissimilar values, beliefs, or convictions that are independent of evidence. As an example, some teachers may believe that all students can learn whereas others do not. The difference in their conviction leads to conflict over ability grouping and grading.
- *Tangible disputes.* Conflict often evolves in relation to scarce resources (e.g., time, money, supplies, and technology). Categorized as tangible disputes, they are political in nature. As an example, the social studies and English departments may be at odds over scheduling a computer lab because sufficient lab space is unavailable.
- *Interpersonal disputes.* This form of conflict involves strong feelings of dislike between or among individuals. Often, these disputes become malevolent and are very harmful if left unmanaged or unresolved.
- *Territorial disputes.* Territorial conflict results from actual or perceived territorial intrusion. As an example, a principal and superintendent may disagree over control of the school newsletter. These disputes are common in highly bureaucratic systems

where authority is distributed across subsystems with the expectation that each subsystem will not intrude into others.

- *Perceptual disputes.* Individuals and groups in conflict may have distorted images of one another that lead to conclusions about motives and goals that may not be accurate. Often, the parties involved see themselves as having positive intentions and their adversaries as having negative intentions. For example, consider a dispute between first and second grade teachers over retaining students in first grade. The first grade teachers are opposed to retentions; the second grade teachers favor them. Both groups believe they are acting in the best interests of students; both groups believe the other group is acting out of self-interest. Certain factors contribute to or exacerbate conflict.

## Conflict and Employee Unions

Employee unions and collective bargaining frequently generate tensions between administrators and employees. For example, principals are susceptible to experiencing role conflict in dealing with teacher associations. On the one hand, they want to be members of the administrative team, loyal to the superintendent, school board, and district policy. On the other hand, they want to build and retain positive relations with teachers (Kowalski, 2003).

Evidence regarding the effects of unionism on schools has been conflicting. For example, critics argue that collective bargaining has led to greater centralization, less principal autonomy, and animosity between principals and teachers. Proponents counter that unionism has made boards and superintendents less bureaucratic and more attentive to real problems in the schools (Shedd & Bacharach, 1991). Regardless of which position one embraces, virtually everyone agrees that unionism produces conflict that often has negative consequences on a school's climate. In an effort to diminish negative effects, two alternatives to traditional collective bargaining have gained popularity: collaborative bargaining and consensus bargaining. Whereas conventional negotiations almost always place teachers and administrators in an adversarial relationship, the alternative approaches are designed to build trust and promote shared decision making. Collaborative bargaining seeks to focus on real problems affecting schools; consensus bargaining strives to increase rationality by reducing emotion and extreme positions (Misso, 1995). Some labor relations specialists, however, caution that collaborative approaches often result in goal displacement; that is, the participants focus more on the process of collaboration than on outcomes they produce (Harrington-Lueker, 1990). Collaborative approaches also increase the likelihood that administrators will be required to participate directly in the bargaining process (Attea, 1993).

Even when principals are not directly involved in collective bargaining, they may encounter conflict related to managing a master contract. Factors that make disputes more likely include (a) new provisions (changes from the previous agreement) that are not understood by employees or administrators, (b) dissimilar interpretations of master contract provisions, and (c) perceptions of unfair practices by administrators. Principals need to be aware of grievance procedures and their specific role in resolving disputes.

## Managing Conflict

Conflict is inherently neither constructive nor destructive; its effect on schools depends on how it is managed (Kowalski, Petersen, & Fusarelli, 2007). Regardless of whether it occurs internally (e.g., between or among school employees) or externally (e.g., between community stakeholders and school employees), it provides change opportunities—occasions when principals can pursue improvements that might not otherwise be tolerated (Hanson, 2003). Conversely, viewing conflict as being predominately or exclusively negative often deters change by intensifying personal animosity and distrust (Daresh & Playko, 1995).

A variety of techniques can be used to manage conflict and selecting an effective one depends on your ability to diagnose the type of conflict in question. Table 8.1 includes possible management techniques. The techniques are presented in alphabetical order and their effectiveness varies, especially in relation to the type of conflict being addressed. Table 8.2 identifies several of the more effective techniques for each type of conflict.

In the past, principals were often socialized to believe that conflict was inherently counterproductive because it reduced school efficiency by forcing administrators and teachers to take time away from their normal responsibilities. Acting in this frame of mind, principals often opted either to avoid conflict or to make instant accommodations so that they personally would not have to deal with unpleasant situations. As Hanson (2003) points out, ignoring and accommodating are ineffective managerial responses that squander opportunities to use conflict as a change catalyst.

*Table 8.1*  Conflict Management Techniques

| Technique | Description | Advantage | Disadvantage |
|---|---|---|---|
| Appealing to higher-level values | Often applied in transformational leadership, the technique appeals to values, beliefs, or goals (e.g., professionalism and service to students) deemed more important than the immediate conflict. The intent is to have individuals diminish their focus on self-interest | It is an ethical and professional strategy | It may be viewed as idealistic and ineffective |
| Compromise | The technique entails parties making concessions in order to resolve an issue | It is relatively efficient and considered politically acceptable | It often produces poor or mediocre decisions |
| Conciliatory gestures | The technique entails getting one party to make a gesture aimed at reducing tensions (e.g., a conciliatory statement, act of good faith) and getting the other party to reciprocate. The intent is to move toward cooperation through recurring conciliatory acts | It allows the parties to the dispute to reduce tensions incrementally as they work toward resolution | Its effects are often attenuated by perceptions that the gestures are either insincere or manipulative |

*Table 8.1  cont.*

| Technique | Description | Advantage | Disadvantage |
| --- | --- | --- | --- |
| Direct order | The technique entails the principal making a ruling and ordering the parties to comply | It provides the quickest and most efficient resolution | It does not usually resolve the underlying causes of conflict |
| Empirical interventions | The technique entails using data and other forms of evidence to clarify the issue in dispute | It provides a rational approach that is considered normative in professions | It fails if the parties are unwilling or unable to respond rationally to evidence |
| Group dynamics | This technique entails interventions intended to develop higher levels of mutual understanding and respect. Common activities include team building, personality inventories, and trust building | It can result in improved collaboration and mutual respect | It fails if the parties are unwilling or unable to engage in the process with an open mind |
| Interdependence analysis | This technique entails parties understanding and accepting a systems perspective; that is, they recognize interdependence and their need to be collaborative rather than combative | It can strengthen bonds among persons and school subsystems | It fails if the parties do not understand schools as social and political systems |
| Mediation | This technique entails interventions carried out by an impartial third party—typically, a qualified professional who is not a school employee. It is often used to settle disputes related to union master contracts | It is a relatively fair intervention and often acceptable when parties are no longer willing to communicate with each other | It creates a dependency on third parties to settle disputes and can be expensive and time-consuming |
| Resource intensification | This technique entails the infusion of either human or material resources. It is most effective when conflict is centered on competition for scarce resources | It is highly effective for settling conflict involving resource allocation | It creates an expectation that future conflict will result in added resources |
| Restructuring | This technique entails rearranging parts of the school (e.g., moving an elementary school teacher to a different grade level or revamping the structure of academic departments in a secondary school) | It usually can be controlled by the principal and is an indirect solution | It typically does not address the underlying causes of conflict |
| Role clarification | This technique entails efforts to establish an accurate and mutual understanding of roles as established by the district or school (i.e., legitimate roles) | It reinforces organizational structure and roles | It fails if the parties reject legitimate roles |
| Voting | This technique entails conducting a democratic vote to determine which side in a dispute will prevail | It is quick, efficient, and acceptable in a democratic society | It produces winners and losers, and the conflict often resurfaces |

*Table 8.2*  Interface of Types of Conflict with Management Techniques

| Type of conflict | More effective techniques |
| --- | --- |
| Interpersonal | Direct order, group dynamics, conciliatory gestures |
| Perceptual | Empirical interventions, role clarification |
| Tangible | Resource intensification, compromise, restructuring |
| Territorial | Role clarification, resource intensification, mediation |
| Value | Interdependence analysis, appealing to higher values, mediation, voting |

## REFLECTIONS

The situation encountered by Principal Marsh in the vignette serves to remind us that the line separating leadership and management is often blurry. In meeting his responsibility to evaluate teacher performance, he either strengthens or weakens personal relationships with teachers—relationships that are critically important to improving school effectiveness. His dilemma also reveals how unexpectedly and quickly problems can occur.

Despite mounting expectations that principals devote more time and energy to school improvement, their managerial role generally and their HRA responsibilities specifically have not diminished. In many schools, and especially those without assistant principals, allocating adequate time to all responsibilities is literally impossible. In a study of novice high school principals in Ohio (Woodruff & Kowalski, 2009), for example, trying to commit adequate time to all job responsibilities and trying to manage overall workloads were found to be the two greatest problems of practice.

As you think about a principal's role in the HRA functions described in this chapter, consider how they dovetail with the leadership responsibilities identified in earlier chapters. The notion that a principal can transition between being a professional leader and an organizational manager without affecting relationships is certainly questionable. Likewise, it is myopic to believe that a principal, even if highly successful as an instructional leader, can disregard his or her managerial responsibilities and maintain a successful practice.

## Knowledge-Based Questions

1 What responsibilities do principals commonly assume in the recruitment function?
2 Why is teacher selection considered a process rather than an event?
3 What is the difference between a structured and an unstructured interview?
4 Why has staff development often failed to affect overall school effectiveness?
5 What are the similarities and differences between summative and formative performance evaluation?
6 What is the difference between teacher competency and teacher performance?
7 Why is it important for principals to apply management techniques to conflict in schools?

## Skill-Based Activities

1 Assume you are a new principal and the superintendent has asked you to evaluate previous staff development programs in your school and to recommend changes. Identify the facets of staff development you would examine.
2 Take a position for or against using selection committees that include some teachers to employ new teachers and provide a rationale to support your decision.
3 Assume you are a new high school principal, and the faculty and staff are divided over the use of a $25,000 gift from a former student. One group wants to use the money to purchase additional media center materials and the other group wants to use the money to purchase additional physical education equipment. Develop a strategy you would use to manage the conflict.
4 In the vignette at the beginning of the chapter, the mathematics teacher believes that the principal, a former physical education teacher, is unqualified to evaluate her performance. Develop a position statement regarding her claim.
5 In the past, principals have relied entirely or primarily on classroom observations they conduct to evaluate teacher performance. Critique this practice and indicate what you would do differently as a principal.

## CHAPTER 9

# Managing Pupil Services

*Over the past several years, Maria Zappata, principal of Jackson Middle School, has made a concerted effort to help teachers accumulate and use data to inform their important decisions about students. With the assistance of district personnel, she created a computer network that allowed teachers to access and insert data in student records. At first, many of the teachers were skeptical, in part because they were not comfortable using the technology. Gradually, however, they learned the system and began using it rather extensively.*

*Several weeks ago, a student with a history of behavior problems was suspended from school for 10 days as a result of igniting a fire in a waste basket in the cafeteria. The boy's parents appealed the suspension; and after they did not prevail, they retained an attorney who notified Principal Zappata that the parents had consented to him having access to their son's records. After checking with the superintendent, she allowed the attorney to view the file. As he examined the content, the attorney found a number of teacher comments had been inserted in the record. For example, a language arts teacher wrote, "He shows no respect for female students and his anti-social behavior toward girls is both disruptive and troubling." A physical education teacher had inserted the following comment: "I don't trust this student; he's got sticky fingers."*

*After reading these and several similar comments, the attorney asked Principal Zappata if she had evidence to support the judgments that had been placed in the file. She responded that the teachers' comments were data provided by competent professionals who observed the student on a daily basis. The attorney indicated that he disagreed and would advise the parents to pursue legal action against the principal and teachers who had inserted what he called "unsubstantiated condemnations" of his client.*

## INTRODUCTION

Principals have some responsibilities not readily recognized by teachers, parents, and other stakeholders. Many managerial duties related to students fall into that category. As examples, principals must ensure that proper student records are maintained and protected; they must ensure that students are appropriately supervised outside of classrooms; and they are expected to administer a broad activities program that meets student needs and interests. Though these tasks may seem rather inconsequential in relation to instructional leadership, they actually consume a considerable amount of a principal's time and energy. And, as portrayed in the opening vignette, they may lead to legal problems.

This chapter examines four pervasive managerial responsibilities assumed by principals: maintaining student information, providing an effective student activities program, providing supervision outside of classrooms, and managing a food service program. Though these functions do not constitute the full range of responsibilities pertaining to student management, they are among the most pertinent duties. Student discipline, clearly another function in this category, is discussed in the next chapter, which focuses on school safety. The four primary objectives for this chapter are:

- Describing the legal and educational dimensions of maintaining student records and using student data
- Identifying the nature of a student activities program and detailing pertinent issues related to shaping, managing, and evaluating it
- Describing principal responsibility for ensuring proper supervision outside of classrooms with focused attention given to outdoor aspects of a school campus and student transportation
- Identifying the fundamental aspects of managing a school food service program

After reading this chapter, you should be able to demonstrate the ability to do the following correctly:

- Articulate basic legal requirements for maintaining student records
- Discuss how legal requirements pertaining to student records and the use of data to improve decision making interface
- Identify the purposes of a student activities program and a principal's responsibility for managing it
- Develop an outline for evaluating a school activities program including criteria for evaluating individual activities
- Identify effective measures a principal can take to ensure student safety outside of classrooms
- Detail a principal's responsibilities for managing a food service program

## STUDENT INFORMATION

The management of student information has become a two-edged sword for many principals. On the one hand, they must protect the privacy rights of students as specified by federal law, state law, and district policy. On the other hand, they must develop data management systems so that schools can accumulate, store, and make data available to teachers making important decisions affecting students and other professional staff making decisions affecting both students and the entire school.

## Student Privacy Rights

Student records are protected by privacy provisions in two federal laws: the Family Education Rights and Privacy Act (FERPA) and the Individuals with Disabilities Education Act (IDEA). Fundamentally, FERPA, subject to several exceptions, grants parents access to their children's educational records and prohibits school officials from divulging student educational records to third parties without the consent of either parents or students beyond the age of 17 (FERPA, 2000). Schools found not to be in compliance could lose federal funding.

Data covered by the law include records, files, documents, and other materials that contain information directly related to a student (FERPA, 2000). Student discipline records, though covered, may be shared with school professional staff (including teachers) who have a legitimate interest in a student's behavior that poses a significant risk to the safety or well-being of that student, other students, or other members of the school community (Potter & Stefkovich, 2009).

Principals and other school officials are responsible for establishing policy and rules related to the FERPA. For example, they determine "who, other than a parent or eligible adult student, has access to educational records; when a legitimate interest in reviewing those records exists, and what directory information will be made available without parental consent" (Clark, 2001, p. 40). The following specific suggestions for principals are offered by Shoop (2008):

- Explain to parents and eligible students (those 18 or older) their rights under FERPA. Such explanation must be provided annually.
- Maintain accurate records that describe all examinations of student files and provide information stating why the file was examined.
- All corrections or adjustments to student records should be dated and initialed by the person making the changes.
- Students and parents should be permitted to add materials to the record.
- Disciplinary information placed in a student record should describe the infraction, including time, place, witnesses, and other pertinent information.
- Confidential information contained in a student's data file should not be discussed with third parties.
- Student records should be kept in a safe and secure place and never removed from the school without proper authorization.

According to Essex (2004), principals and other school officials are vulnerable to legal problems for acts of omission and commission. The following are the acts of omission:

- Failing to inform parents, guardians, or eligible students of their FERPA rights annually

- Failing to provide parents, guardians, or eligible students opportunities to inspect and challenge the accuracy of information contained in the student's file
- Failing to secure and safeguard confidential records
- Failing to provide parents, guardians, or eligible students notice of a court-ordered subpoena before releasing all or part of a student's confidential records
- Failing to warn authorized third parties (a) that personally identifiable information disclosed cannot be released to any other party without proper consent, (b) that released information must be destroyed when it is no longer needed for the purpose for which it was disclosed, and (c) that non-compliance results in the third party being denied identifiable information from educational records for at least a 5-year period
- Failing to inform school employees of the law of libel and slander in relation to FERPA

The following are the acts of commission:

- Allowing persons to view student files when no legitimate educational interest is involved
- Sharing confidential information with others who have no legitimate need of such information
- Making categorical statements that unjustly stigmatize students (e.g., placing a statement in a student's file indicating that the student is unstable or dishonest)
- Communicating confidential information to authorized persons or agencies based on opinion rather than fact (e.g., making a reckless statement about a student that is not supported by evidence in the student's file)

Whereas FERPA is pertinent to all students, IDEA focuses on students with disabilities. Section 504 of the Rehabilitation Act of 1973 does not have provisions regarding records confidentiality and access; however, school districts must have a 504 policy stipulating that parents must have an opportunity to examine relevant records and detailing how this can be done. According to Clark (2001) FERPA influenced IDEA regarding "transfer of rights and protection of the collection and confidentiality of student records and their maintenance, disclosure, and destruction" (p. 42). Clark adds that, even though students covered by IDEA are included in the privacy protections of FERPA, several notable differences should be recognized.

- Transfer rights from the parents or guardian to the student at age 18 are not automatic under IDEA. However, IDEA allows a state legislature to enact a law that provides for the transfer of IDEA procedural rights to a competent student with a disability who has reached the state's legal age of majority.
- IDEA requires a designated special education records custodian to ensure confidentiality.
- IDEA requires training and instruction for persons (e.g., teachers, principals, counselors, and paraprofessionals) who collect or use personally identifiable information.

Though FERPA does not afford private citizens a private right to legal action (i.e., parties may not sue for damages if school officials violate the law), this does not mean that principals are protected against negative consequences if they violate the law. Parents, guardians, or eligible students can file complaints with the U.S. Department of Education through the Family Policy Compliance Office (Daggett & Huefner, 2001). This agency investigates complaints, and works with the parties to provide a remedy if the complaints are found to be valid. If a school is found to be in non-compliance, a principal may be blamed or implicated. In addition, most states have statutes that protect privacy rights and provide a right to legal recourse—and these state laws can result and have resulted in suits being filed against districts and schools (Stuart, 2005).

In summary, principals need to be fully aware of three types of restrictions pertaining to student records: federal law, state law, and district policy. Building on this framework, they should add a fourth dimension—school rules and regulations. As shown in Figure 9.1, these four sets of control criteria determine how school personnel develop, maintain, and store student records.

## Data Management

Over the past few years, considerable attention has been given to the data collection and data-based decision-making requirements in the No Child Left Behind Act

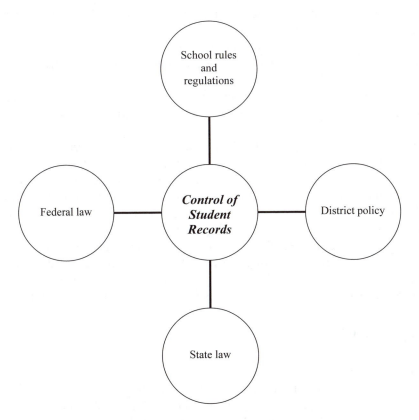

*Figure 9.1* Controls and Restrictions for Managing Student Records.

(NCLB). Though schools always have acquired and maintained considerable data, the information was usually unorganized and inaccessible, especially to teachers. Being data rich but information poor partly explains why accumulated data often were not used to inform important decisions. Lamenting this fact, Carroll and Carroll (2002) noted that, at best, decision making in schools prior to NCLB was based on raw data from a single source (e.g., from a test administered by a teacher) and at worst on hunches and untested hypotheses. Unmistakably, NCLB was designed to change this condition. At the same time, however, NCLB has raised concerns about protecting privacy rights, especially relating to student records and, thus, about the extent to which it is congruent with FERPA and IDEA (Torres & Stefkovich, 2005). Principals not only need to understand provisions in these three federal laws pertaining to student records and data, they also need to know how schools can comply with all of them at the same time (Potter & Stefkovich, 2009).

Specifically, NCLB requires schools to have a Management Information System (MIS) that can be used effectively by educators to convert data into information and then transform information into knowledge (Petrides & Guiney, 2002). Regardless of its quality design and capacity, such a system has limited utility if it (a) cannot be used by employees who require data, (b) contains the wrong types of data, or (c) provides the right types of data in the wrong form (Kowalski, Lasley, & Mahoney, 2008). According to Sarmiento (2006), an MIS should be:

- *Timely.* Data are made available when they are needed and they are continuously updated to ensure they remain relevant.
- *Accessible.* Data can be retrieved and used by professional staff requiring them.
- *Usable.* Data provided are valid, accurate, and presented in a form that is understood by users.
- *Multidirectional.* Data are able to move downward, upward, and horizontally in a school and from the school outward to community and vice versa.

Properly structured, an MIS should provide two types of evidence that inform educators. The first is professional evidence, including theoretical knowledge (e.g., research studies and theories) and craft knowledge (e.g., collective wisdom accumulated by practitioners). This form of evidence is most readily found in professional books and journals. The second category of evidence consists of facts specific to a school. Included are data about (a) students (e.g., individual test scores, grades), (b) the community (e.g., demographic profiles), (c) the school (e.g., policy, aggregate student data), and (d) government (e.g., federal or state mandates, legal requirements). Both types of evidence inform decision making and problem solving; by integrating them, an educator enhances the probability that he or she will make an effective decision (Kowalski et al., 2008).

## STUDENT ACTIVITIES

When the topic of school activities is addressed, most persons immediately think of athletics. In fact, the range of programs under this heading is quite broad. As examples, participation in student government, student publications, clubs, plays, convocations, and band also fall into this category. Activities occur outside of regular classes and they are intended to benefit students educationally and socially. Some programs are extensions of a school's curriculum and are often called *co-curricular activities*; an example is marching band, which is typically an extension of instrumental music courses. Other programs have a less direct nexus to regular courses and they are commonly called *extracurricular activities*; athletic teams are an example.

The scope of activity programs increases as students move upward in grade levels; therefore, elementary school principals typically have the lowest level of responsibility in this area and high school principals have the highest level. The actual amount of time a principal is required to spend managing student activities depends on several variables. The most notable are the size of the school, the number and types of activity programs, and human resources. In many secondary schools, assistant principals, athletic directors, coaches, and faculty sponsors help manage many of the programs; but, even with these resources, principals usually spend a considerable amount of time attending events and dealing with problems related to activities.

The purported benefits of student participation in school activities have been discussed by myriad authors. The more commonly identified advantages have included:

- Improving participant self-esteem (Fredricks & Eccles, 2006)
- Improving participant academic performance (Black, 2002)
- Preventing students from dropping out of school (McNeal, 1995)
- Elevating student motivation to do well in school (Holloway, 2002)
- Increasing community pride and participation in schools (Kennedy, 2008)

In their analysis of research on student activities, Feldman and Matjasko (2005) concluded that program structure was an important variable affecting outcomes. They wrote:

> School-based, structured, extracurricular activity participation, in contrast to participation in unstructured activities (sometimes including school-based activities), is associated with positive adolescent developmental outcomes, namely (a) higher academic performance and attainment; (b) reduced rates of dropout; (c) lower (to a degree) rates of substance use; (d) less sexual activity among girls; (e) better psychological adjustment, including higher self-esteem, less worry regarding the future, and reduced feelings of social isolation; and (f) reduced rates of delinquent behavior, including criminal arrests and antisocial behavior. (p. 193)

In order to be effective, however, activities need to be relevant; that is, they should address needs and interests of students. Moreover, they should be planned, shaped by essential policy and rules, properly supervised by qualified personnel, and evaluated periodically to determine if and how they can be improved.

In recent years, four aspects of activity programs have been relevant for many principals:

- *Cost.* Because of limited resources, some schools now charge students a participation fee. This decision has raised a number of questions and protests, especially in relation to possibly excluding students. Voicing concerns about activity fees, Hoff and Mitchell (2007) note that waiving fees for students from lower-income families is advisable if charging activity fees is unavoidable.

- *Academic performance.* The proper balance between academics and activities has been a perennial topic of debate. Responding to what they view as a growing imbalance, some state legislatures have enacted what are commonly known as "No Pass/No Play" laws—legislation that prohibits students receiving a single failing grade from participating in extracurricular activities. Such action should be considered legally and educationally. Legally, such laws have been challenged, primarily on Fifth Amendment due process and Fourteenth Amendment equal protection grounds. Though the courts generally have found that students have the right to participate in school-sponsored activities, they have ruled that the right may be limited by a state's compelling interest. Thus, No Pass/No Play legislation has been found to be acceptable if it is rationally related to a state's legitimate interest in increasing the academic performance of its children (Burnett, 2000). Educationally, proponents argue that exclusion from activities will serve as an incentive to improve grades; opponents argue that students participating in activities do better academically than those who do not.

- *Supervision.* Finding faculty to sponsor, coach, or supervise activities can be a problem for some principals. Often teachers initially taking these assignments opt to not continue after a few years because the time commitments and problems are thought to exceed compensation. In athletics, specifically, this condition, coupled with the fact that coaching is not a separately licensed profession, has led to rule changes in many states concerning the employment of coaches. Though the changes allow principals to hire coaches who are neither licensed teachers nor school employees, they also increase the potential for lawsuits against schools and administrators (Knorr, 1996). As an example, abuses by part-time coaches who lack teaching credentials may result in charges of negligence against those who hired them and those who had responsibility to supervise them.

A school's student activities should be evaluated annually to determine if programs are meeting their goals and if programs need to be added, deleted, or modified. Overall, the school's activities should meet or exceed student needs and interests. Moreover, each program should be evaluated using the following criteria (also see Figure 9.2):

- *Statement of purpose*—identifies a program's mission and contribution to the school
- *Relevant board policy*—provides parameters for operating programs
- *Effective school rules*—provide standards for participation and conduct
- *Supervision requirements*—identify the extent to which an activity must be supervised, the qualifications of the supervisor, and the supervisor's identity (by position or name)
- *Participation level*—provides information relative to the number of students being served
- *Fiscal requirements*—identify required expenditures and anticipated revenues (e.g., admissions charges, student fees)
- *Summative assessment*—determines if an activity has met its goals and should be continued
- *Formative assessment*—determines how an activity should be improved

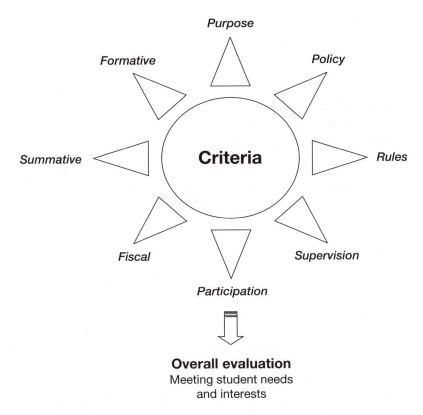

*Figure 9.2* Criteria for Evaluating Individual Activities Leading to an Overall Evaluation of School Activities.

## SUPERVISING STUDENTS OUTSIDE CLASSROOMS

Between 10 percent and 25 percent of all child and adolescent injuries occur at school, and the average award given to plaintiffs filing lawsuits against district and schools related to these injuries has been in excess of $500,000. Contrary to popular belief, most injuries occurring in and around schools do not occur in athletics, laboratories, or shop classes. Rather, most take place during recess, in physical education, and on school vehicles (Barrios, Jones, & Gallagher, 2007). Given these statistics, providing proper supervision to ensure student health and safety is an imperative for principals.

### Playgrounds and Athletic Fields

Schools should have safety plans that identify potential hazards, especially in areas where injuries are most likely to occur. Kaldahl and Blair (2005) recommend the following steps:

- Record and validate the locations and causes of injuries
- Evaluate policy, rules, and regulations pertinent to common injuries (e.g., playground rules and district policy concerning using school property outside the regular school day)

- Conduct an analysis of the entire school site and identify potential hazards
- Inspect hazardous areas periodically to determine if they are being controlled properly

Outcomes of litigation against districts and schools not only call for principals and other school officials to act responsibly; they also demonstrate the importance of ensuring that conditions contributing to accidents are identified and rectified. As an example, plaintiffs seeking damages due to injury occurring during recess as a result of faulty playground equipment often have successfully sued school officials (Young, 2004). Accordingly, principals should ensure both that outdoor areas on a school campus have appropriate and safe equipment and surfaces and that these areas are subject to appropriate inspections, maintenance, and supervision (O'Neill, 2000).

## Pupil Transportation

At more than a few schools, the time periods during which students arrive at and depart from school are hectic. The reasons for the condition vary, but several problems are often contributing factors:

- *Poorly designed ingress and egress routes.* Some schools are located in congested areas and vehicles, including school buses, find it difficult to enter and leave school property. Stalled traffic presents a safety concern and frustrates persons affected by it.
- *Poorly designed or inadequate loading and unloading areas.* Once buses and automobiles enter school property, they should park in safe areas where students can leave the vehicles. Inadequate safe parking increases the need for supervision and elevate the probability of accidents.
- *Inadequate supervision.* The quantity and quality of supervision required vary depending on grade levels. As an example, elementary school students, especially those in the primary grades, often need supervision so that they go to the correct room or the correct bus in a timely manner. In a high school, supervision of student parking lots may be an issue.

While students are on school property, principals and other staff members have a responsibility to take reasonable measures to protect their safety. Though direct supervision by school personnel during the periods when students wait for and ride buses is not practical, principals nevertheless are expected to advise bus drivers and assist them when necessary (Dawson & Sanders, 1997). Discipline problems occurring on buses do not always mirror those occurring in schools. Commenting on this point, an elementary school principal (Dillon, 2001) said, "I was always amazed to have children whom I regarded as model students show up at my door with behavior referrals from bus drivers for outrageous behavior or inappropriate language" (p. 39). This principal added that he and colleagues concur that teasing, bullying, and violence are more likely to occur on buses than in elementary schools. From a legal perspective, a principal's responsibility for students being transported to and from school is not perfectly clear. Analyzing this topic, Zirkel (2007) provided the following insights:

- School buses are a fertile area of negligence liability.
- Off-campus student injury or death can occur before the bus arrives (e.g., vehicular accidents at poorly located pickup locations), during the bus trip (e.g., assaults by other students or collisions with other vehicles), or after the drop-off (e.g., the school bus accidentally strikes a student).
- The applicable statutory and common law, including governmental immunity, also varies widely.
- A principal cannot leave the safety of students entirely to the school bus driver and cannot leave knowledge of the applicable law entirely to the district lawyer. Preventing student injuries is part of the principal's professional responsibility. (p. 13)

Clearly, principals cannot prevent all disruptive behavior and accidents, but they can provide structure that reduces the number of incidents. To do this, they must first and foremost let others know that they are focused on pupil transportation issues and will intervene to help bus drivers and to ensure student safety during arrival and departure times (George, 1995). Moreover, they must have a basic understanding of the issues involved. The following are points of information that should be known:

- A principal's responsibility for aspects of pupil transportation as specified in law and policy
- The recent history (at least past 3 years) of discipline problems and accidents
- Effective measures taken at schools that face similar conditions
- Policy and rules governing student behavior on school buses and when leaving and boarding school buses
- Policies and rules governing parents bringing children to school and picking them up from school in their own vehicles
- In secondary schools, policy and rules governing students driving their own vehicles to school
- Policy and rules concerning departure from campus during the school day (e.g., allowing students to eat lunch outside the campus)

## FOOD SERVICES

Often overlooked is the fact that most principals essentially oversee the operation of a restaurant. With a few exceptions, school districts provide student lunch programs, and an increasing percentage, prompted by federal subsidies, also provide breakfast programs. In 2000, for example, more than 71,000 schools did so (Coles, 2000). Like all food service operations, schools are vulnerable to lawsuits when accidents, such as food poisoning, occur. Incidents of food-borne illness in schools increased by about 10 percent a year during the 1990s (Fitzgerald, 2002). Though the extent to which principals are directly responsible for operating a food service program varies, every one of them needs to understand the fundamental aspects of this process.

One objective of a school food service program is to provide nutritious, desirable, and reasonably priced meals. This seemingly simple goal has become increasingly difficult over time because of higher government standards and diverse consumer demands.

As examples, many parents demand that their children have an option to have regular school meals, and the number of students requiring or requesting special menus, such as vegetarians, has increased substantially (Jones, 1996). Consequently, a very large percentage of schools now offer salad bars and à la carte options in addition to their traditional lunch menu.

A second goal is to avoid risk. Risk entails vulnerability to negative situations, such as accidents and lawsuits. A small rural district in Washington, for instance, had to pay a nearly $5 million judgment to the families of eleven children who became ill after being served undercooked taco meat in an elementary school cafeteria (Cook, 2003). Districts routinely purchase insurance to transfer risk to third parties, but the cost of doing so often is affected by the quality of management provided and a school's safety record. Many schools allow community groups to use cafeterias outside the school day and, even when district policy specifically provides parameters for such use, principals incur an added responsibility (Kowalski, 2002).

Historically, school district officials have treated food services programs with a polite indifference; if a school's program did not have a serious deficit, it was left alone. As a result, long-term planning rarely was executed, and critical issues such as equipment replacement typically were ignored until they became unavoidable problems. Today, management of food services programs is more sophisticated. For example, cost controls, cost–benefit analysis, and a reinvestment of resources to fund necessary improvements are considered standard procedures (Boehrer, 1993).

The issue of supervising a food service program is especially noteworthy for principals because, in many schools, first-level management is provided by employees without formal management training—for example, a cafeteria supervisor or head cook (Anderson & Durant, 1991). Consequently, in districts that have a highly decentralized food services approach (i.e., each school operates its own program with little or no district-level supervision), principals retain substantial responsibility for overseeing the management aspects of the program. Recognizing the demands placed on principals and seeking greater uniformity of practices across schools, some districts have reduced the need for school-level management by either centralizing operations or outsourcing. In the former, food services are managed at the district level, with food often being prepared at one or more centralized sites and being delivered to schools just prior to when it is served. The latter involves contracting with a private company to operate food services.

# REFLECTIONS

In the vignette at the beginning of this chapter, Principal Zappata is challenged because she allowed teachers to insert comments about students into official records. Her motives are defensible in that she was encouraging teachers to develop and access data to inform the important decisions they made about students. However, in the realm of managing functions directly affecting students, principals usually learn quite quickly that good intentions do not prevent legal or political problems.

Studies of novice principals (e.g., Woodruff & Kowalski, 2008) often reveal a disjunction between what is foreseen and what occurs. That is, first-time principals are often surprised to learn how much time they devote to doing things they prefer to avoid—or at least to doing things they see as relatively unimportant. As you contemplate your future as a principal, keep two facts in mind. First, no matter how effective you may be as an instructional leader, your inability to manage is likely to result in serious problems. Second, learning to manage after you become a principal can be precarious because serious problems resulting from poor management can occur before you have had the time to hone your skills.

This chapter is intended to provide knowledge about several of the pertinent management functions assumed by principals. It is to be hoped that other graduate courses, such as school law, human resources management, and school finance, augment your knowledge base on these subjects and ensure that you to enter practice with adequate managerial skills.

## Knowledge-Based Questions

1   What legal restrictions must a principal follow in managing student records?
2   In what ways may NCLB conflict with FERPA and IDEA in relation to student data?
3   Many authors argue that student activities enhance overall school effectiveness. In what ways can activities have a positive effect?
4   What criteria should be used to evaluate activities? How often should they be evaluated?
5   What can a principal do to ensure that students remain safe when being transported to and from school?
6   What responsibilities are commonly assumed by a principal in relation to a food service program?

## Skill-Based Activities

1   Explain how a principal can develop and use a management information system to enhance data-based decision making without violating student privacy rights.

2   Assume you are a high school principal, and the superintendent in your district is planning to recommend a "No Pass/No Play" policy to the school board. Take a position favoring or opposing his intention and provide a rationale for your position.

3   Take a position for or against employing persons who are neither licensed teachers nor school employees as coaches. If you oppose employing such individuals, explain why. If you support employing such individuals, indicate what measures you would take to screen and supervise them.

4   Accidents on playgrounds or athletic fields resulting in student injuries frequently result in lawsuits against districts and schools. As a principal, detail what you would do to prevent accidents in these areas.

5   Assume you are an elementary school principal and the superintendent is contemplating whether to centralize food services for the district's seven elementary schools. Specifically, she is looking at preparing all the food at the district's high school and then delivering it to the elementary schools. She estimates that the centralized program would eliminate seven positions and save the school district approximately $100,000. Identify the possible advantages and disadvantages of the superintendent's plan for an elementary school.

## CHAPTER 10

# Providing a Safe School Environment

On July 1, Dr. Rosemary Sullins became principal of Calumet River High School, an institution enrolling just over 1,700 students in four grades. Previously, she had been principal of a much smaller middle school. By November 1, conflict between Dr. Sullins and the school's professional staff (including the two assistant principals) over rules and student discipline was evident.

The previous principal, Jack Hossup, had a reputation as a stern disciplinarian—a positive status in a community where both crime rates and unemployment were increasing. The school's former football coach, Principal Hossup had taken a "no nonsense" approach to dealing with students who violated school rules; and he administered punishment swiftly, even if the offenders were athletes. His self-imposed role as the school's disciplinarian made him popular both with teachers and with the assistant principals, largely because they appreciated having as little involvement as possible in carrying out this responsibility.

The staff quickly learned that Dr. Sullins had a different philosophy toward student discipline—one that she articulated to them during a mid-September meeting. Without disparaging her predecessor, she respectfully disagreed with the school's prevailing practices for at least two reasons. First, she argued that effective discipline required a school-wide approach in which all professional staff assumed some responsibility; second, she was opposed to dealing with behavior problems solely by punishing offenders. She pointed out that, in the school where she previously served as principal, punishment was always tied to remedial actions intended to prevent negative behavior from recurring.

In many high schools, assistant principals are relegated to handling student discipline; but at Calumet River, the inverse was true. One assistant was assigned to instructional programs and the other was assigned to managerial functions (e.g., facility management, cafeteria program). Principal Hossup devoted much of his time to managing student discipline and extracurricular activities. Both assistant principals liked the arrangements, and they openly opposed the new principal's intent to have them and the faculty play a more active role in managing discipline.

*Sensing resistance and not inclined to force her ideas on others, Principal Sullins attempted to convince others that the prevailing practice was counterproductive and incongruent with practices found in highly effective schools. At faculty meetings, she presented statistics for discipline patterns prior to her arrival at Calumet River. She focused most directly on figures for out-of-school suspensions. During each of the 7 years that Mr. Hossup was principal, the number of suspensions had increased. Correspondingly, the total number of reported discipline problems also had increased. Dr. Sullins pointed out that the data clearly showed that harsh and swift action by the principal had failed to curtail behavior problems—and, arguably, excluding students from school had resulted in more not fewer discipline cases.*

*Her efforts to persuade the staff to support her recommended changes for student discipline, however, were unsuccessful. Moreover, some teachers and the two assistant principals were suggesting privately that she wanted to involve others in discipline management simply because she lacked the expertise to assume the assignment.*

## INTRODUCTION

Schools not only help students learn, they have a responsibility to keep students safe. These two missions are inextricably intertwined. Affirming this point, Marzano (2003) posits that providing a safe and orderly school environment is essential to student learning. Though most educators readily agree with his position, they do not necessarily agree with how such an environment can or should be maintained. As illustrated in the opening vignette, many of the employees at Calumet River High School believe that simply excluding trouble makers from school is an effective approach.

This chapter addresses two broad dimensions of school safety. The first is student discipline. This topic is examined from both philosophical and managerial perspectives. The other topic is school crisis planning and management. In the aftermath of violent and fatal events at several schools during the 1990s, states have required schools to develop and practice crisis plans as means of making schools even more safe environments. After reading this chapter, you should be able to demonstrate the ability to do the following correctly:

- Understand differing philosophical dispositions toward student discipline, especially dissimilarities between control and cooperation approaches
- Identify positive and negative actions in relation to structuring a school discipline program
- Identify the concept of manifest determination and explain how it must be applied in schools
- Discuss the advantages and disadvantages of zero-tolerance policy and rules
- Describe a school safety audit and its value to crisis planning
- Detail the essential aspects of a school crisis plan
- Identify positive actions to ensure that the plan is understood and applied properly
- Detail how communication should be managed during and after a crisis situation

## MANAGING PUPIL CONDUCT

Principals and assistant principals devote substantial time to developing and enforcing rules of conduct for students. Standards for student discipline in a school are rooted in laws, district policy, and philosophy as shown in Figure 10.1. Federal and state laws define student rights and universally unacceptable behavior; statutes pertaining to the treatment of students with disabilities and to bringing weapons to school are examples. State policy (promulgated by state boards of education) and district policy (promulgated by local school boards) reaffirm laws and provide other guidelines for pupil conduct. Community values and beliefs are instrumental in determining how discipline is actually managed by school employees.

Generally, a school's discipline philosophy can be viewed on a continuum ranging from a cooperation disposition to a control disposition as shown in Figure 10.2. A control disposition is nested in the conviction that fear of punishments causes students to comply with rules (Jones, 1987); a cooperation disposition is nested in the conviction that students comply because they accept rules as essential to maintaining a safe and orderly school environment. The two opposing beliefs illuminate the fundamental difference between a punishment-centered approach to student discipline and a collaborative approach to student discipline (Henley, 1997).

In public schools, principals and other administrators are granted authority to develop rules and regulations to ensure that all persons comply with laws and policies. Concurrently, however, they are expected to take a positive approach toward student discipline. That is, they should forge rules and implement them in a manner that is fair, reasonable, and beneficial to student social growth. The intent in this chapter is to stress

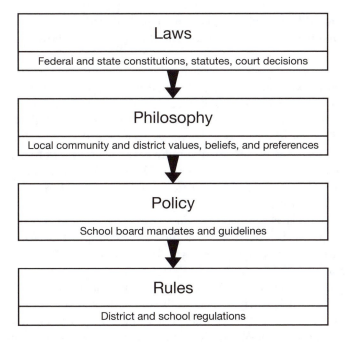

*Figure 10.1* Factors Determining Student Discipline.

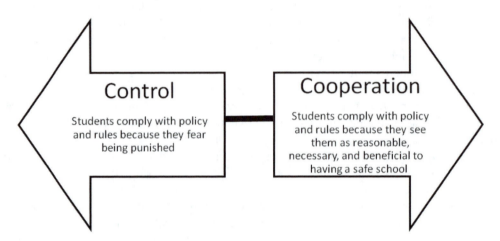

*Figure 10.2* Opposing Philosophies for Student Discipline.

the need for developing a school discipline plan grounded in an acceptable philosophy. In relation to this general task, focused attention is given to adopting rules (or regulations), student due process, disciplining special needs students, and zero-tolerance policy.

## School Discipline Plan

Every school should have a written plan for managing student conduct. The document should be tailored to a specific school and should answer the following basic questions:

- *What values and beliefs guide school employees with respect to pupil conduct?* Even though all school employees must obey laws, local policy and rules pertaining to student discipline are not identical, largely because local communities and educators do not have uniform values and beliefs about student conduct. Both the community's expectations (typically expressed by the school board) and a school's philosophy (typically shaped by professional employees) provide a framework for setting behavior standards and disciplinary action (Walker, Colvin, & Ramsey, 1995).
- *Who is responsible for enforcing laws, policy, and rules pertaining to student conduct?* Ideally, the responsibility for student social development and discipline is shared by school employees. This is because both issues are pervasive and too demanding to be handled adequately by one or two staff members (Campbell, 1999). A discipline plan should clearly identify employee responsibilities in the areas of social development and discipline.
- *What specific responsibilities are assumed exclusively by administrators?* Some laws and policies identify the principal specifically as the person responsible for managing certain aspects of student discipline. Thus, the school's disciplinary plan should clearly identify the responsibilities assumed exclusively by administrators (Campbell, 1999).

- *How do employees and students learn rules and expectations?* A principal should never take for granted that all parties will take the initiative to learn what is expected of them. Planned learning experiences (e.g., employee orientation, student convocations) should be scheduled to inform employees and students about the rules, procedures for enforcing them, and possible consequences for breaking rules (Walker et al., 1995).
- *How are discipline data collected, stored, and analyzed?* Under the No Child Left Behind Act, schools are required to maintain and report discipline-related data (Dunklee & Shoop, 2006). Principals need to determine how they meet this requirement.
- *How is the discipline program evaluated?* Principals should conduct both summative and formative evaluations of the school's discipline program to determine if it has been successful and to determine how it can be improved (Walker et al., 1995).

Students have a right to know policy, rules, and regulations that address their behavior. This information needs to be communicated to them and their parents in school *student handbooks*; but, ideally, information is provided and reinforced in other ways as well (e.g., at convocations, in classrooms, newsletters, and school Web sites). Student handbooks should be revised annually and submitted to the superintendent and ultimately to the school board for approval prior to the start of each new school year. Some schools require students (or their parents) to sign a statement attesting that they have read the handbook and understand the rules of conduct included in them.

## Establishing and Enforcing Rules

Principals establish rules to facilitate the implementation of laws and district policy. Exercising authority in this area should be coordinated with the superintendent (or designee) to ensure that school rules neither violate district policy nor conflict with laws or rules established at a higher level (e.g., by state departments of education). Rules developed by a principal should be congruent with the school's stated philosophy, mission, and vision.

When setting rules, principals should consider the extent to which the discretion of school employees will be restricted. Reiterating a typology presented earlier, Clemmer (1991) identifies four types of rules:

- *Mandatory.* These rules identify an issue requiring action and do not allow decision-maker discretion. They are intended to ensure absolute consistency; the emphasis is on following a prescribed action, not on encouraging professional judgment. Zero-tolerance policies and rules are in this category. The following regulation is an example: *Smoking is prohibited on school property and student offenders shall be suspended for 3 days.*
- *Directory.* These rules identify an issue requiring action and allow a limited level of decision-maker discretion. They are intended to promote consistency but allow decision makers to weigh contextual variables (conditions surrounding an incident). The following regulation is an example: *Smoking is prohibited on school property and student offenders shall be suspended for 3 days unless extenuating circumstances merit a lesser or more severe punishment.*

- *Discretionary*. These rules identify an issue requiring action and give the decision maker considerable discretion. The following regulation is an example: *Smoking is prohibited on school property and student offenders shall be disciplined as deemed appropriate by school officials.*
- *Proscriptive*. These rules identify an issue requiring action and give the decision maker complete discretion. The following regulation is an example: *Smoking is prohibited on school property and school personnel are expected to enforce this policy and determine if student offenders should be disciplined.*

When establishing rules, principals should weigh carefully the amount of discretion allowed by district policy. Then they need to determine the amount of discretion they actually give to school staff.

## Practical Guidelines

Because of the nexus between student discipline and academic performance, management of student behavior is a pivotal factor in school improvement. Therefore, a school's philosophy should detail underlying values and beliefs about behavior and the school's vision statement should provide an image of ideal student behavior (Kowalski, Petersen, & Fusarelli, 2007).

Research and experiences in schools provide a rich body of knowledge about effective and ineffective student discipline practices. This knowledge offers a framework for a school's discipline plan. The following are positive actions principals should embrace:

- *Focus on correcting behavior problems*. Changing negative behavior always should be a primary goal. Even when punished, students should receive counsel or remediation intended to induce behavioral changes (Skiba & Sprague, 2008).
- *Focus on positive social behavior*. In addition to eliminating problem behavior, school personnel should teach positive social behaviors, such as respecting the rights of others, self-control, and resolving conflict fairly (Yell & Rozalski, 2008).
- *Deal with problem behavior quickly*. Behavior requiring disciplinary action should be addressed immediately or at least as soon as possible. A prompt response enhances the probability that relevant information about the behavior will be reported accurately and that the student and his or her peers will perceive the importance of the matter.
- *Involve parents*. Parents need to be informed as soon as possible when disciplinary action is deemed necessary and involved in efforts to prevent the behavior from recurring (Ruder, 2006).
- *Involve teachers and other professional staff*. In effective schools, student discipline is a school-wide and shared responsibility (Horner, Horner, & Sugai, 2005). Every school employee ought to assume responsibility for modeling proper conduct and for correcting improper conduct. Teachers referring students for disciplinary action, for example, should complete an official referral form that clearly describes the nature of the behavior requiring attention and they should remain involved in the resolution of a situation.

- *Exhibit care, respect, and support for students.* Because behavior change and teaching positive social behavior are primary objectives, principals and other school employees should demonstrate that they care about students and are willing to assist them to become responsible citizens.
- *Promote self-discipline.* Self-discipline involves assuming social and moral responsibility for personal actions as opposed to controlling behavior through either punishment or extrinsic rewards (Bear & Duquette, 2008). The value of self-discipline has been made even more apparent by research (e.g., Raffaele-Mendez, 2003; Tobin, Sugai & Colvin, 1996) reporting that imposed punishment, such as out-of-school suspensions, appears to increase behavior problems rather than reducing them.
- *Model positive behavior.* Principals and other school employees need to model the behavior they expect from students (Spitalli, 2005).

Conversely, some actions commonly pursued in schools have proven to be counterproductive. The following are among the most notable:

- *Do not use academics to punish students.* Penalizing students academically (e.g., by making them write a paper or do additional homework, or lowering their grades) establishes a negative link between punishment and learning.
- *Do not punish a student in front of other students.* When punishment is necessary, the action is detailed and explained in a private meeting.
- *Do not bully students.* Corporal punishment, ridicule, threats, and similar aggressive actions rarely have a positive effect on student behavior; more likely, they symbolically suggest to students that the principal and other educators do not care about their welfare (Spitalli, 2005).
- *Do not ignore policy and rules.* Many teachers are prone to criticize principals who either ignore discipline policy and rules or apply them selectively. If you cannot support an existing policy or rule, strive to change it (Kowalski, 2006).
- *Do not confuse discipline with punishment.* Discipline, properly pursued, focuses on promoting positive behavior (e.g., citizenship and caring for others) and student cooperation; punishment focuses on negative behavior and imposed controls (Henley, 1997).
- *Do not ignore the overall consequences associated with excluding students from school.* Students who are punished by being excluded from school usually do not find other alternatives to continue learning. Though certain behaviors cannot be tolerated, long-term suspensions and expulsion should not be used freely to rid the school of behavior problems. Preventive programs and inclusive approaches to teaching positive behavior are often effective as alternatives (Skiba & Sprague, 2008).
- *Do not set unattainable standards.* Unrealistic rules often become mock rules—that is rules that are not enforced (Hanson, 2003). In addition, they fuel skepticism about the intent of school personnel to enforce rules (Thompson & Walter, 1998).

## Student Due Process Rights

Students have rights that stem from the Due Process Clause in the U.S. Constitution. The legal clause serves several purposes including guaranteeing fairness and producing more accurate results. The requirement has two dimensions: substantive due process and procedural due process. The former generally refers to the reason or cause why school officials seek to take disciplinary action that may deprive a student of liberty or a property right and the reasonableness of such action. The latter refers to the process that must be followed before the proposed punishment can be imposed (Yell & Rozalski, 2008). Procedural due process includes notifying the individual of infraction and intended punishments, an opportunity to have a hearing, and an opportunity to appeal disciplinary decisions. Legal decisions involving student discipline have established that students have a property right to an education; and this right may not be taken away without due process—even for suspensions that cover a few days (Seyfarth, 1999).

Under due process, students are entitled to the following:

- Receiving a timely notice of the reasons for the recommended discipline
- Having opportunities to prepare and present a defense
- Being represented by legal counsel
- Having a fair and impartial hearing
- Having opportunities to examine witnesses and present evidence
- Receiving an impartial and fair decision
- Having an opportunity to appeal a decision

## Students with Disabilities

Principals must be especially cautious when disciplining students with disabilities. A student with a disability is defined by eligibility criteria of state regulations for implementing the Individuals with Disabilities Education Act (IDEA) as amended, or as a person with a qualifying disability for the purpose of Title II of the Americans with Disabilities Act or Section 504 of the Rehabilitation Act. A student in this category may not be suspended or otherwise excluded from school for more than 10 days if his or her individualized education program (IEP) team determines that a violation of law, policy, or rules is related to the diagnosed disability. A manifest determination must be conducted before the long-term suspension is imposed. In making this determination, the student's IEP team must review relevant evidence and then determine if the infraction in question was (a) a manifestation of the student's disability, (b) caused by or had a direct and substantial relationship to the student's disability, or (c) the direct result of the local educational agency's failure to implement the student's IEP (Amberger & Shoop, 2006). If any of these conditions are found to be valid, the student may not be expelled or suspended for more than 10 days.

Excluding a student with a disability for a shorter period of time is another matter. Addressing shorter-term suspensions, Yell and Rozalski (2008) wrote:

> When students with disabilities violate a school's code of student conduct, school officials may unilaterally suspend the students or place them in an alternative educational program for up to 10 school days, to the same extent that such sanctions are used with students without disabilities. In such situations, school officials must provide students their due process rights. (p. 12)

Because of the complexity of manifest determination, principals need to be fully aware of laws and district policy pertinent to this issue. In addition, they need to ensure that proper procedures are in place to deal with such matters when they occur.

## Zero Tolerance

After 1990, zero-tolerance policy and rules emerged as a critical topic for administrators, both because they restricted discretion and because they raised legal concerns. The concept mandates predetermined consequences, usually severe and punitive, for a serious offense regardless of mitigating circumstances, or situational context. Arguably, the most extensive analysis of zero tolerance and exclusionary policy was conducted by the American Psychological Association (APA) Zero Tolerance Task Force (2008). Though the task force admitted that evidence was insufficient "to evaluate the impact of zero tolerance policy and practices on student behavior and school climate" (p. 857), the group emphasized that the "overwhelming majority of findings from the available research on zero tolerance and exclusionary discipline tend to contradict the assumptions of that philosophy" (p. 857). As an example, the report concludes that simply excluding students from school had little or no effect on changing unacceptable behavior. Equally notably, excluding students without providing remediation appears to have had long-term negative consequences for both students affected and society. Moreover, data suggest that not only did suspensions and expulsions fail to deter inappropriate behavior but the frequency of reported discipline problems in a school often increased as the number of exclusions increased. Last, the report notes zero-tolerance policy and rules have affected students of color and students with disabilities disproportionately—though the reasons for this outcome have not been sufficiently analyzed.

Zero tolerance is concurrently an asset and a liability for principals. On the one hand, they are responsible for maintaining a safe school environment; and excluding students who present a danger to others or who continuously disrupt the education process is sometimes necessary. On the other hand, this concept prevents administrators, counselors, and teachers from exercising professional judgment when managing student conduct. Likewise, students are sometimes excluded from school without being provided alternatives for continuing their education and without remediation that may be needed to alter unacceptable behavior (Peterson, 2005). Consequently, principals are expected to maintain a delicate balance between school safety and the rights and needs of individual students (Essex, 2000).

## SCHOOL CRISIS PLANNING AND MANAGEMENT

In the aftermath of a series of tragic shootings on school campuses during the late 1990s, states have required districts and schools to develop school crisis plans. *Merriam-Webster's Collegiate Dictionary* (1993) defines *crisis* as a "turning point for better or worse," as a "decisive moment" or "crucial time," and goes on to reveal that crisis is a "situation that has reached a critical phase." Crises in schools range in scope and intensity. As examples, they can affect only one person or an entire community; they can occur before, during, or after school; and they can occur on or off campus as is the case with a bus accident (U.S.

Department of Education, 2003). Situations that qualify as a school crisis include violent acts, natural disasters (e.g., fires, tornadoes, hurricanes, snow storms, and earthquakes), accidental deaths, suicide, chemical spills, accidents, structural failures in the facility (e.g., collapsed wall or roof), fire, and acts of terrorism. The extent to which any of these negatively affect a school depends in part on the quantity and quality of management provided by principals and other school staff members (Fink, 1986).

## Developing a School Crisis Management Plan

A school crisis management plan (SCMP) should be conceived as a living document that is updated and improved periodically (Clarksean & Pelton, 2002). The U.S. Department of Education (2003) proposes a four-stage process that covers both planning objectives and process:

- *Prevention and mitigation*. This stage has three parts: a safety audit of the school; identification of local resources/agencies (and their plans); and analysis of traffic patterns that may be pertinent to emergencies. In addition, administrators attempt to coordinate information with local businesses and government agencies.
- *Preparedness*. In this phase, administrators develop site plans so that they are available to first responders. This information includes items such as floor plans, building elevations, information about entry ways, windows, utilities, and communication/ alarm systems, and control panels. Plans for communicating during a crisis and for conducting drills are also addressed at this phase.
- *Response*. This phase addresses issues such as locating and equipping a command center, identifying evacuation routes, a strategy for disseminating crisis planning information to relevant stakeholders, determining how reporters, parents, and spectators will be managed, and security of the school site during a crisis.
- *Recovery*. This phase details strategies for returning the school to normal operations. Provisions for aftercare services by psychologists, counselors, and other health providers need to be included.

The overall task of preparing to deal with possible crises is discussed here in relation to five functions: creating a school crisis team, conducting a school safety and security audit, developing an SCMP, preparing employees to implement the plan, and evaluating the plan. The linear associations among these functions are shown in Figure 10.3 and the specific nature of each is provided in the following sections.

### Creating a School Crisis Team

Crisis planning and management are time-consuming and difficult tasks, and principals should not attempt to do them alone. The first step in the process is creating a school crisis team "responsible for developing a plan and coordinating activities during an actual crisis" (Quinn, 2002, p. 6). Kowalski (2008) suggests that principals appoint persons who meet the following criteria:

*Figure 10.3* Linear Approach for Developing a School Crisis Management Plan (SCMP).

- They possess effective communication skills
- They are interested in serving on the committee and are available to do so
- They possess knowledge pertinent to planning
- They possess knowledge pertinent to crisis management

Almost always, the principal will chair the committee, and he or she certainly should if the school does not employ an assistant principal. Other persons to be considered as committee members include assistant principals, security personnel, custodians, the school nurse, counselors, a coach or athletic trainer, and several teachers (Quinn, 2002).

After the committee is construed, the chair should assign members to the following specific roles:

- *Vice-chair.* This person assists the chair and conducts the chair's responsibilities when necessary. An assistant principal is usually appointed to this role; but, if such a person is unavailable, a responsible individual willing and able to provide essential leadership and management can be appointed.
- *First responder coordinator.* This person meets all first responder personnel when they arrive at the school during a crisis. He or she provides first responders with pertinent data (e.g., provides maps, floor plans), and directs them to the crisis area.
- *First-aid responders.* These persons must have first-aid training. They render emergency medical assistance until emergency personnel arrive. If no such person is employed in a school, the principal should select one willing to receive the necessary training.
- *Sweep team coordinators.* These persons are the last ones out of the building when an evacuation is ordered. They check hallways, restrooms, and other non-classroom areas to determine if all persons have left the facility and to see if suspicious items (e.g., unusual-looking packages) are in the building.
- *Communication coordinator.* Ideally, one person is designated to coordinate all communication during a crisis. This person works directly with the principal and the school district's communication coordinator (or superintendent). In smaller schools, the principal often assumes this role.
- *Staff liaison.* This person communicates with school employees about the committee's activities and seeks concerns that need to be shared with the entire committee.
- *Student liaison.* This person performs the same duties as the staff liaison but his or her target audience is the student body.

- *Parent liaison*. This person performs the same duties as other liaisons but his or her target audience is parents.

In addition to its regular meetings, a school crisis team should conduct at least one open forum regarding crisis planning each year allowing stakeholders an opportunity to voice concerns or offer suggestions for improving crisis management. The committee needs to maintain minutes and other records of their activities.

## Conducting a School Safety and Security Audit

A safety and security audit provides information about existing conditions that constitute vulnerabilities and risks (Trump, 1998). According to Gillens (2005) an audit addresses the following issues:

- Pertinent policy, rules, and regulations to determine if they are sufficiently comprehensive and adequate
- Infrastructure and assets to determine if they provide sufficient protective measures
- Infrastructure continuity and contingency planning to determine if they provide sufficient protection against major disruptions to normal operations
- Security systems and controls to determine if they provide a sufficient first line of defense

Trump (1998) also recommends two other assessments: discipline data, especially those related to incidents involving crimes, and pertinent safety data obtained from employees through surveys or interviews.

Several states have developed safety audit programs that are made available to school districts (Brickman, Jones, & Groom, 2004). Trump (1998) cautions, however, that the use of these checklists or prepackaged programs is not foolproof. As examples, the instruments may not include all relevant subjects or they may be used by unqualified individuals unable to make necessary assessment decisions.

The reason why the safety and security audit needs to be completed prior to drafting an SCMP is that the outcomes of this process are essential to effective planning (Rettig, 1999). The audit report also has symbolic significance because it demonstrates to employees, students, and the public that school officials are acting responsibly by using evidence to develop an SCMP (Kowalski, 2008).

## Developing an SCMP

At the point that a school crisis committee begins to develop an SCMP, it should have (a) identified potential crisis situations, (b) described the characteristics of each potential crisis, and (c) assigned members of the crisis team to specific roles. Even if the principal does not chair the school crisis committee, he or she should play an active part in facilitating the development of this document (Duke, 2002). In particular, a principal must ensure a collaborative environment in which the school crisis committee is able to work with representatives of various government agencies and services such as police departments and local hospitals (Thompson, 2004).

Often, it is tempting to simply copy an SCMP that has been developed elsewhere because doing so would save a great deal of time. But, as Trump (1998) warns, a plan is unlikely to be effective unless it is written to meet a school's specific needs that have been validated through a safety audit.

The U.S. Department of Education (2003) recommends the following activities for developing an SCMP:

- Identify and involve all relevant stakeholders who are concerned about safety and security and likely to be involved if a crisis occurs
- Consider all existing plans and information including those developed by first responders (e.g., local fire department and police department)
- Identify the types of crises that need to be anticipated
- Define roles and responsibilities that have been assigned to school personnel and to other agencies
- Develop communication processes and explain how they should be deployed to exchange information with stakeholders
- Identify necessary equipment and supplies and measures necessary to obtain them
- Identify immediate crisis responses, such as lockdowns, evacuation, and relocation
- Collect maps, floor plans, and other pertinent facility-site information
- Identify measures to account for students during a crisis and to subsequently release them to their parents

Trump (1998) suggests the following additional actions related to developing the SCMP:

- Identify an area of the school that will be the command center during a crisis. When selecting this area, the planners should consider the area's security, accessibility, size, and appropriateness to accommodate the material that must be stored there.
- Appoint alternates to assume responsibilities for key roles in the event that one or more committee members are absent during an actual crisis.
- Determine the role and responsibilities for school employees who are not members of the school crisis committee.
- Establish emergency codes for communicating during a crisis (e.g., a code that instructs staff to lock down the school).
- Make sure backup equipment is available to conduct communication.

Managing the aftermath of a crisis is probably the most ignored element of a school plan. Once the crisis is under control, licensed mental health workers, counselors, social workers, and clergy may be able to make important contributions. Aftercare needs depend on the nature of the crisis; therefore, contingencies for dealing with the aftermath of a crisis should be included in the plan.

## Implementing the SCMP

The initial implementation aspect involves communicating the plan to stakeholders, especially to school employees who must directly follow it. Once informed, a principal conducts periodic simulations to ensure that the plan is effective and being interpreted correctly (Smiar, 1992). Principals who have had firsthand experience with a crisis (e.g., Baker, 2005) also emphasize that it is essential to determine if school employees have the requisite skills to carry out the plan. Crisis plans should be revised annually; therefore, at least one practice drill needs to be conducted each time the plan is altered.

### Evaluating the SCMP

The SCMP should be treated as a living document; that is, it is revised periodically as conditions warrant. The evaluation serves two purposes: to determine if the plan is meeting its stated objectives and to determine how the plan can be improved. With respect to the latter goal, an annual safety and security audit is recommended. This inspection identifies (a) new concerns, (b) continuing concerns, and (c) resolved concerns. As part of the evaluation process, administrators should have legal counsel review the SCMP for liability and privacy issues (Jones & Paterson, 1992).

## Communicating During a Crisis

The manner in which school personnel respond to a crisis puts a human face on the institution (Rollo & Zdziarski, 2007). Administrators who have experienced a school crisis have learned that reporters and parents arrive at the school quickly. In this information age, there is little lag time between an incident and public disclosure. The noted school safety expert Kenneth Trump identifies communication as a

> thorn in the side of school officials in a crisis situation. Relevant problems include the mechanical aspects of communication, such as overloading of telephone systems, having non-functioning public address systems, or having too few or poor quality two-way radios. Emergency notification of parents, internal staff communications, and media aspects of communication often represent the "crisis after the crisis" for school leaders. (Kowalski, 2005, p. 48)

Therefore, principals should consider appropriate communication practices and integrate them into the SCMP.

The following facets of communication need to be included in the SCMP:

- *A communication plan.* Ideally, school districts have coordinated district and individual school communication plans detailing how communication is to be carried out during and after a crisis.
- *Designated spokesperson(s).* Designating a district spokesperson to communicate during a crisis is considered the ideal because this option reduces the likelihood of conflicting messages reaching the public. In larger districts, however, it may be more practical to have a district coordinator and a spokesperson in each school. Spokespersons need to be knowledgeable of schools, knowledgeable of and comfortable with the media, credible, confident, calm, and good communicators (Kowalski, 2002).
- *Identified key stakeholders.* For each potential crisis listed in the SCMP, key stakeholders should be identified. For elementary and secondary schools, these audiences typically

include government agencies (e.g., police, fire, and other emergency services), school district administration (e.g., the superintendent, school board members), school employees, students, parents, other community members, and the media.

- *Anticipated difficult questions.* The principal, communication director, and other members of the school crisis team should identify possible difficult questions they are likely to be asked during a crisis. By doing this, they are better prepared to answer questions directly.
- *Policy covering employee and student communication.* Reporters usually seek interviews with employees and students who remain on the school campus. District policy and school rules should instruct both groups how to respond to such requests. Typically, they are advised to direct the reporters to the district's official spokesperson.
- *Necessary equipment and supplies.* There are two levels of equipment and supplies for communicating during a crisis: items that are part of the normal school environment and used for daily operations, and items reserved for use during a crisis. Examples in the former category are telephones, internal communication systems, fax machines, and alarm systems. Examples in the latter category are a bull horn, two-way radios, and a "hot line" that is activated allowing parents or other parties to contact school officials.
- *A database containing pertinent information.* As an example, a fact sheet should contain statistical information about the district and individual schools—data that are useful to first responders and reporters.
- *Communication pathways (protocols).* Phone or e-mail trees should be established in order to reach the community and especially parents (U.S. Department of Education, 2003).

Typically, voice commands are the best and most efficient way to notify building occupants that a crisis has occurred or may occur. Codes, such as the following ones, inform employees of the nature of the crisis and direct them to take prescribed actions.

- Code yellow: classroom lockdown; an unauthorized person is in the building
- Code blue: a catastrophic medical event is occurring in the building
- Code red: a weather-related event is imminent; move to your assigned safe area
- Code purple: evacuate the building and proceed to a designated student holding area
- Code green: general all clear; return to your classroom

After school employees are notified of a crisis situation, measures need to be taken to communicate with parents and the media. At this phase, principals must know what to do and what to avoid. The following are things they should do:

- Get as many facts as possible before communicating with stakeholders
- Inform student families of the actions being taken
- Use consistent terminology that can be understood by stakeholders (U.S. Department of Education, 2003)
- Be open and honest when communicating (Warner, 1994)
- Develop messages you want the public to receive and be consistent in delivering them
- Activate the crisis hotline so stakeholders can contact school officials

- Communicate what is being done to deal with the situation
- Issue press releases when appropriate (Kowalski, 2008)
- Keep school staff informed, especially those assigned to manage students (Heath & Sheen, 2005)
- Maintain a log of media inquiries, responses, and press releases (U.S. Department of Education, 2003)
- Respond to rumors immediately

The following are things they should not do:

- Do not answer hypothetical questions
- Do not disclose the names of students and employees unless legal approval to do so has been granted (Fiore, 2002)
- Do not be evasive when contacted by the media
- Never respond to a question by answering, "no comment"
- Never get angry when asked questions

Media coverage does not end when a crisis is brought under control. Anticipate that reporters will analyze causes, critique management responses, and then ask questions about both. Thus, according to the U.S. Department of Education (2003), principals should be prepared to discuss the following issues:

- What had been done to prevent the crisis and why the preventive measures were not successful
- What was done to manage the crisis once it occurred
- What effects the crisis had on students and employees and what is being done to deal with those consequences
- What was done to bring the school back to normal operation
- What postcrisis procedures and aftercare services were available and deployed
- What forms of debriefings were provided for employees, students, and parents
- What school officials have done to analyze the cause of the crisis
- What lessons were learned from having experienced the crisis
- What measures are being taken to ensure that the crisis will not recur or to reduce its effects if unavoidable

## REFLECTIONS

Maintaining a safe school environment is one of a principal's most important and demanding assignments. Some aspects of this responsibility are embedded in managerial responsibilities discussed previously. As an example, ensuring that the school facility is clean and free from environmental hazards is an aspect of safety that falls under facility management. The purpose of this chapter is to examine two of the most comprehensive and difficult aspects of school safety: managing student conduct and managing crisis situations.

You should consider the content of this chapter in relation to your experiences in schools. What type of discipline programs have you encountered? Is your school prepared to manage a crisis situation? By interfacing the knowledge provided in this chapter with the realities of your practice as an educator, you are likely to develop a deeper understanding of key concepts.

### Knowledge-Based Questions

1   From a philosophical perspective, what is a "control" disposition toward managing student conduct?
2   How does a control disposition differ from a cooperation disposition?
3   What is manifest determination?
4   What is a zero-tolerance approach to student discipline?
5   What are the primary underlying assumptions of zero tolerance?
6   What is student due process?
7   How may rules affect the extent to which educators can exercise discretion in managing pupil conduct?
8   In a crisis situation, who are first responders? Why should first responders be familiar with a school's crisis plan?
9   What is a school safety audit? At what point in crisis planning should the audit be completed?
10   What should a principal do to ensure that staff and students know the crisis plan and are able to implement it?

## Skill-Based Activities

1   Obtain a copy of the crisis plan for a school, preferably the one in which you work. Identify its strengths and weaknesses.

2   Identify the advantages and disadvantages of zero-tolerance policy and rules.

3   Obtain a student handbook for a school, preferably the one in which you work. Evaluate the quality of the publication with respect to detailing policy and rules for student conduct.

4   Assume you are a principal who has been invited to speak to a local service club on the topic of student discipline. Outline what you would tell the group about the appropriate roles for teachers and families in regulating pupil conduct.

5   Develop a list of qualifications you would use as a principal to appoint persons to the school crisis team.

# PART IV

# Vital Aspects of Practice

## CHAPTER 11

# Problem Solving and Decision Making

*Joe Stajen has been principal of Walker Middle School for 11 years, and previously he was a teacher in the district for 14 years. Last year, his close friend and the district superintendent, Bob Quince, retired. Mr. Quince's departure was prompted by criticism from parents who were alarmed by steadily declining student test scores in every school in the district. Mr. Stajen and the other principals felt that the former superintendent was made a scapegoat for problems that were beyond the control of administrators and teachers. They also believed that the arrival of a new superintendent would dampen public criticism, at least for a couple of years.*

*The school board replaced Mr. Quince with Dr. Juanita Jones—a veteran educator who had little in common with her predecessor. Though she knew little about the Walker district when she accepted the position, she was aware of the declining student test scores and the mounting public criticism that they had spawned. Moreover, the school board bluntly informed her during her interviews that they expected the next superintendent to be a "visionary change agent."*

*Two weeks after officially assuming her new position, Superintendent Jones spent 2 days with the administrative staff at a planning retreat. On the first day, she informed the group that, prior to moving to Walker, she had examined the district's state report cards, read all of the minutes for the previous year for both school board and administrative staff meetings, and had telephone conversations with several community leaders who had been recommended to her by the board president. She then shared three observations regarding the analysis she had completed.*

- *Not only had scores on the state achievement tests declined for 5 consecutive years, the year-to-year rate of decline had accelerated.*

- *The administrative staff, led by the previous superintendent, repeatedly took the position that the underlying problem in the district was declining social and economic community conditions, not the quality of instruction. Hence, no effort was made to engage in systematic school improvement.*
- *Though never publicly disclosed by school board members, the board actually had urged Mr. Quince to develop a school-improvement strategic plan. After he failed to do so for 3 consecutive years, he was asked to resign or face dismissal.*

*Superintendent Jones acknowledged that social and economic factors were relevant, but she took the position that school personnel had to make successful interventions to counteract them. She then said that she was initiating an aggressive plan to improve school performance in the district and that the details for the first stage would be presented to them the next day. Most of the administrators, especially those who were anticipating a few years of political tranquility, were surprised by their new superintendent's candor. And though they disagreed with findings of fact, none took exception with them.*

*The next morning, Superintendent Jones unveiled the first stage of her district improvement plan. It required each principal to develop a school-based report that (a) explained test scores for the past 5 years in a manner that would be understood by stakeholders, (b) identified possible reasons for extended and accelerated test score declines, and (c) identified alternative actions that could be considered in relation to reversing the trend. Further, principals had to work collaboratively with staff to develop the reports and the documents had to be submitted to her by end of the first semester.*

*Again, the administrators were stunned; but this time, Principal Stajen, acting as the self-appointed spokesperson for the principals, responded.*

*"First, many of us do not agree with the analysis you shared yesterday. Regardless of what the minutes may contain, we spent a great deal of time in our administrative meetings discussing the test score issue. All of us were in agreement then and continue to believe now that the primary problem is outside of schools—and we understand that parents and politicians don't like to hear this. In my opinion, what you're asking us to do is problematic for three reasons. First, I and my fellow principals spend about 10 hours a day at school; and, despite such a long work day, we can't get everything done. If we do these reports, who is going to do our work? There's no way we can continue to meet our responsibilities and write the reports. Second, these reports are very likely to reveal that Mr. Quince was right about this matter all along. Telling the public that they are being developed may only raise false hopes. Last, if the reports are necessary, why are district administrators not writing them? You and the two assistant superintendents are supposed to be the experts on district improvement."*

*Staring at Principal Stajen, Dr. Jones replied, "The problem of declining school performance is our problem, and we will address it together. Simply blaming the community and taking the position that school personnel can do nothing to ameliorate the situation is no longer acceptable. My directive about the reports is non-negotiable. You will do them; you will do them collaboratively; and you will be held accountable for the product."*

## INTRODUCTION

Tensions surrounding demands for school improvement magnify the reality that contemporary principals are expected to lead and manage. More specifically, principals are being required to diagnose problems in their schools and to make recommendations or final decisions about what should be done to address them. For many veteran principals, changes in role expectations have produced conflict and anxiety—a condition illustrated by reactions of the middle school principal in the vignette about the Walker school district.

This chapter addresses problem solving and decision making from the principal's perspective. Though the two responsibilities are different, they are intertwined. Problem solving, the broader task, involves a series of decisions. Thus, competent decision making is essential to competent problem solving. After reading this chapter, you should be able to do the following accurately:

- Identify and describe the common stages of problem solving
- Engage in defining (or framing) problems that occur in schools
- Identify factors that can deter problem solving
- Explain the relationship between problem solving and decision making
- Describe rational approaches to decision making and their underlying assumptions
- Differentiate between ideal and satisfactory decisions
- Describe the advantages and disadvantages of group decision making in schools

## PROBLEM SOLVING AND THE PRINCIPAL

A principal's work is surrounded by possible and actual problems. Some are not especially consequential and demanding. Others, however, are quite important because they may lead to negative end results for the school, staff, students, or principal. In all professions, the most proficient practitioners are those able to deal with these difficult and atypical dilemmas, quandaries that usually defy textbook solutions (Schön, 1987).

Though a variety of approaches can be applied to problem solving, linear paradigms are easier to pursue because they provide a sequential path that is easier to follow. The problem-solving model proposed here has five stages and is illustrated in Figure 11.1. In the context of contemporary practice, problems are addressed collaboratively by administrators, teachers, and others. References in this chapter to the principal's responsibilities in problem solving are not intended to imply that he or she should act alone. Often, a school-improvement committee involving the principal makes the required critical decisions.

### Comprehension Stage

A problem definition (or frame) is based on your assumptions and attitudes concerning a situation requiring attention. As a principal, how you frame a problem determines how you deal with it; as examples, it influences criteria for managing the situation, a preferred solution, and the constituent decisions you make in dealing with the situation. If your

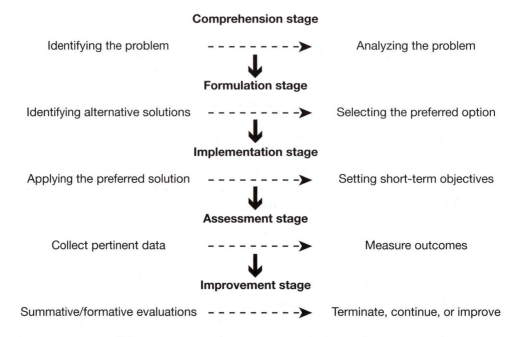

*Figure 11.1* Linear Model for Problem Solving.

definition is narrow, your response is apt to be limited; if your definition is inaccurate, your response is apt to be ineffective and possibly aggravating.

Though principals quickly learn that managing serious problems is difficult and time-consuming, many do not understand how problem framing helps or hinders their responses to these situations. As a result, the manner in which they have approached problems has not been the same. Behavioral dissimilarities are largely explained by the following realities:

- Principals differ in their ability to frame problems (e.g., some lack requisite knowledge or skills).
- Principals differ in their willingness to frame problems (e.g., some prefer to react intuitively or routinely).
- Principals do not have identical values and experiences; therefore, they often interpret contextual variables (conditions surrounding the situation) and other evidence differently (Kowalski, 2008; Kowalski, Lasley, & Mahoney, 2008).

Thus, not all principals define difficult problems correctly and sufficiently.

Cognitive psychologists focus on three aspects of a problem as illustrated in Figure 11.2. They are (a) a current state, (b) a desired state, and (c) the absence of a direct obvious way to eliminate a gap between the current and desired state (Mayer, 1983). For example, assume that a school currently has only 60 percent of its students scoring at or above grade level in mathematics. The state benchmark is 90 percent; however, the principal and staff are unsure what they should do to reach this level. According to Reitman (1965), there are four possible combinations of current and desired states of knowledge:

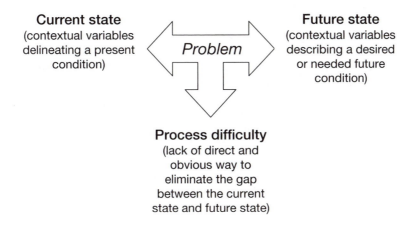

*Figure 11.2*  Basic Elements of a Problem.

- *A well-defined current state; a well-defined desired state.* For example, a principal knows the current level of student performance and the state benchmark.
- *A well-defined current state; a poorly defined desired state.* For example, a principal knows the current level of student performance but does not know the state benchmark.
- *A poorly defined current state; a well-defined goal.* For example, the principal does not know the current level of performance but knows the state benchmark.
- *A poorly defined current state; a poorly defined goal.* For example, the principal knows neither the current level of performance nor the state benchmark.

Before the principal could frame the problem correctly, both the current and desired states must be known. If this knowledge is missing, he or she must acquire it. At that point, some principals may act intuitively and define the problem as the gap between the current and desired state. In fact, however, the problem is likely to be absence of a clear path to reducing and eventually eliminating the gap. That is, a problem exists when something is needed or wanted but a principal is unsure what to do in order to attain it (Reys, Lindquist, Lambdin, Smith, & Suydam, 2003).

After a problem is framed, the principal needs to analyze it. This process adds vital information making it more probable that appropriate actions will be considered, evaluated, and selected. According to Kowalski et al. (2008), analysis entails determining:

- The seriousness of the problem (e.g., possible consequences of not meeting the accepted benchmark)
- Possible causes (e.g., poor textbooks, inadequate instruction)
- Manageable components (e.g., incremental, plausible interventions)

## Formulation Stage

Ideally, principals would have all the time and information they need to select an ideal solution to a pending problem. In schools, neither asset is common. Consequently, administrators typically identify only a few obvious possibilities and select one that is satisfactory rather than foolproof (Hanson, 2003). Using the previous example, the principal needs to identify and consider possible alternatives for improving math test scores. Based on analysis, they may include better instructional materials, higher teacher expectations, more diversified instructional approaches, more direct parental involvement, supplemental instruction, and teacher aides.

Once identified, alternatives are evaluated using three criteria: potential, application, and context. Information about the criteria is provided in Table 11.1. Based on the objective analysis of the identified alternatives and the timeframe available, the principal then decides to pursue one or more of the possible solutions, either sequentially or simultaneously.

## Implementation Stage

After the preferred solution is identified, it is applied. This stage often includes securing and improving resources to ensure that the preferred solution is pursued as intended. As examples, teachers may need staff development, the instructional environment may need to be reconfigured, and new equipment may be required. Therefore, effort must be made to provide a climate conducive to pursuing the preferred solution. Unfortunately, change initiatives often are pursued even though known barriers have not been removed.

Setting short-term objectives—that is, incremental steps related to achieving the long-term goal—also are important at the implementation stage. Standing alone, the long-range goal (to eliminate or sufficiently manage the problem) is insufficient because it often is not evaluated until the entire implementation period is finished (e.g., 3 or more years). By that time, resources and time may be wasted, largely because the principal and others ignored compelling evidence indicating that the solution was not functioning as anticipated. Short-term goals should provide incremental and assessable objectives.

## Assessment Stage

The summative assessment of a short-term objective should be conducted at least annually. The intent is to determine if an objective has been met. Problem solving often gets derailed at this stage because the objective in question is (a) not measurable, (b) not measured, or (c) measured inaccurately. The assessment process also should include

*Table 11.1* Criteria for Evaluating Alternatives

| Criterion | Definition | Example |
| --- | --- | --- |
| Potential | An alternative's capability to achieve a desired condition | Does an alternative have the potential to raise student test scores to the state benchmark? |
| Application | The extent to which a school possesses the technical attributes to apply an alternative appropriately | Do teachers and administrators have the knowledge, skills, and resources necessary to apply an alternative as intended? |
| Context | The extent to which a school's climate is conducive to applying an alternative appropriately | Are the staff's shared underlying assumptions about education congruent with an alternative? |

collecting data that can be used to improve elements of the problem-solving approach being used. For example, qualitative data collected from teachers often provide insights for making periodic adjustments.

## Improvement Stage

Improvement efforts should be based on evaluation decisions that have been derived from assessment data and pertinent knowledge. The summative aspect of this function includes drawing conclusions as to whether a short-term objective has been met. The formative aspect requires reflection in an effort to analyze the summative outcome and to determine if adjustments are necessary. Formative evaluation is especially critical when a judgment is made that a short-term objective has not been met. In these instances, the planners need to determine the reasons for this outcome and to make improvement decisions. Generally, failing to achieve a short-term objective may be attributable to one or more of the following conditions:

- *The problem was framed (defined) incorrectly or inadequately*. If this is deemed to be the fundamental issue, the problem-solving cycle reverts to the Comprehension Stage and a new problem definition is developed.
- *The preferred solution is invalid or less than adequate*. If this is deemed to be the fundamental issue, the cycle reverts to the Formulation Stage and a new preferred solution is selected.
- *The application of the preferred solution is flawed*. If this is deemed to be the fundamental issue, the cycle reverts to the Implementation Stage and necessary adjustments are identified.

Figure 11.3 illustrates options after the summative and formative evaluations are completed.

## DECISION MAKING AND THE PRINCIPAL

In attempting to solve problems, principals make numerous decisions, each having the potential of thwarting a positive outcome. Every decision is characterized by the following elements:

- *A goal* – the decision maker has an objective he or she intends to accomplish
- *More than one option* – the decision maker has two or more choices he or she can make in pursuing the goal
- *Selection of a preferred option* – the decision maker selects one of the options (Welch, 2002)

Principals actually make dozens of decisions every day, but most are made instinctively and instantly—that is, little or no thought is given to identifying multiple choices and to evaluating them objectively. Typically, such behavior is not problematic because the issues involved are relatively inconsequential. For example, deciding to talk to a

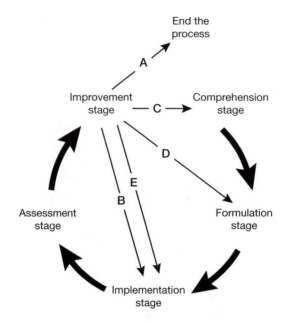

A = Short-term objective is met and the problem is resolved or sufficiently managed
B = Short-term objective is met and the process moves to the next short-term objective
C = Short-term objective is not met because the problem was framed incorrectly
D = Short-term objective not met because of the ineffectiveness of the preferred solution
E = Short-term objective not met because of ineffective implementation

*Figure 11.3* Alternative Choices Post Summative and Formative Evaluations.

teacher after school rather than during her preparation period as she requested may not have any negative implications for a principal. Difficulties in the realm of decision making usually occur when administrators fail to distinguish between important and unimportant decisions and when they make important decisions the same way they make unimportant decision (Kowalski et al., 2008; Kowalski, 2009a).

## Principal Behavior

Persons who have had an opportunity to work with principals recognize that these administrators usually differ both in their willingness to make decisions and in their approaches to making them (Kowalski, 2008). This variance is explained by two factors: a principal's personal disposition toward decision making and workplace expectations. With respect to the former, some principals are naturally inclined to make decisions and some are not; and those with an aversion to decision making prefer to enforce decisions made by others. In the context of a school, a principal's behavior also is affected by role expectations—both formal (i.e., those identified in a job description and emphasized by the superintendent) and informal (i.e., those established and pursued by means of the school's culture). The intersection of these factors is illustrated in Figure 11.4.

Conflict emerges when personal dispositions toward decision making are incongruent with formal or informal role expectations. As an example, a principal may prefer to avoid making important decisions but his superintendent expects him to determine what

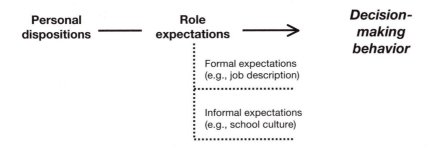

*Figure 11.4* Factors Influencing Principal Decision-Making Behavior.

needs to be done to improve student achievement test scores. When experiencing this discord, some administrators have chosen to allow personal disposition to trump role expectations; others have attempted to change personal dispositions; and still others have attempted to change the role expectations. As a result, principals, even those employed in the same district and having the same role expectations, often respond differently when faced with the need to make important decisions.

Generally, principals are more inclined to either avoid failure or take risks. Those in the former category focus on preventing mistakes; as a result, they usually are reluctant to initiate innovations—even when schools clearly need to be restructured. This behavior is most likely to be rewarded when there is limited pressure for schools to change. Risk takers on the other hand focus on institutional improvement. They are willing to experiment with new ideas and the prospect of occasional failures does not deter them from experimenting (Schein, 1996). The latter behavior is most likely to be rewarded when demands for school reform are high. As discussed earlier in this book, formal and informal principal role expectations historically have tilted toward failure avoidance; as examples, principals rarely were given incentives to take risks and they were threatened with punishment if they made mistakes (Kowalski, 2003). In the context of such an institutional climate, principals were usually rewarded if they did not cause problems for the superintendent and school board. Today, the political climate surrounding schools is less tranquil. In the midst of stakeholder dissatisfaction, many school districts are seeking principals who can build learning communities and shape school-improvement initiatives.

## Decision Complexity and Difficulty

Situations requiring principal decisions vary in complexity and difficulty; and, because of time and resource limitations, a principal needs to be able to separate situations that require extensive analysis from those that do not. Simon (1960) identified the three following criteria that help administrators to do this:

- *Frequency.* This criterion pertains to the rate at which a matter requiring a decision occurs. Routine matters occur daily; unique matters occur rarely.
- *Structure.* This criterion pertains to the degree to which a matter requiring a decision can be defined (or framed) accurately. Structured situations are easy to define; unstructured situations are not.

- *Significance.* This criterion pertains to the degree to which a matter requiring a decision is important. Important decisions have meaningful consequences; unimportant decisions do not.

By analyzing a situation using these criteria, a principal can determine whether a programmed, semi-programmed, or unprogrammed decision is required (Kowalski et al., 2008).

- *Programmed decisions* require little or no analysis because the situation is routine, structured, and relatively unimportant; and existing policy, rules, and procedures prescribe a decision.
- *Semi-programmed decisions* require a moderate level of analysis because conditions are mixed (e.g., the situation occurs periodically, is somewhat structured, and is moderately important). Though existing policy, rules, and procedures address aspects of the situation, they do not specifically prescribe a decision.
- *Unprogrammed decisions* require extensive analysis because conditions are unique, unstructured, and relatively important; and existing policy, rules, and procedures do not prescribe a decision.

The three criteria and their relationships to decision programming are explained in Table 11.2.

Principals not only need to understand the differences between types of decisions; they need to know why those in the unprogrammed category present substantial risk to the school and to them. Situations requiring unprogrammed decisions usually are characterized by substantial uncertainty. In the context of organizational decision making, uncertainty refers to a condition in which the precise outcomes of identified alternatives are unknown and the types of information needed to ameliorate this condition are unknown (Simon, 1960; Cray, Haines, & Mallory, 1994). If uncertainty is high, the risk that a decision may affect the school or principal negatively is high.

## Data-Based Decisions

In the aftermath of the No Child Left Behind Act (NCLB) passed in 2001, principals have had to address another dimension of decision making—using quantitative or qualitative information sources to inform their choices (Picciano, 2006). Though using data to make important decisions affecting clients and society has been a normative standard

*Table 11.2* Characteristics and the Types of Decisions Required

| Conditions favoring programmed decisions | Conditions favoring semi-programmed decisions | Conditions favoring unprogrammed decisions |
| --- | --- | --- |
| Situation occurs routinely | Situation occurs periodically | Situation occurs rarely |
| Situation is easy to define | Situation is moderately difficult to define | Situation is difficult to define |
| Situation is unimportant | Situation is moderately important | Situation is important |

in most human services professions, the process was not required of most educators in the past. Supporters of the decision requirements embedded in NCLB want to change this condition. Most notably, they want principals to "view data as the axis around which school improvement revolves" (Parsley, Dean, & Miller, 2006, p. 39).

Many educators, including principals, recognize the potential value of considering data, but they believe that data alone are insufficient to make effective decisions. This position was articulated by Doyle (2002) shortly after NCLB became law.

> Today's education leader, whether the leader of the school district, the school building or the classroom, must change data into knowledge, transform knowledge into wisdom and use wisdom as a guide to action. But if data-driven decision making and scientifically based research are the necessary preconditions to wise decision making, they not sufficient. True, without data and solid evidence the modern decision maker is helpless, but simply possessing data and evidence is no guarantee of success. (p. 30)

Other education analysts have criticized the concept of data-based decision making because of its potential effects on democratic decision making. Specifically, they argue that it bypasses civic engagement by allowing educator expertise to trump stakeholder interests (e.g., Bridges, 2008) and limits the influence of shared social values on important education decisions (e.g., Biesta, 2007). Opposition to the concept from within the education profession stems primarily from the perception that the process is in reality "research-based decision making"—a positivist approach that purposefully denigrates educator expertise, artistry, and values (Pring, 2004).

Several arguments have been used to defend the application of data-based decision making in schools. The following are among the more prominent ones.

- There has been a substantial increase in the quantity and quality of research conducted in and for professions (Howard, McMillen, & Pollio, 2003); therefore, practitioners in all professions are expected to use empirical evidence to inform their practice.
- Technological developments have removed barriers to apply empirical data to practice. Today, tools such as the internet and computers make it possible for practitioners to access, organize, and store massive amounts of data, including those derived from research (Eraut, 2004).
- In the past, many educators thoughtlessly rejected empirical evidence, preferring to rely on intuition, politics, or emotions. In the current environment of accountability, this behavior is unacceptable (Whitehurst, n.d.).

Principal behavior is not only shaped by dispositions; it also is affected by knowledge and skills. Thus, skepticism toward data-based decision making is enhanced when an educator has not been prepared adequately to make assessments and to use assessment data in decision making (Popham, 2006). Though principals typically take at least one graduate-level course in research or evaluation, many of them complain that the content they experienced was abstract and unrelated to their practice (Kowalski, Petersen, & Fusarelli, 2009). Doyle (2003) adds that both administrators and teachers often see data as a liability, largely because statistics such as student test scores have been used skillfully by critics to blame them for public education's shortcomings. In truth, however, data-based decision making applied appropriately does not specify that a decision should be based solely on empirical evidence; rather, it specifies that empirical and other forms of data should be weighed in conjunction with tacit knowledge and values (Kowalski, 2009b).

Building, maintaining, and using information systems to facilitate decision making has become a high priority for principals. The responsibility has three dimensions as shown in Figure 11.5. The value of an information system (often called a database management system) is determined by the extent to which it allows school personnel to generate, gather, and use data effectively (Wayman, 2005). Beyond resource acquisition, a principal has two important responsibilities: fostering a school culture that treats information systems and data as essential elements of professional practice, and ensuring that professional staff members are proficient in generating and using data (Kowalski, et al., 2008).

## DECISION PARADIGMS

Three types of paradigms inform principals about decision making. Normative models provide direction as to how decisions should be made; they assume rationality and their goal is an ideal decision. Prescriptive models also are linear and also assume rationality; however, their goal is to produce a satisfactory decision. Descriptive models provide information about how decisions have actually been made; they reveal how personal values, bias, politics, and emotions often lessen rationality.

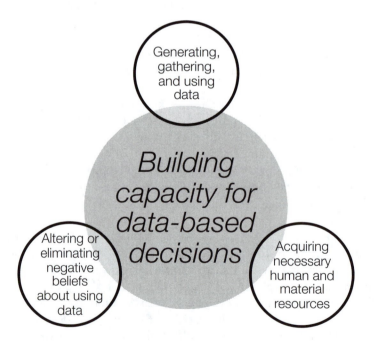

*Figure 11.5* Facilitating Data-Based Decision Making in Schools.

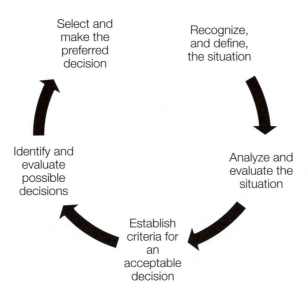

*Figure 11.6* Common Components of Rational Decision-Making Models.

## Normative and Prescriptive Models

Normative models—that is, paradigms based on rationality and intended to produce an ideal decision—are concurrently attractive and offsetting. They are linear approaches analogous to recipes; hence, they appeal to inexperienced administrators. Virtually all rational models share the sequential steps shown in Figure 11.6. According to Simon (1960), such approaches are nested in the assumption that a decision maker can (a) identify all decision alternatives, (b) view every alternative in a panoramic fashion before choosing one of them, (c) know all consequences that would follow each choice, (d) assign values to each alternative, and (e) select one based on its quantitative superiority. Rarely, if ever, is an administrator able to meet these conditions. For instance, principals can never be totally objective; they rarely can access all pertinent information; they rarely can identify all pertinent alternatives; and they typically have neither the time nor the financial resources to apply the model as intended (Kowalski et al., 2008). In light of these limitations, most principals either do not apply a normative model or apply it in modified form.

The most frequent modification to a normative model is to lower the benchmark for an acceptable outcome—that results in a prescriptive model. Most notably, administrators resign themselves to making a satisfactory rather than ideal decision (Hellreigel & Slocum, 1996). This adjustment, known as "satisficing," stems from the realization that assumptions underlying normative models are imperfect. March and Simon (1958) described the distinction between pursuing an ideal decision and a satisfactory decision as "the difference between searching a haystack to find the sharpest needle in it and searching the haystack to find a needle sharp enough to sew with" (pp. 140–1). As previously described, requirements for data-based decision making are making behavioral approaches more common in schools. As a result, principals are showing greater interest in linear prescriptive models.

## Descriptive Models

Much of the research on decision making in schools has focused on how decisions actually have been made. Findings and conclusions from these investigations provide insights about principal behavior, especially in situations where principals elect not to follow either normative or prescriptive models. Moreover, this body of research reveals the pervasiveness of subjectivity and politics in schools and their effects on consequential decisions affecting students and society.

The exercise of political power is inevitable in public schools because local districts are the point in government where individual rights and societal rights intersect most directly (Levin, 1999). For example, special interest groups and individuals have often confronted school officials when policy decisions are viewed as being unacceptable. In a democracy, conflict is considered inevitable and compromise is common; hence, principals often were socialized to pursue political approaches to making decisions. According to Giesecke (1993), political decision making is grounded in the following realities:

- Often, no individual (e.g., the principal) or group (e.g., a school council) has sufficient power to ensure that their decisions will be accepted consistently and broadly.
- Power is usually dispersed among individuals and groups; and frequently the most powerful have no legitimate power (i.e., those with the greatest influence are neither school board members nor administrators).
- In order to advance their interests, individuals and groups often forge coalitions—a process that often requires them to modify their demands to acquire added power.
- Compromise is widely accepted as a suitable way to make a difficult decision—even when the choice made is clearly not the most effective.

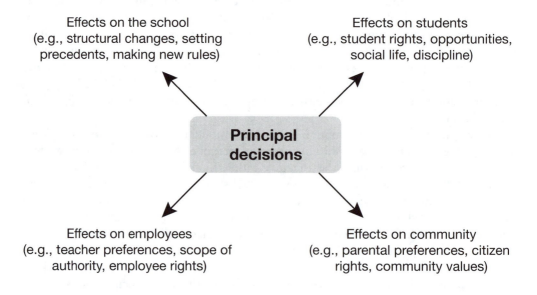

*Figure 11.7* Entities Affected by Principal Decisions.

The effects of a principal's decision can be viewed in four dimensions as shown in Figure 11.7. Because the interests of students, school employees, the school or district as an organization, and the community at large are often dissimilar, any decision is likely to be opposed by some stakeholders and likely to benefit some parties more than others. Consider, for example, a principal who must decide whether to keep a school operational during a teachers' strike. If he succeeds, his behavior may be viewed positively by the superintendent, school board, and parents; however, his relationships with teachers may be destroyed. If the principal acts politically, he weighs the power of both groups and then makes a decision favouring the one with the greater power.

Principals also commonly engage in incremental decision making, sometimes referred to as "muddling through." Basically, it is a pragmatic approach reflective of political influences found in organizations (Lindblom, 1993). The intentions of this behavior are to minimize organizational change produced by decisions and reduce conflict among stakeholders. Consequently, the value of a decision alternative is determined by two criteria: the extent to which an alternative requires changes in the school and the extent to which an alternative is acceptable to stakeholders. An alternative that is lower in anticipated change and higher in acceptability is more attractive than an alternative that is higher in anticipated change and lower in acceptability (Hoy & Tartar, 1995).

Some important decisions are driven by a principal's personal beliefs and bias. When this occurs, the administrator essentially inverts a traditional problem-solving model; that is, instead of framing a problem and searching for a solution, he or she searches for a problem allowing him or her to apply a preferred solution (Cohen, March, & Olsen, 1972). Consider a new elementary school principal who advocates block scheduling as a way to improve student test scores. Teachers reject his idea, in part because the concept is not widely used in elementary schools and because they have had no previous experience with it. The principal knows that the teachers have the power to thwart; so he remains patient and waits for an opportune moment to pursue block scheduling. A year later, a drop in student test scores prompts the superintendent and school board to demand changes at the school. Under pressure to improve student performance, teachers drop their resistance to block scheduling and the concept is implemented. Though the change may have a positive effect, the manner in which the decision was made is questionable because the principal failed to (a) analyze the problem (decline in test scores), (b) consider other plausible alternatives, and (c) evaluate the alternatives using data that are available (e.g., research findings about block scheduling in elementary schools).

In summary, our knowledge of how principals make important decisions should enhance our appreciation of using prescriptive models to increase decision quality. Though factors such as politics and personal values are inevitable and possibly beneficial, they should not be the sole factors determining important choices about education. Principals have a responsibility to protect those who have little or no power (e.g., students) and to make fair and balanced decisions that are in the best interests of students and the broader community.

## GROUP DECISION MAKING

Many important decisions in districts and schools are made by committees because group processes are thought to be effective and democratic. Estler (1988), for example, pointed out that this decision-making approach produced both pragmatic and philosophical benefits. As examples, participation usually has a positive effect on school productivity, reinforces democratic values, and elevates employee consciousness of individual rights. The prevalence of this approach in districts and schools also is rooted in the following realities:

- On the one hand, stakeholders expect principals to perform as professionals; for example, they are told to make leadership decisions determining what should be done to improve schools. On the other hand, stakeholders expect them to behave democratically; for example, they are to ensure that public values and interests are integrated into consequential decisions (Wirt & Kirst, 2001).
- Experiences with failed reforms have prompted policymakers to conclude that local support for change is critical to restructuring poorly performing schools. As a result, democratic decision making has been promoted as an effective process for increasing political and economic support (Ogawa, Crowson, & Goldring, 1999).
- Group decision making is generally accepted as a positive process that produces distributed intelligence, shared leadership, and communal learning (McBeath, 2001). As an example, groups usually provide a spectrum of viewpoints in relation to a problem (Razik & Swanson, 2002).
- Group decision making is an effective process for managing inevitable conflict that emerges from the intersection of individual citizen rights and societal rights (Cooper, Fusarelli, & Randall, 2004; Levin, 1999).

Principals often discover that relying on groups to solve problems can result in second-level problems (difficulties that emerge when attempting to solve a primary problem). The following are some of the more notable concerns:

- Group decisions typically are less efficient than principal decisions; that is, they require more time and resources (Clark, Clark, & Irvin, 1997).
- Preferences expressed by the group participants are often competing or even incompatible, resulting in conflict (Kowalski et al., 2008).
- Educators focus on self-interests rather than problems affecting a school (Malen & Ogawa, 1992).
- Group members often focus more on social acceptance than on making quality decisions (Reitz, 1987).
- Group members often are not held accountable for the decisions they make. Accordingly, groups are more likely to make mediocre or poor decisions (Luthans, 1985).
- Groups often are controlled by one or two influential members; thus, they do not function democratically as intended (Janis, 1982).

Given these potential pitfalls, a principal's role is pivotal in group decision making, especially in relation to structuring groups (e.g., size, member selection) and intervening (e.g., conflict management) when necessary. The following are practical steps principals can take to make decision groups more productive:

- Ensure that group members are sufficiently diverse to represent the spectrum of stakeholders.
- Select members who have relevant expertise or who will be directly affected by the decision.
- Select members who have the emotional maturity and disposition to be collaborative.
- Provide an environment that is conducive to the group's work. As an example, the arrangement should reinforce the equal standing of each group member.
- Provide clear expectations so that the group understands its assignment and time parameters.
- Address conflict impartially and quickly if it emerges.
- Promote decision ownership; that is, the members should be encouraged to accept accountability for the decision made.

In light of the prevalence of group decision making in schools, Kowalski et al. (2008) posit that principals are most effective when they understand the professional, philosophical, and political aspects of this process, and readily recognize conditions that facilitate successful outcomes.

## REFLECTIONS

Problem solving and decision making are at the core of a principal's practice. Yet these two demanding assignments are often taken for granted. Perhaps more than other factors, the pursuit of school improvement at the local level and efforts to professionalize teaching and school administration have set new expectations for these requirements over the past few decades.

Content in this chapter distinguishes between problem solving and decision making. Though they are separate functions, the former is inextricably tied to the latter; that is, problem solving requires a series of decisions. Moreover, each decision made in relation to a problem has the potential of attenuating outcomes. Yet the manner in which principals respond to problems, the extent to which they accept responsibility for making decisions, and the manner in which they make decisions continue to vary considerably.

In contemporary practice, certain competencies related to problem solving and decision making have become pivotal. The following are examples:

- Being able to define or frame a problem accurately
- Being able to determine whether a situation requires a structured, semi-structured, or unstructured decision
- Being able to produce, manage, and apply data to problem solving and decision making

- Creating a school infrastructure that facilitates the use of data
- Knowing when it is advantageous to engage in group decision making

After reading the chapter, reflect on principal behavior you have observed. To what extent did the principals exhibit these competencies? Did they accept responsibility for making important decisions? To what extent did they make effective decisions?

## Knowledge-Based Questions

1   What must you know in order to define or frame a problem?
2   What are short-term objectives in relation to problem solving? How do these objectives differ from the problem-solving goal?
3   What is the difference between assessment and evaluation?
4   What are the differences among structured, semi-structured, and unstructured decisions? Under what conditions should each be pursued?
5   What is the relationship between uncertainty and risk in decision making?
6   What arguments can you make to defend group decision making in schools?
7   What is the difference between pursuing an ideal decision and pursuing a satisfactory decision? Why do many principals pursue the latter?
8   What is a linear approach to decision making? What is the perceived advantage of this approach?
9   How can a principal control the extent to which political influence affects an important decision?

## Skill-Based Activities

1   Identify possible reasons for the conflict between the new superintendent and principals in the vignette at the beginning of this chapter. After analyzing the reasons, select the one that you believe is most prominent.

2   Assume you are an elementary school principal and have been considering three alternative programs for teaching science in the intermediate grades. Identify criteria you could use to evaluate the merits of these alternatives.

3   Develop a description of a situation in which a new principal experiences conflict between her personal disposition toward decision making and the prevailing school culture.

4   Assume you are a high school principal and the school board has approved a policy that simply states "every school in the district must have a curriculum committee." Identify questions you would pose to the superintendent before attempting to comply with the policy.

5   Principals commonly make decisions related to student discipline. Describe circumstances that prompt you to make structured, semi-structured, and unstructured decisions regarding student suspensions.

6   Assume that you are a high school principal and a group of teachers in the school has proposed the adoption of a "No Pass/No Play" rule that prevents any student failing a class from participating in athletic programs. Further assume that the athletic booster club has signed a petition opposing the idea. Develop a process that you would use to make a decision on this matter.

CHAPTER 12

# Collaborative Efforts for School Improvement

*When recommending Nina Shaw to be the new middle school principal, Superintendent George Simpson told the school board, "She is a proven visionary leader and change agent who will institutionalize real reforms in our middle school." Less than 2 years later, the board members were asking him how he could have been so wrong.*

*The Clear Springs School District is a relatively small system serving an affluent suburban community. Before being employed as principal, Dr. Shaw served as a middle school principal in a large urban district. During her tenure there, she had acquired a reputation as a reformer. Specifically, she had created teacher teams and initiated supplemental programs for low-performing students. Her accomplishments were highly publicized by the media.*

*Dr. Shaw accepted the position in Clear Springs knowing that the superintendent and board demanded excellence and continuous improvements—even though student performance in the district, at least as measured by test scores, was already well above average. Specifically, they wanted a principal who would develop a vision and strategic plan to ensure continuous growth—tasks that already had been accomplished in the district's other four schools. Convinced that Dr. Shaw's predecessor was incapable of and unwilling to provide the necessary level of leadership, Superintendent Simpson recommended that the previous principal's contract not be renewed.*

*Shortly after beginning her new position, Dr. Shaw reviewed what had been done previously to develop a vision statement for the middle school. In essence, the previous principal had appointed a committee of teachers and parents and elected to not participate directly in their deliberations. The committee's progress was stalled by unresolved conflict, much of it stemming from disagreements over values pertaining to an ideal middle school experience. Dr. Shaw told Superintendent Simpson that she was not surprised by her finding, because she believed that the committee members probably lacked the requisite knowledge and skills to complete their assignment. Applying a different strategy, she unilaterally developed a vision statement and convinced the superintendent and board to approve it. She then developed a strategic plan that set goals to achieve her vision. After the two documents were made public, some stakeholders were openly critical—not of the documents but of the manner in which Dr. Shaw had developed them. Specifically, they resented that neither faculty nor parents had been given opportunities to provide input or to critique the documents before they were approved. They also chastised the superintendent and school board for being undemocratic. Some teachers began to challenge the principal's leadership style, contending that her dictatorial approach to visioning and planning was indicative of how she handled all matters.*

*Though Clear Springs Middle School now had a vision and a strategic plan, controversy surrounding the development of documents cast a cloud over the school's future. Attendance at board meetings was increasing and so was the negative tone of the sessions. Speaking on behalf of disgruntled citizens at a recent board meeting, a parent said, "In a progressive community such as Clear Springs, one would expect that the superintendent and school board members know and be sensitive to the fact that, in a democratic society, process and product are equally important. The manner in which visioning and planning was conducted at our middle school causes us to question whether our district leadership team meets this benchmark."*

## INTRODUCTION

Lessons learned from failed school reforms verify that process is exceedingly important in institutionalizing change in public schools. Even the best policies are ineffective if they are rejected or ignored. This point is exemplified by what occurred in Clear Springs Middle School. Even if a visionary principal can detail a school future and develop effective goals for reaching the destination, stakeholders may reject the products if they believe their rights as citizens have been usurped.

This chapter examines strategies principals can apply to achieve school improvement. The argument is made that change initiatives are unlikely to be institutionalized if they are incongruent with the prevailing culture. This point is examined in relation to both rational and coercive tactics that have been used in an attempt to change schools. Conversely, reforms are far more likely to be institutionalized if they are developed collaboratively—that is, if they are forged cooperatively by principals, other internal stakeholders (e.g., teachers and support staff), and external stakeholders (e.g., parents and the media) and if they are congruent with shared values.

After reading this chapter, you should be able to demonstrate the ability to do the following correctly:

- Explain why change has been resisted in schools
- Identify the consequences of student failure in contemporary society
- Explain why continuous improvement is beneficial to all schools
- Differentiate among rational, coercive, and reconstructive strategies of improving schools
- Identify the advantages of pursuing collaborative approaches to school improvement
- Identify different approaches to civic engagement and their advantages and disadvantages

# NEED FOR CONTINUOUS IMPROVEMENT

## Consequences of Student Failure

Many citizens are surprised to learn that the failure rate in public elementary and secondary education (defined in terms of the percentage of students who either do not graduate from high school or graduate despite being functionally illiterate) remained amazingly constant at around 35 percent through the second half of the previous century. An optimist might look at this statistic and argue that schools are as effective or more so than they were in the "good old days," especially as they now enroll substantially more students with problems that constrain learning (e.g., learning disabilities, the effects of living in poverty or in a dysfunctional family). Such a conclusion, however, is myopic because school failure rates have become increasingly consequential. Addressing this point, Schlechty (1990) explained that a student dropping out of high school five or six decades ago usually found gainful employment in a factory. He or she earned a decent salary, was able to acquire personal property, and paid taxes to support governmental services. Today, students who do not graduate from high school or who do so despite being functionally illiterate are more likely than ever before to be incarcerated or to collect welfare. Thus, their disappointing performance in school not only diminishes the quality of their lives, it affects society negatively.

## Resistance to Change

Schools historically have not been inclined to initiate or encourage change, a disposition resulting from public education's traditional role as an institution of social stability (Spring, 1990). Until the mid-twentieth century, efforts to radically change education policy were uncommon. After that point, however, the judicial and legislative branches of the federal government took a more direct role in public education by addressing constitutional issues. Arguably, the two most pervasive and enduring examples of system-wide change in public education were initiated by the U.S. Supreme Court and the U.S. Congress.

- As a result of *Brown* v. *Board of Education* in 1954, de jure racial segregation was ruled a violation of the Equal Protection Clause of the Fourteenth Amendment of the United States Constitution; consequently, states were prohibited from establishing separate race-based public schools.
- In 1975, Congress passed the Education for all Handicapped Children Act (P.L. 94-142), the first law that clearly defined the rights of students with disabilities to free appropriate public education. The law mandated that every student with a disability had to have an individualized education program (commonly called an IEP) and had to be placed in a least restrictive environment (initially referred to as mainstreaming and later as inclusion).

Both the *Brown* decision and P.L. 94-142 explicate two realities about public schools: most significant change is initiated by forces outside schools and lasting change is more probable if legal penalties or other sanctions for non-compliance are established and enforced.

Resistance to change also is nested in traditional roles developed for administrators and teachers. Until recently, educators were neither especially well prepared academically nor socialized culturally to assume responsibility for adapting their work environments to evolving societal needs (Hall & Hord, 2001). As described in the previous chapter, principals and teachers often learned quickly that personal rewards were more likely if they avoided failure and that penalties were more likely if they took risks (e.g., experimented with new ideas). In fact, policymakers working with business elites initiated the vigorous quest for school reform circa 1983 based on the conviction that educators could not and would not independently improve schools (Metz, 1990; Rubin, 1984). The primary strategy applied by state legislatures was intensification mandates; specifically, states provided additional funding for schools and required teachers and students to do more of what they were already doing (Kirst, 1988). This approach to school reform was "simple, uniform, universal, and abrupt" (Finn, 1991, p. 42).

By 1990, it became apparent that generic mandates and more funding, at best, had been only moderately successful in raising student test scores (Hawley, 1988). Analysts concluded that reform had failed because intensification disregarded variations in real student needs (Passow, 1988), underestimated the power of educators to circumvent mandates (Fullan, 2001; Hall & Hord, 2001), and ignored prevailing change-resistant cultures in schools (Sarason, 1996). Circa 1990 states began moving to a new strategy, the concept of *directed autonomy*. According to Weiler (1990), the new line of attack was characterized by four actions:

- State policymakers set broad improvement goals for local districts and schools
- Local officials were given leeway to determine how they would meet these goals
- State departments of education periodically assessed progress and evaluated districts and schools
- Local officials were held accountable for district and school outcomes

This arrangement required principals to lead and facilitate efforts to improve schools, including the restructuring of school cultures and instructional delivery systems. Today policymakers and education critics expect principals and their teacher colleagues to continuously challenge routines, roles, and school culture (Belasen, 2000).

## CHANGE STRATEGIES

In simple terms, a strategy is an action plan for achieving one or more goals. Broadly, there are three strategies for changing organizations: rational, coercive, and reconstructive (see Table 12.1). The intent here is to summarize the approaches and to demonstrate how they have been applied to school reform.

*Table 12.1* Change Strategies for Principals

| *Rational strategies* | *Coercive strategies* | *Reconstructive approaches* |
| --- | --- | --- |
| Acting on the conviction that employees behave rationally | Acting on the conviction that educators will not initiate change | Acting on the conviction that school culture is a deterrent to reform |
| Providing employees evidence of why change is necessary and educating them to institutionalize a new norm | Using power to force them to change | Building a vision and altering fundamental assumptions that influence behavior |

## Rational Approaches

There are two subcategories of rational approaches to change. The first is the *empirical–rational* method. It is predicated on two convictions: change should be based on empirical evidence demonstrating the need for change, and employees will act rationally after being exposed to this evidence (Chin & Benne, 1985). Assume that a high school principal wants to implement block scheduling. Following this model, he would accumulate data indicating that the current traditional schedule deters student learning. He then would explain why he believes block scheduling eliminates or at least attenuates these deterrents. After presenting his evidence and supporting argument to the faculty, he anticipates they will act rationally by accepting the change.

The empirical–rational strategy has two fundamental deficiencies. First, as discussed in the previous chapter, many educators are dubious of empirical evidence—especially data that contradict their values and beliefs. Second, people are not always rational, even in the face of compelling evidence. Juries in criminal cases, for example, have nullified a law by acquitting a defendant regardless of the weight of evidence presented; in essence, juror emotions, philosophy, or political dispositions trumped the evidence. In the case of a school, evidence that contradicts shared values and beliefs embedded in school culture may be rejected regardless of its validity or reliability (Kowalski, Petersen, & Fusarelli, 2007).

The second approach in this category is known as the *normative–educative* method. It is predicated on the belief that an existing norm (e.g., program or process standard) needs to be replaced with a more effective norm. In order to institutionalize the new norm, however, the principal must ensure that employees understand it and have the skills and dispositions necessary to implement it (Chin & Benne, 1985). In schools, the strategy is commonly called staff development. Assume an elementary school principal wants to implement cooperative learning. Rather than trying to persuade faculty using the empirical–rational approach, she arranges for some or all teachers to attend workshops that promote the proposed change and prepare them to implement it.

The normative–educative strategy, however, has often been derailed by school culture. Though teachers may return from the workshops enthused and eager to implement the program or process, their fervor and interest wane quickly if the new norm is found to be incongruent with the prevailing culture (Hall & Hord, 2001). Consider a school culture that promotes competition. In such a school, teachers are likely to resist cooperative learning—a socially collaborative process. In summary, normative–educative approaches are usually ineffective if they are used to promote process or programs that contradict shared values and assumptions (Kowalski et al., 2007).

## Coercive Approaches

Coercive approaches are rooted in the conviction that educators are either unwilling or unable to initiate change. Therefore, external (e.g., governors, state legislators, state boards of education) or internal (e.g., school board, superintendent, or principal) power figures must force them to change (Chin & Benne, 1985). The No Child Left Behind Act exemplifies this approach. Consider a middle school principal who wants teacher teams to develop collaborative lesson plans. Rather than trying to convince them with data or trying to build enthusiasm for his preference through staff development, he simply sends a memorandum to the faculty that states: "As of the beginning of the next semester, all teacher teams must develop collaborative lesson plans."

The obvious advantage of coercive approaches is efficiency. They require less time and energy than the other models. Nevertheless, they have serious drawbacks. As examples, persons most directly affected by a proposed change (e.g., teachers) typically have no "buy-in"; that is, they lack a vested interest in seeing that the change succeeds. Moreover, they resent being pressured to do something they are not naturally inclined to do. Consequently, principals and teachers at best may be spitefully obedient and at worst may ignore or even sabotage mandates. Coercion is most successful when accompanied by rigorously enforced sanctions (as previously noted in relation to school desegregation and students with disabilities). And, unless the pressure for change is sustained, teachers can be expected to revert to their traditional practices when they have the opportunity to do so (Kowalski et al., 2007).

## Reconstructive Approaches

Both rational and coercive approaches are thwarted by change-resistant school cultures. Recognizing this fact, advocates of reconstructive approaches posit that institutionalizing necessary improvements is improbable unless basic elements of an organization are altered. Senge (1990) argues that highly effective organizations succeed by replacing change-resistant cultures with *learning cultures*—an institutional environment "where people continually expand their capacity to create the results they truly desire, where new and expansive patterns of thinking are nurtured, where collective aspiration is set free, and where people are continually learning to see the whole together" (p. 3). The extent to which schools move in the direction of learning cultures depends largely on the quality of leadership provided by principals.

Traditionally, principals have been socialized to function as instruments of change—managers who ensure that laws, policies, and reform mandates get implemented even when teachers oppose them. Moreover, principals in the past have been neither prepared nor encouraged to challenge the status quo in their schools. In a learning culture, these conditions change radically. Collaboratively with teachers and other stakeholders, a principal forges a vision and diagnoses the prevailing culture to determine the extent to which it aids or prevents the school from achieving its intended future state (see Table

12.2). Without a shared vision, efforts to rebuild culture are apt to fail as stakeholders disagree about what the school can and should become. A reconstructive approach, however, may take 3 or more years (Fullan, 2001), and it is not possible unless a principal has credibility as an educator and is trusted by school employees and stakeholders generally (Kowalski et al., 2007).

Three competencies are especially critical for principals who seek to erect a learning culture (see Figure 12.1):

- A principal must understand school culture conceptually (Sarason, 1996).
- A principal must know how to function as a change agent (Murphy, 1994).
- A principal must have the competence to build trusting relationships and engage others in open and candid discussions (Kowalski, 2005).

Even if principals are knowledgeable and competent, they require dispositions that prompt them to build a learning culture. This includes proclivities to be a democratic (e.g., Blase & Blase, 1999; Hoyle, 1994) and transformational (e.g., Marks & Printy, 2003; Silins, Mulford, & Zarins, 2002) leader who treats teachers as peer professionals.

## SCHOOL–COMMUNITY COLLABORATION AND SCHOOL IMPROVEMENT

The concept of a learning organization, explained earlier in chapter 5, addresses how principals collaborate with teachers and other staff members to identify and solve problems that limit school effectiveness. The purpose here is to extend that discussion by examining collaboration between external stakeholders and school personnel.

### Importance of School–Community Collaboration

Generally, there are two reasons why school–community collaboration is potentially beneficial. Philosophically, citizens support the value of liberty; therefore, they believe they have a fundamental right to participate in deliberative democracy—a process in which individual rights and interests intersect directly with espoused societal interests (Levin, 1999). Denied opportunities for democratic discourse, stakeholders are inclined to distrust both elected officials and the professional administrators employed by them (Lan, 1997). Politically, experience has taught us two important lessons: any proposed change probably will be opposed by one or more groups (Bauman, 1996; Stone, Orr, &

*Table 12.2* Stages for Building a Culture Conducive to Change

Build a vision
Identify deficiencies
Diagnose culture
Evaluate culture
Alter/replace negative assumptions

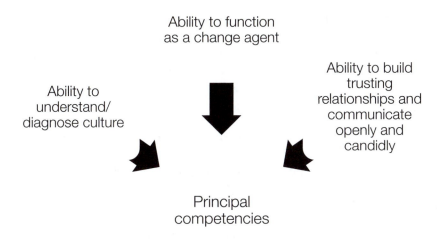

*Figure 12.1* Principal Competencies for Reconstructing School Culture.

Worgs, 2006), and even the best-designed reforms can be scuttled by opponents (Björk & Gurley, 2005).

All organizations, including schools, are most effective when they maintain equilibrium with their external environment—that is, they are most successful when they identify and address social and individual needs (Hanson, 2003). In a democratic society, principals are expected to provide stakeholders opportunities to state and test their views, especially in relation to proposed changes that affect the community generally and them specifically (Fusarelli, 1999). Meeting this expectation, however, has become increasingly difficult in schools serving diverse stakeholder groups (i.e., groups expressing dissimilar and often competing values, beliefs, and priorities). As communities, districts, and schools have become less homogeneous, citizen participation in policy decisions has diminished. Though detachment occasionally results from citizen satisfaction with schools (Tracy & Durfy, 2007), more often it is a sign of alienation or apathy (Eliasoph, 1998; Putnam, 2000). Simply put, citizens opt to remain silent rather than to become embroiled in controversial issues (Hodgkinson, 2002), and this tendency is most pronounced in schools where groups are sharply divided philosophically and politically.

Direct citizen participation in government also declined for other reasons. After World War II, population growth and the development of new communities (e.g., suburbs) resulted in fewer but larger school systems (Kowalski, 2006). Gradually, town hall meetings, such as the one depicted in the movie *Hoosiers*, became rare and democratic localism was replaced with representative democracy—a concept in which school board members and professional administrators make consequential decisions on behalf of the community. Arguably, this governance model works well for many issues but its effectiveness in relation to school improvement at the local level has been drawn into question. Scholars examining attempted reforms have concluded that most of them were never institutionalized (Datnow, 2005), partly because they were not tailored to address the real need of individual schools (Hall & Hord, 2001) but also because they were not widely supported by local stakeholders (Bauman, 1996).

## Collaborating with External Stakeholders

An important first step to ensuring external stakeholder collaboration is considering the nature of citizen participation. Civic engagement is framed in several dimensions, and the following four identified by Cooper, Bryer, and Meek (2006) are especially pertinent for principals (also see Figure 12.2):

- *Involvement.* What stakeholders should be involved? How deeply will they be involved?
- *Initiation.* Who will be responsible for igniting collaboration?
- *Purpose.* What are the motives and goals for involving stakeholders?
- *Approach.* What process or participation method will be used for collaborating?

How civic engagement is pursued is especially important because not all approaches are initiated by school officials.

### Adversarial Approach

The adversarial approach, prevalent across America, is based on the assumption that the most effective way for citizens to pursue their personal interests is to confront government officials (Cooper et al., 2006). It often occurs either because stakeholders are not given other options or because they do not have faith in the options provided. Although certainly accepted as a legitimate process in a democracy, the method frequently damages

## *Involvement*

Defining external stakeholders, ensuring diversity,
determining depth of involvement

## *Engagement*

Taking the initiative to ignite collaboration, inviting
stakeholders to participate

## *Purpose*

Determining the motives and goals for external
stakeholder collaboration

## *Approach*

Determing the methods used to engage external
stakeholders in collaboration

*Figure 12.2* Four Dimensions of Collaborating with External Stakeholders.

relationships among stakeholders because the ensuing conflict is not managed properly (Feuerstein, 2002). This negative outcome can incrementally destabilize districts and schools, ultimately making school improvement virtually impossible. In their seminal research on the politics of public education, Lutz and Iannoconne (1978) found that adversarial approaches fueled citizen discontent leading to the defeat of incumbent board members, the dismissal of superintendents, and internal volatility in schools.

## Elections

In public education, elections commonly are used to select school board members and to decide tax-related issues (Edelman, 1985). The method's value in relation to making important school reform decisions, however, is questionable. Elections are rarely preceded by meaningful discourse so citizens of different persuasions are not provided a formal opportunity to state and test their views. Moreover, many stakeholders may opt not to vote; however, that lack of participation does not diminish the possibility that non-voters will object to the outcome. Experiences with school-related elections indicate that in many communities fewer than 20 percent of eligible voters participate (Feuerstein, 2002).

## School Councils

During the late 1980s, school councils became a popular way to engage citizens in school reform. The extent to which these groups have succeeded, however, has varied; studies (e.g., Leithwood, Jantzi, & Steinbach, 1999) often reveal that they have had limited influence on relevant structural and instructional issues. Their potential effectiveness has been reduced by both internal and external problems. Internally, for example, councils have been created without a clear and shared statement of purpose; and, once operational, power struggles between teachers and other council members have evolved (Flinspach & Ryan, 1994). Externally, many stakeholders may view councils as another layer of bureaucracy, especially if they believe council members do not represent their views (St. John & Daun-Barnett, 2008).

## Deliberative Democracy

A form of communitarianism, deliberative democracy provides opportunities for broad civic engagement. In this approach, school officials recognize and accept that citizens have "the obligation and the right to participate in the educational decisions which most affect their lives" (Fusarelli, 1999, p. 98). The method emphasizes "social responsibility, democracy, and collective commitment to the common good" (Kowalski et al., 2007, p. 129) and includes "candid, two-way communication, especially the exchange of ideals that could radically alter the organization of public schools" (St. John & Daun-Barnett, 2008, p. 66). Principals and other school officials encourage stakeholders to state their opinions, to test their and other opinions, and to collaborate to reach consensus (Medearis, 2005). Combining deliberative democracy with the activities of school councils provides a hybrid approach that could be highly advantageous in many schools.

## Collaborating with the Media

The manner in which school-improvement efforts are portrayed by reporters in the print and electronic media influences public opinion. Therefore, collaboration with journalists is another factor principals need to consider. Historically, however, administrators have been inclined to typecast reporters as troublemakers interested only in negative news (McQuaid, 1989). In an information-based society, being able to hide from the media is not only an improbability; it is precarious. If efforts to achieve school reform are a focal issue in the community, the question is not whether the media will cover the topic but rather what sources they will use in doing so.

Obviously, the importance of media relations extends beyond matters related to school improvement. Thus, it is one of the first issues a new principal should address. Keep in mind that the issue is not whether relationships between principals and the media should exist, because they always do. The real concern is whether the relationship will be positive, and administrators have a responsibility to make sure that it is (White, 1998). A positive relationship, however, does not require principals to behave unprofessionally. Providing information secretly or otherwise speaking to reporters off the record is never a good idea. A principal should never say anything to a reporter he or she would not want presented in the public domain (Howard & Mathews, 2000). Table 12.3 provides suggestions for building and maintaining relationships with journalists.

*Table 12.3*  Collaborating with the Media: Factors Contributing to Positive Relations with Journalists

| Factor | Importance |
| --- | --- |
| Taking the initiative to become acquainted | Waiting for a reporter to initiate the first contact is not a good idea because it is probable that initial contact will center on a negative issue. Inviting reporters to the school to get acquainted is a productive idea (Kowalski, 2008) |
| Developing mutual understanding and respect | Principals and journalists need to understand and respect each other's responsibilities (Raisman, 2000) |
| Being cooperative | Journalists expect principals to be cooperative. Thus, accepting or returning phone calls and providing requested data prior to deadlines fortifies relationships (Frohlichstein, 1993) |
| Answering reporter questions | Principals who refuse to answer questions or do so by saying "no comment" are not behaving effectively. A principal should explain why a question cannot be answered; and, if applicable, indicate who may be able to answer the question (Million, 2000) |
| Being honest | An administrator who lies or obscures facts rarely prevents a good reporter from finding the truth (Posner, 1994). A principal caught lying loses credibility, public trust, and positive relationships (Howard & Mathews, 2000) |
| Recognizing positive contributions | Journalists, like other professionals, appreciate receiving recognition. When stories are reported accurately and help the school, students, or employees, principals should make an effort to express appreciation (Kowalski, 2008) |

## REFLECTIONS

School reform is often viewed as an event rather than a continuous process; this is an unfortunate perception in a world where the rate of societal change keeps accelerating. Contemporary principals have a greater responsibility to initiate and facilitate change than at any previous time in history. How they decide to assume this responsibility is, therefore, critically important. As long as the concept of local control is sustained, many of the pivotal reform decisions will need to be made at the school level.

The content of this chapter is intended to underscore the importance of school culture in relation to school improvement. Time and time again, educators have proven that they can prevent new ideas from being institutionalized; therefore, most traditional reform strategies eventually prove to be disappointing. This is why scholars now focus on the need to move from change-resistant cultures to learning cultures as a prelude to normalizing structural, curricular, and instructional changes.

As you reflect on what you read in this chapter, consider how you felt when others made important decisions that affected you. Did you feel good about being included? Or did you resent being excluded? Also think about why teachers and principals have resisted mandates imposed on them by state officials and school boards.

### Knowledge-Based Questions

1   Why have public schools been highly resistant to change?

2   What factors have made continued resistance to change unacceptable?

3   What is the difference between a rational and a coercive change strategy?

4   What negative effects can occur as a result of adversarial approaches to civic engagement?

5   What is democratic localism? Why has the issue regained importance in public education?

6   What benefits are likely if principals elect to collaborate with internal and external stakeholders?

7   Educators have relied heavily on staff development to implement new ideas. Why does this approach to school improvement often fail?

8   What are the advantages and disadvantages of relying on school councils to develop vision statements and strategic plans?

9   Why is it important to collaborate with the media?

10  What is deliberative democracy? Why is this process considered to be effective with respect to pursuing school improvement at the local level?

## Skill-Based Activities

1   Develop an argument as to why principals should or should not independently develop a school vision statement.
2   Assume you are a new principal. Explain to your staff why you would or would not diagnose the school's culture before developing or revising a vision statement.
3   Create a rationale for operating a school council in conjunction with deliberative democracy.
4   Critique the behavior of Dr. Shaw as described in the opening vignette.
5   Describe the characteristics of an ideal visionary principal.

# CHAPTER 13

# Commitment to Being a School Administrator

*Bill and Nancy Coal are both employed by the Summit City School System. She teaches language arts at the middle school and he is the vice-principal of the high school, a position he assumed 3 years ago. After teaching and coaching for 8 years, the principal, Ernie Bogs, convinced Bill to become an administrator.*

*Initially, Bill liked being vice-principal. But more recently he was having second thoughts. He had expected that, with experience, his typical work day would be less demanding and shorter. He discovered that he was wrong on both counts. His work load kept increasing and he was getting home later and later—he often got home 3 or 4 hours later than his wife. Last spring, he shared his concerns with Principal Bogs and told him that he was thinking about returning to the classroom. Not wanting to lose his vice-principal, Principal Bogs convinced the superintendent and school board to give Bill a 13 percent salary increase—a raise that dissuaded him from resigning as vice-principal.*

*As the new school term began, Bill again was having doubts about remaining an administrator. As a result of his salary increase, however, he felt obliged to remain in the position for at least 1 or 2 more years. In mid-October, the superintendent contacted him requesting a meeting later that day. At 4:30 p.m., Bill arrived at the superintendent's office. He was immediately told that the middle school principal had been diagnosed with a serious illness and would be retiring unexpectedly in 5 weeks. The superintendent then told Bill that he wanted him to be the interim middle school principal.*

*Immediately after that conversation, Bill returned to the high school and spoke with Principal Bogs. He learned that Principal Bogs had recommended him to be the interim principal. He told Bill, "You know I don't want to see you leave the high school. But in the best interests of the school district and community, you are the person to take over at the middle school. The superintendent and school board have a great deal of confidence in you. If you do as well as you have in your current position, I'm sure they will want you to take the position on a permanent basis. And if that doesn't work out, you can come back as my vice-principal. I'll name an interim replacement for you until your job status is permanent."*

*That evening, Bill told his wife, Nancy, about his conversations with the superintendent and Principal Bogs. She had heard that the middle school principal was ill, but his impending retirement had not been announced publicly. She also told Bill that she would support any decision he would make but admitted that she might be uncomfortable having him as her principal.*

*The next morning, Bill arrived at school tired and confused. He had not slept more than 3 hours, and the decision he had to make had generated considerable anxiety. As he sat at his desk trying to decide what he should do, dozens of questions raced through his mind. Could he be successful as a middle school principal? Would he enjoy the job? What effect would the new job have on his personal life? How would Ernie Bogs and the superintendent react if he declined to take the position? Would he appear ungrateful, especially after receiving such a high salary increase? He suddenly realized that he did not have any of the answers.*

## INTRODUCTION

Administrative stability in schools is important because frequent leadership changes lessen the probability of improving school cultures and otherwise elevating school performance (Lashway, 1999). Yet approximately one-third of all principals are replaced each year (Doud & Keller, 1998) and turnover rates are higher than those for teachers (Fuller, n.d.). Most resign voluntarily and accept another principal position or a district-level administrative position; however, about 10 percent of all principals exit administration annually.[10] In part, instability is explained by the career options principals have. As examples, they are often tenured teachers and can return to the classroom; some are attractive candidates for management positions in the private sector; and many qualify for early or regular retirement.

As demonstrated in the preceding vignette, administrators often must make pivotal career decisions. In Bill's case, he must decide whether to be a principal without the benefit of career goals to guide him. His anxiety stems largely from not knowing whether he is committed to being an administrator. His lack of knowledge stems from a lack of planning. Like many educators, he has allowed fate to determine his future.

This final chapter addresses personal commitment to becoming a principal. The content is based on two convictions. First, highly committed principals engage in authentic practice. That is, their behavior is moral, ethical, transformational, and participative; and they concurrently serve others and set high expectations. Second, they develop and rely on a personal plan to make important career choices. As such, they have (a) an objective awareness of their strengths and weaknesses, (b) measurable career goals, and (c) a strategy for meeting career goals. The four primary objectives for this chapter are:

- Describing authentic practice in relation to moral–ethical behavior
- Describing authentic practice in relation to serving others
- Explaining the importance of career planning
- Providing a model for career planning

After reading this chapter, you should be able to demonstrate the ability to do the following correctly:

- Identify the nature of ethics within professions and ethical standards for administrators
- Discuss the concept of servant leadership and apply it to the principalship
- Explain why many educators do not engage in career planning and identify the possible negative effects of not doing so
- Develop an outline for a personal career plan
- Develop examples of measurable career goals

## AUTHENTIC PRACTICE

Authentic practice is a metaphor for exemplary behavior exhibited by practitioners in a recognized profession (Begley, 2006). Several dimensions of authentic leadership for principals were discussed earlier in the book. As examples, being democratic and transformational and engaging in reflective practice are characteristics of this benchmark. Here, authentic practice is examined in two other domains: moral–ethical conduct and service to others.

### Moral and Ethical Practice

Professions emphasize moral character and ethical practice for good reason. Society trusts professionals to act legally and to not abuse or otherwise take advantage of their patients or clients. At the same time, practitioners are expected to abide by ethical standards specific to their expertise and service to society. Delineating the importance of moral leadership in schools, Quick and Normore (2004) wrote:

> Leadership in any endeavor is a moral task but even more so for educational leaders. Not only are educational leaders responsible for the success of their particular institution, but their work also can impact various other institutions now and in the future because those who they lead now will be tomorrow's leaders. (p. 337)

Though a principal's morality is developed individually, it plays a pivotal role in determining whether he or she behaves ethically. Ethics are embedded in codes of conduct maintained by groups to which a principal belongs. Hodgkinson (1991) posits that "Values, morals, and ethics are the very stuff of leadership and administrative life" (p. 11). Minimally, principals are expected to comply with the ethical standards of their profession and community (most principals also are influenced by religious and family ethics).

Two aspects of ethics are pervasive across professions. The first pertains to legal behavior; simply put, professionals are expected to obey the law; consequently, an illegal act (stealing from your employer) is also unethical. Some authors (e.g., Howlett, 1991), however, separate illegalities and unethical behavior, contending that professional ethics begin where laws end. The second pervasive aspect of ethical behavior pertains to making balanced decisions. Any act that purposefully favors one party over others is considered unethical (Blanchard & Peale, 1988).

In school administration specifically, ethics extend to other unacceptable behaviors such as bias, discrimination, nepotism, violating confidentiality, and shirking work responsibilities (Howlett, 1991; Kimbrough & Nunnery, 1988). According to Greenfield (1991), administrative ethics are framed by the use of power and decision choices. Sergiovanni (1992) described moral and ethical principals as being committed to representing all stakeholders fairly and equally; they are administrators who resist temptations to behave politically. Possibly the most widely referenced clarification of ethics in school administration is provided by Starratt (1991, 1995). His typology has three foundational themes: the ethic of critique, the ethic of justice, and the ethic of caring.

- *Critique.* This theme involves the use of power. For example, a principal who uses his authority to force teachers to perform personal favors would be violating this ethic. Critique is highly relevant to school improvement because it addresses a principal's moral dispositions about empowerment and collaboration.
- *Justice.* This theme demands attention to both individual rights and the common good. The primary foci are democratic participation and equal access to programs and resources. For example, a principal who arbitrarily allocates resources without allowing faculty to have input or who unfairly distributes resources to reward his supporters and to punish his critics would be violating the ethic of justice.
- *Caring.* This theme acknowledges the right of individuals "to be who they are" and requires those who care for them to encounter them "in their authentic individuality" (Starratt, 1991, p. 195). It focuses on human relationships such as cooperation, shared commitment, and friendship. A principal who dislikes a teacher and treats her unfairly simply because of her personal views would be violating the ethic of caring.

Ethical behavior is continuously challenged by a pervasive reality of the principalship, explained by Wirt and Kirst (2005): principals concurrently are expected to be professionals (making important decisions based on empirical evidence) and public employees subservient to the will of the people. In essence, they are challenged to apply professional knowledge in political contexts so that they can be politically effective while remaining moral and ethical.

In summary, morality and ethics are complex but highly relevant issues for principals. The degree to which practitioners are moral individuals who behave ethically determines whether schools are moral institutions—social agencies that honor and respect the needs and interests of every student (Greenfield, 1995).

## Serving Others

The philosophical conviction that administrators should serve others was formally introduced into management literature in the late 1970s. One of the first models, known as servant leadership, was constructed by Robert Greenleaf (1977). He posited that administrators who embraced this concept deliberately served others, primarily by placing the needs, aspirations, and interests of others above their own. Some conceptualizations of servant leadership, however, have been controversial—both because empirical evidence supporting effectiveness is missing (Washington, Sutton, & Field, 2006) and because they put forward the idea that employee needs and interests supersede organizational interests (e.g., Graham, 1991). The position espoused here is that service-oriented principals are also ethical principals; they neither are selfish nor serve only school employee interests. Instead, they are ethical practitioners committed to serving student, employee, community, and school interests (e.g., protecting institutional integrity) concurrently. They consciously evaluate multiple needs and interests and seek to make fair, balanced, and effective decisions (see Figure 13.1).

The concept of principal as servant leader is framed by ethical and transformational leadership and the creation of learning communities. Burns (1978) noted that transformational leadership occurs "when one or more persons engage with others in such a way that leaders and followers raise one another to higher levels of motivation and morality" (p. 20). He describes the style as being moral because it elevates the conduct and aspirations of all those involved. Application of transformational leadership by principals has been advocated by many leading scholars (e.g., Leithwood & Jantzi, 1997, 2000; Silins, 1994) who claim that the style improves teacher motivation, commitment, and innovation—and ultimately school effectiveness.

Learning communities were discussed previously in chapter 5. In schools that function in this manner, principals and teachers practice as peer professionals, collaborate to challenge the status quo, engage in self-expression, and experiment with new approaches that may improve school performance. By doing these things, they make collective learning the cornerstone of school improvement (Giles & Hargreaves, 2006) and institutionalize effective new ideas and constructive assumptions about teaching and learning (Rait, 1995). Most notably, they are able to transform change-resistant cultures into learning cultures.

Seeking to describe successful principals internationally, Day (2007) noted that those who are most effective "lead in ways which enable all staff in their schools to raise

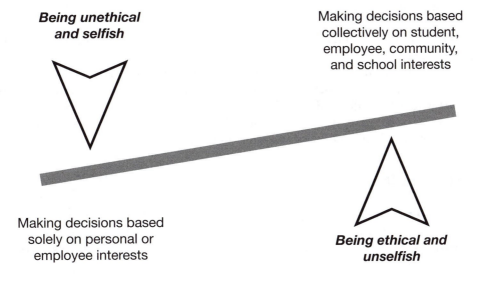

*Being unethical and selfish*

Making decisions based collectively on student, employee, community, and school interests

Making decisions based solely on personal or employee interests

*Being ethical and unselfish*

*Figure 13.1* Serving Others by Making Ethical and Unselfish Decisions.

rather than dampen their aspirations of success for themselves and those in their care. They nurture cultures of care with achievement" (p. 22). He concluded that successful principals have a passion for teaching and learning and for teachers and learners. Though building trust and serving others are critically important, they should never be used to protect incompetence, under the guise of servant leadership or otherwise. Emphasizing the importance of competence to learning communities, Fullan, Bertani, and Quinn (2004) wrote:

> Organizations with a high level of trust among participants combine respect, personal regard, integrity, and competence—yes, competence. We cannot trust even well-intentioned people if they are not good at what they do. Effective, highly interactive cultures incorporate high pressure and high support. (p. 45)

Thus, serving the needs and interests of employees should never justify ineffective schools that fail to meet the needs of some students.

## CAREER PLANNING

A person's career consists of an evolving sequence of jobs (Zunker, 1990) and work experiences in them (Arthur, Hall, & Lawrence, 1989). Unfortunately, relatively little is known about the extent to which principals plan their careers. Generally, however, they have three options:

- They can elect not to develop a career plan in which case they rely on good fortune and react to opportunities as they may occur.
- They can rely on others (e.g., mentors or sponsors) to develop a career plan for them. Though such assistance is usually beneficial, it does not diminish the need to take personal responsibility for career planning (Graen, 1989).
- They can develop a personal career plan and assume responsibility for updating it periodically.

Personal commitment and being proactive rather than reactive make the third alternative the best choice.

Career planning has become increasingly essential for principals because the position across schools is less homogeneous and broader than it was just three decades ago. Both leadership (e.g., visioning and initiating change) and management (e.g., completing state accountability reports) tasks have been added, largely as a result of protracted efforts to achieve school reforms (DiPaola & Tschannen-Moran, 2003).

### Deciding to Plan

In deciding whether to develop a career plan, you need to consider two issues: the advantages of planning and the reasons why persons usually opt to forgo these advantages. Properly developed, a career plan is both an instrument and a process; that is, it contains pertinent data and provides a pathway for moving into the future (McDaniels & Gysbers, 1992). Plans provide many benefits as demonstrated by the following examples:

- *Getting to know you.* Career planning requires self-assessment; that is, you must objectively look in the mirror and determine your interests, capabilities, knowledge, skills, values, beliefs, and goals. This information then allows you to evaluate job opportunities in relation to your characteristics (Lyon & Kirby, 2000).
- *Reducing uncertainty and risk.* Decision uncertainty depends on the extent to which you know the effects of your possible choices. Career plans reduce uncertainty because they allow you to evaluate your options objectively; for example, you can determine if a position complies with your goals and strategy. The lower the level of uncertainty the less risk that your decision will have negative effects (Kowalski, Lasley, & Mahoney, 2008).
- *Providing peace of mind.* Career decisions usually generate stress because of their potential consequences. Though planning does not eliminate stress, it does reduce the negative effects of stress by providing a framework for making decisions (Buskirk, 1976).
- *Monitoring progress.* A plan makes it more likely that periodically you will assess progress toward your career goals and adapt your objectives and strategies when necessary (Buskirk, 1976).
- *Preventing complacency.* Administrators can easily become complacent, especially when they believe they have job security. Yet settling to remain in your current position instead of exploring other opportunities can cause remorse at a later time (Kowalski, 2003b). Having a plan makes it more likely that you will weigh what you have to gain in relation to your current comfort level when given an opportunity to advance your career.

Despite these advantages, many persons, including college graduates, fail to develop career plans. Studying this issue, Steele and Morgan (1991) found that the following excuses are especially prevalent:

- *I know what I want to be.* Individuals offering this explanation claim that they have known since childhood what they want to be. Therefore, considering career alternatives would have been a waste of time.
- *I'm comfortable letting life decide my fate.* Individuals offering this explanation have a fatalistic attitude toward their careers; that is, they believe that fate cannot be altered by planning.
- *I will make decisions when I need to.* Individuals offering this explanation believe they will have many opportunities and, when they arise, they will make an appropriate decision.
- *I don't have the time.* Individuals offering this explanation believe the potential benefits of career planning are outweighed by the time and effort required.
- *I don't have enough information.* Individuals offering this explanation typically are unsettled regarding a preferred career. They suggest that they might develop a career plan at some future point when they know more about possible careers.

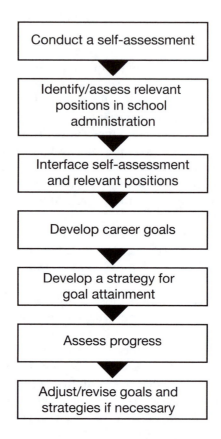

*Figure 13.2* Linear Career Planning Model.

Career planning is especially important for principals, because the normal career progression for administrators has been to leave teaching to become an assistant principal, to later become a principal, and eventually to become a district-level administrator (an assistant superintendent or superintendent). Yet relatively little is known about factors that generate job satisfaction at each stage and the extent to which job satisfaction in a current position influences the decision to seek a higher-level position (Kwan, 2009). Having a plan allows you to set a personal career ladder.

## Developing a Plan

Various approaches can be applied to personal career planning but, for those without extensive knowledge of the subject, a linear paradigm is recommended. A seven-step process is illustrated in Figure 13.2, and explanations of each step are provided in Table 13.1.

The most effective career plans are characterized by the following attributes:

- *Being continuous*. The planning process is perpetual and goals and strategies are periodically adjusted (preferably annually) to account for new or unforeseen circumstances.
- *Being purposeful*. The plan is goal-driven; that is, it identifies linear (sequential) objectives.
- *Being directive*. The plan provides a framework for decision making; that is, career opportunities are evaluated in relation to linear objectives.
- *Being flexible*. Goals and strategies can be adjusted when necessary.
- *Being realistic*. The goals are attainable and the tactics for achieving them are doable.
- *Being influential*. The plan can and does influence important career-related decisions.

## Career Portfolios

A career portfolio provides a tangible record of evidence with respect to formal education, career goals, and work experiences (Pond, Burdick, & Yamamoto, 1998). Having one enhances career planning, because essential evidence and other forms of data are maintained. Thus, the content can be used to determine personal growth (e.g., job skills), progress toward existing goals, job satisfaction, and readiness for more challenging positions.

A typical portfolio is organized around a career plan. As an example, the first section may include self-assessment data, such as writing samples, performance evaluations, and test scores (e.g., Graduate Record Examination, PRAXIS exam). A career portfolio also can facilitate ongoing reflection (Brown & Irby, 1995), a process discussed in chapter 11.

*Table 13.1* Career Planning Steps

| Step | Explanation |
| --- | --- |
| Conduct self-assessment | Requires introspection to determine strengths and weaknesses and personal requirements and preferences |
| Identify relevant administrative positions | Requires identification of various types of assistant principal and principal positions (e.g., level and size of school) and assessments of responsibilities typically associated with them |
| Interface self-assessment and positions | Requires analysis of personal attributes in relation to types of assistant principal and principal positions |
| Develop career goals | Establish chronologically the administrative positions you intend to acquire and realistically have opportunities to acquire |
| Develop a strategy | Establish tactics for meeting career goals |
| Assess progress | Periodically, and at least annually, objectively assess progress toward meeting the next unmet goal |
| Adjust/revise goals | Make judgments regarding progress toward goals and determine if the goals should be revised, if the strategy should be revised, or both |

## REFLECTIONS

Instability in the principalship remains a primary concern in relation to school reform because frequent leadership changes deter school improvement. Less recognized are the effects of instability on career choices related to entering this position. As you finish your academic studies for a principal's license and contemplate pursuing the position, reflect on factors that draw you to and push you away from being an administrator. As explained previously in this book, studies of novice principals (e.g., Woodruff & Kowalski, 2009) often reveal a disjunction between what is anticipated and what is encountered. That is, first-time principals are often surprised to learn how much time they devote to doing things they prefer to avoid.

Also consider why highly committed principals embrace authentic practice. Specifically, think about the nexus between authentic practice and job satisfaction. The most dedicated principals tend to be guided by a moral–ethical compass and they feel passionately about serving others. Equally notable, they are concurrently caring and demanding; that is, their devotion to authentic practice does not deter them from setting high expectations and from dealing with incompetence.

Those who exit the principalship often cite long hours, unrealistic demands, incessant conflict, and low remuneration as problems (Johnson, 2005; Norton, 2003). Though these factors are prevalent in most districts and schools, they have less negative influence on highly committed practitioners. Thus, knowing why you want to be principal and knowing what aspects of the job you find satisfying are advantages—not only for you but for your employer. Principals who develop and apply a personal plan are likely to possess this knowledge; and they usually make more effective choices than their peers when they encounter career peaks and valleys.

## Knowledge-Based Questions

1    What is the difference between ethical and moral practice?
2    Why do professions have codes of ethics?
3    What is servant leadership?
4    What are the common criticisms of servant leadership?
5    How can a principal concurrently serve employees and students?
6    Why do many college graduates avoid career planning?
7    What are the consequences of entering administration without a career plan?
8    What types of data are relevant to a personal career plan?
9    Why is commitment an important consideration in relation to school-level administrative positions?
10   Why is it important to have measurable goals in your career plan?

## Skill-Based Activities

1    Identify forces that constrain principals from being moral and ethical.
2    Using Starratt's typology, identify unacceptable behavior in the ethic of critique, the ethic of justice, and the ethic of caring.
3    Describe at least three behavioral differences between principals who exhibit service to others and principals who do not.
4    Assume you are developing a career plan. Outline what you would do to evaluate your strengths and weaknesses.

# Notes

1. School district wealth is commonly determined by assessed valuation per pupil—a statistic calculated by dividing the district's assessed valuation (total of property value) by the district's enrollment.
2. An example of democratic localism can be found in the movie *Hoosiers*. Dissatisfied with a new high school basketball coach, a group of citizens holds a town hall meeting in a local church to vote whether the coach should be retained.
3. The cost of human and material resources increases because of inflation. Thus, when a school district's revenue is frozen, it actually is reduced by inflation. In some instances, the problem is averted if a district is experiencing an enrollment decline.
4. Though this research was not conducted with school administrators, it has been referenced repeatedly in school administration texts. The study referred to task-orientation as initiating structure and people-orientation as consideration. Administrators could rank low, moderate, or high in each.
5. Since their original work, a sixth type of power, information control, has been considered (Raven, 1992). This form of influence pertains to controlling needed data and information. Because its influence in schools has not been examined extensively, it was not added to the original list. Many authors continue to focus on the original five types of power.
6. Cult leaders, for example, have often used referent power that was detrimental to society and individuals.
7. The Carnegie unit was developed in 1906 as a measure of the amount of time a student has studied a subject. For example, if a student studied a subject for a total of 120 hours, he or she would earn one unit of high school credit. Some states use "credits" rather than units, and two credits are the equivalent of one unit.
8. Block periods are typically 90 minutes and traditional class periods are usually 50 or 55 minutes.
9. Value-added assessments focus on student growth over a specific period (typically two semesters). They entail a pre-test at the beginning of the period and a post-test at the end of the period. Growth is measured by the differences in pre- and post-test scores.
10. The terms *turnover* and *exits* are often confused. The former refers to a change of personnel in a position for any reason whereas the latter refers solely to a person leaving a position without returning to it (Kowalski, 2003a).

# References

## PREFACE

Bennis, W. B. (1984). The four competencies of leadership. *Training and Development Journal, 38*(8), 14–19.

## CHAPTER 1

Alexander, K. M. & Alexander, D. (2009). *American public school law* (9th ed.). Belmont, CA: Wadsworth.

Anderson, J. E. (1990). *Public policymaking: An introduction.* Boston: Houghton Mifflin.

Bauman, P. C. (1996). *Governing education: Public sector reform or privatization.* Boston: Allyn and Bacon.

Beck, L. G. & Murphy, J. (1996). *The four imperatives of a successful school.* Thousand Oaks, CA: Corwin Press.

Björk, L. G. & Keedy, J. L. (2001). Politics and the superintendency in the U.S.A.: Restructuring in-service education. *Journal of In-service Education, 27*(2), 275–302.

*Brown* v. *Board of Education,* 347 U.S. 483 (1954).

Butts, R. F. & Cremin, L. A. (1953). *A history of education in American culture.* New York: Henry Holt and Company.

Campbell, R. F., Cunningham, L. L., Nystrand, R. O., & Usdan, M. D. (1990). *The organization and control of American schools* (6th ed.). Columbus, OH: Merrill.

Clemmer, E. F. (1991). *The school policy handbook.* Boston: Allyn and Bacon.

Coyle, L. & Witcher, A. (1992). Transforming the idea into action: Policies and practices to enhance school effectiveness. *Urban Education, 26*(4), 390–400.

Crampton, F. & Whitney, T. (1996). *The search for equity in school funding.* NCSL Education Partners Project. Denver, CO: National Conference of State Legislatures.

Cuban, L. (1988). *The managerial imperative and the practice of leadership in schools.* Albany: State University of New York Press.

Cuban, L. (1998, January 28). A tale of two schools: How progressives and traditionalists undermine our understanding of what is "good" in schools. *Education Week,* p. 48.

Downer, D. F. (1991). Review of research on effective schools. *McGill Journal of Education, 26*(3), 323–31.

Edmonds, R. (1979). Effective schools for the urban poor. *Educational Leadership, 37,* 15–27.

Ellis, J. (1983). Since 1965: The impact of federal funds on public education. *Education and Urban Society, 15,* 351–66.

Fowler, F. C. (2000). *Policy studies for educational leaders.* Upper Saddle River, NJ: Merrill, Prentice Hall.

Fuhrman, G. C. (2004). The ethic of community. *Journal of Educational Administration, 42*(2), 215–35.

Greenfield, W. D., Jr. (1995). Toward a theory of school administration: The centrality of leadership. *Educational Administration Quarterly, 31*(1), 61–85.

Hanson, E. M. (2003). *Educational administration and organizational behavior* (5th ed.). Boston: Allyn and Bacon.

Hoy, W. K. & Miskel, C. G. (2005). *Educational administration: Theory, research, and practice* (8th ed.). New York: McGraw-Hill.

Imber, M. & Van Geel, T. (1993). *Education law*. New York: McGraw-Hill.

King, R. A., Swanson, A. D., & Sweetland, R. G. (2003). *School finance: Achieving high standards with equity and efficiency* (3rd ed.). Boston: Allyn and Bacon.

Knezevich, S. J. (1984). *Administration of public education: A sourcebook for the leadership and management of educational institutions* (4th ed.). New York: Harper & Row.

Kowalski, T. J. (2003). *Contemporary school administration: An introduction* (2nd ed.). Boston: Allyn and Bacon.

Kowalski, T. J. (2006). *The school superintendent: Theory, practice, and cases* (2nd ed.). Thousand Oaks, CA: Sage.

Kowalski, T. J., Lasley, T. J., & Mahoney, J. (2008). *Data-driven decisions and school leadership: Best practices for school improvement.* Boston: Allyn and Bacon

LaMorte, M. W. (1996). *School law: Cases and concepts* (5th ed.). Boston: Allyn and Bacon.

Levin, H. M. (1987). Education as a public and private good. *Journal of Policy Analysis and Management, 6*, 628–41.

Levin, H. M. (1999). The public–private nexus in education. *American Behavioral Scientist, 43*(1), 124–37.

Noblit, G. W. & Dempsey, V. O. (1996). *The social construction of virtue: The moral life of schools.* Albany: SUNY.

Protheroe, N., Shellard, E., & Turner, J. (2003). *A practical guide to school improvement: Meeting the challenges of NCLB.* Arlington, VA: Educational Research Service.

Purkey, S. & Smith, M. (1983). Effective schools: A review. *Elementary School Journal, 83*(3), 426–52.

Radin, B. A. & Hawley, W. D. (1988). *The politics of federal reorganization.* New York: Pergamon Press.

Razik, T. A. & Swanson, A. D. (2001). *Fundamental concepts of educational leadership* (2nd ed.). Upper Saddle River, NJ: Merrill, Prentice Hall.

Rebell, M. A. (1999). CFE v. State: Sound basic education and racial justice. *Equity & Excellence in Education, 32*(3), 6–24.

Reutter, E. E. (1985). *The law of public education* (3rd ed.). Mineola, NY: The Foundation Press.

Robelen, E. W. (2005, April 13). 40 years after ESEA, Federal role in schools is broader than ever. *Education Week*, pp. 1, 42.

Schlechty, P. (1990). *Schools for the 21st century.* San Francisco: Jossey-Bass.

Sergiovanni, T. J. (2009). *The principalship: A reflective practice perspective.* Boston: Allyn and Bacon.

Sergiovanni, T. J., Kelleher, P., McCarthy, M. M., & Fowler, F. C. (2009). *Educational governance and administration* (6th ed.). Boston: Allyn and Bacon.

Singer, J. D. (1985). Educating handicapped children: 10 years of PL 94-142. *Education Digest, 51*(4), 47–9.

Skocpol, T. (1993). *Diminished democracy: From membership to management in American civic life.* Norman, OK: University of Oklahoma Press.

Spring, J. H. (1991). *American education: An introduction to social and political aspects* (5th ed.). New York: Longman.

Starratt, R. J. (1991). Building an ethical school: A theory for practice in educational leadership. *Educational Administration Quarterly, 27*(2), 185–202.

Stout, R. T., Tallerico, M., & Scribner, K. P. (1994). Values: The "what?" of the politics of education. *Journal of Education Policy, 9*(5–6), 5–20.

Sufrin, S. C. (1963). *Administering the National Defense Education Act.* Syracuse, NY: Syracuse University Press.

Taylor, B. (2002). The effective schools process: Alive and well. *Phi Delta Kappan, 83*(5), 375–8.

Valente, W. D. (1987). *Law in the schools* (2nd ed.). Columbus, OH: Merrill.

Wardekker, W. L. (2001). Schools and moral education: Conformism or autonomy? *Journal of Philosophy of Education, 35*(1), 101–14.

Wirt, F. & Kirst, M. (2005). *The political dynamics of American education* (3rd ed.). Richmond, CA: McCutchan.

Zigarelli, M. A. (1996). An empirical test of conclusions from effective schools research. *Journal of Educational Research*, *90*, 103–10.

## CHAPTER 2

Bauman, P. C. (1996). *Governing education: Public sector reform or privatization*. Boston: Allyn and Bacon.

Bennis, W. G. & Nanus, B. (1985). *Leaders: The strategies for taking charge*. New York: Harper & Row.

Björk, L. G. (1995). Substance and symbolism in the education commission reports. In R. Ginsberg & D. Plank (Eds.), *Commissions, reports, reforms and educational policy* (pp. 133–49). New York: Praeger.

Bruning, S. D. & Ledingham, J. A. (2000). Organization and key relationships: Testing the influence of relationship dimensions in a business to business context. In J. Ledingham & S. Bruning (Eds.), *Public relations as relationship management: A relational approach to the study and practice of public relations* (pp. 159–74). Mahwah, NJ: Lawrence Erlbaum Associates.

Burgoon, J. K. & Hale, J. L. (1984). The fundamental topoi of relational communication. *Communication Monographs*, *51*, 193–214.

Catano, N. & Stronge, J. H. (2006). What are principals expected to do? Congruence between principal evaluation and performance standards. *NASSP Bulletin*, *90*(3), 221–37.

Conger, J. A. (1989). *The charismatic leader: Behind the mystique of exceptional leadership*. San Francisco: Jossey-Bass.

Conrad, C. (1994). *Strategic organizational communication: Toward the twenty-first century* (3rd ed.). Fort Worth, TX: Harcourt Brace College.

Crow, G. M. & Glascock, C. (1995). Socialization to a new conception of the principalship. *Journal of Educational Administration*, *33*(1), 22–43.

Cunningham, W. & Gresso, D. (1993). *Cultural leadership: The culture of excellence in education*. Boston: Allyn and Bacon.

Fullan, M. (2001). *Leading in a culture of change*. San Francisco: Jossey-Bass.

Glasman, N. & Glasman, L. (1997). Connecting the preparation of school leaders to the practice of school leadership. *Peabody Journal of Education*, *72*(2), 3–20.

Grunig, J. E. (1989). Symmetrical presuppositions as a framework for public relations theory. In C. H. Botan (Ed.), *Public relations theory* (pp. 17–44). Hillsdale, NJ: Lawrence Erlbaum Associates.

Hall, G. E. & Hord, S. M. (2006). *Implementing change: Patterns, principals, and potholes* (2nd ed.). Boston: Allan and Bacon.

Hallinger, P. (1992). The evolving role of American principals: From managerial to instructional to transformational leader. *Journal of Educational Administration*, *30*(3), 35–48.

Hanson, E. M. (2003). *Educational administration and organizational behavior* (5th ed.). Boston: Allyn and Bacon.

Hoy, W. K. & Miskel, C. G. (2005). *Educational administration: Theory, research, and practice* (8th ed.). New York: McGraw-Hill.

Johnson, J. P., Livingston, M., & Schwartz, R. A. (2000). What makes a good elementary school? A critical examination. *Journal of Educational Research*, *93*(6), 339–48.

Katz, D. & Kahn, R. (1978). *The social psychology of organizations* (2nd ed.). New York: Wiley.

Kotter, J. P. (1990). *A force for change: How leadership differs from management*. New York: Free Press.

Kowalski, T. J. (2006). *The school superintendent: Theory, practice, and cases* (2nd ed.). Thousand Oaks, CA: Sage.

Kowalski, T. J. (2008). *Public relations in schools* (4th ed.). Boston: Allyn and Bacon.

Kowalski, T. J., Lasley, T. J., & Mahoney, J. (2008). *Data-driven decisions and school leadership: Best practices for school improvement*. Boston: Allyn and Bacon.

Kowalski, T. J., Petersen, G. J., & Fusarelli, L. D. (2007). *Effective communication for school administrators: An imperative in an information age*. Lanham, MD: Rowman & Littlefield Education.

March, J. G. & Simon, H. (1958). *Organizations*. New York: John Wiley.

Milliken, F. J. (1987). Three types of perceived uncertainty about the environment: State, effect, and response. *Academy of Management Review*, *12*(1), 133–43.

National Association of Elementary School Principals. (2009). *Leading early childhood learning communities: What principals should know and be able to do*. Alexandria, VA: Author.

Natriello, G. (1990). Intended and unintended consequences: Purposes and effects of teacher evaluation. In J. Millman & L. Darling-Hammond (Eds.), *The new handbook of teacher evaluation* (pp. 35–45). Newbury Park, CA: Sage.

Nutt, P. C. (1989). *Making tough decisions: Tactics for improving managerial decision making*. San Francisco: Jossey-Bass.

Nyberg, D. A. (1990). Power, empowerment, and educational authority. In S. Jacobson & J. Conway (Eds.), *Educational leadership in an age of reform* (pp. 47–64). New York: Longman.

Portin, B. S. (1998). Compounding roles: A study of Washington's principals. *International Journal of Educational Research*, *29*(4), 335–46.

Protheroe, N. (2004). Professional learning communities. *Principal*, *83*(5), 39–42.

Purkey, S. C. & Smith, M. S. (1982). Synthesis of research on effective schools. *Educational Leadership*, *40*(3), 64–9.

Purkey, S. C. & Smith, M. S. (1983). Effective schools: A review. *Elementary School Journal*, *83*, 427–52.

Robbins, S. P. & Coulter, M. (2007). *Management* (9th ed.). Upper Saddle River, NJ: Prentice Hall.

Schein, E. (1985). *Organizational culture and leadership*. San Francisco: Jossey-Bass.

Schermerhorn, J. (2008). *Management* (9th ed.). New York: Wiley.

Schneider, W. E. (1994). *The reengineering alternative: A plan for making your current culture work*. Burr Ridge, IL: Irwin Professional Publishing.

Senge, P. (1990). *The fifth discipline: Mastering the five practices of the learning organization*. New York: Doubleday.

Sergiovanni, T. J., Kelleher, P., McCarthy, M. M., & Fowler, F. C. (2009). *Educational governance and administration* (6th ed.). Boston: Allyn and Bacon.

Spring, J. H. (2000). *American education* (9th ed.). Boston: McGraw-Hill.

Stufflebeam, D. & Webster, W. J. (1988). Evaluation as an administrative function. In N. Boyan (Ed.), *Handbook of research on educational administration* (pp. 569–602). New York: Longman.

Wimpelberg, R. K., Teddlie, C., & Stringfield, S. (1989). Sensitivity to context: The past and future of effective schools research. *Educational Administration Quarterly*, *25*(1), 82–108.

Winter, P. A. (1995). Vision in school planning: A tool for crafting a creative future. *School Business Affairs*, *61*(6), 46–50.

Yukl, G. (2005). *Leadership in organizations* (6th ed.). Upper Saddle River, NJ: Pearson-Prentice Hall.

# CHAPTER 3

*A framework for success for all students*. (2006). New York: Carnegie Corporation.

Bennis, W. G. & Nanus, B. (1985). *Leaders: The strategies for taking charge*. New York: Harper & Row.

Chance, E. W. (1992). *Visionary leadership in schools: Successful strategies for developing and implementing an educational vision*. Springfield, IL: Charles C. Thomas.

Cunningham, W. & Gresso, D. (1993). *Cultural leadership: The culture of excellence in education*. Boston: Allyn and Bacon.

*Do high school graduation tests measure up? A closer look at high school exit exams*. (2004). Washington, DC: Achieve.

DuFour, R. & Eaker, R. (1998). *Professional learning communities at work: Best practices for enhancing student achievement*. Bloomington, IN: National Educational Service.

Duke, D. (2004). *The challenge of educational change*. Boston: Allyn and Bacon.

Elmore, R. (2003). *Knowing the right things to do: School improvement and performance-based accountability*. Washington, DC: NGA Center for Best Practices.

Firestone, W. A. & Louis, K. S. (1999). Schools as cultures. In J. Murphy & K. S. Louis (Eds.), *Handbook of research on educational administration* (2nd ed., pp. 297–322). San Francisco: Jossey-Bass.

Fullan, M. (1999). *Change forces: The sequel*. Philadelphia: Falmer Press.

Fullan, M. (2001). *Leading in a culture of change*. San Francisco: Jossey-Bass.

Fullan, M. (2004). *Leadership and sustainability*. Thousand Oaks, CA: Corwin Press.

Fullan, M. (2007). *The new meaning of educational change* (4th ed.). New York: Teachers College Press.

Guthrie, J. W. & Schuermann, P. J. (2010). *Successful school leadership: Planning, politics, performance, and power*. Boston: Allyn and Bacon.

Haberman, M. (1994). The top 10 fantasies of school reformers. *Phi Delta Kappan, 75*(9), 689–92.

Hall, G. E. & Hord, S. M. (2006). *Implementing change: Patterns, principles, and potholes* (2nd ed.). Boston: Allyn and Bacon.

Hanson, E. M. (2003). *Educational administration and organizational behavior* (5th ed.). Boston: Allyn and Bacon.

Hoy, W. K. & Miskel, C. G. (2005). *Educational administration: Theory, research, and practice* (8th ed.). New York: McGraw-Hill.

James, J. (1995). Negotiating the grand canyon of change. *School Administrator, 52*(1), 22–9.

Kowalski, T. J. (2003). *Contemporary school administration: An introduction* (2nd ed.). Boston: Allyn and Bacon.

Kowalski, T. J. (2008). *Public relations in schools* (4th ed.). Boston: Allyn and Bacon.

Kowalski, T. J., Lasley, T. J., & Mahoney, J. (2008). *Data-driven decisions and school leadership: Best practices for school improvement*. Boston: Allyn and Bacon.

Leithwood, K., Jantzi, D., & Fernandez, A. (1994). Transformational leadership and teachers' commitment to change. In J. Murphy & K. S. Louis (Eds.), *Reshaping the principalship* (pp. 77–98). Thousand Oaks, CA: Corwin Press.

Martin, J. (2002). *Organizational culture: Mapping the terrain*. Thousand Oaks, CA: Sage.

Marzano, R. J. & Waters, T. (2009). *District leadership that works: Striking the right balance*. Bloomington, IN: Learning Tree Press.

Miskel, C. & Ogawa, R. (1988). Work motivation, job satisfaction, and climate. In N. Boyan (Ed.), *Handbook of research on educational administration* (pp. 279–304). New York: Longman.

Nanus, B. (1992). *Visionary leadership*. San Francisco: Jossey-Bass.

National Commission on Excellence in Education. (1983). *A nation at risk: The imperative for educational reform*. Washington, DC: U.S. Department of Education.

Nutt, P. C. (1985). The study planning processes. In W. G. Bennis, K. D. Benne, & R. Chin (Eds.), *The planning of change* (4th ed., pp. 198–215). New York: Holt, Rinehart & Winston.

Protheroe, N. (2005). Leadership for school improvement. *Principal, 84*(4), 54–6.

Sarason, S. B. (1996). *Revisiting the culture of the school and the problem of change*. New York: Teachers College Press.

Schein, E. H. (1992). *Organizational culture and leadership* (2nd ed.). San Francisco: Jossey-Bass.

Schein, E. H. (1996). Culture: The missing concept in organization studies. *Administrative Science Quarterly, 41*(2), 229–40.

Schlechty, P. C. (2008). No community left behind. *Phi Delta Kappan, 89*(8), 552–9.

Sheldon, S. B. & Epstein, J. L. (2002). Improving student behavior and school discipline with family and community involvement. *Education and Urban Society, 35*(1), 4–26.

Spring, J. H. (2008). *American education* (13th ed.). New York: McGraw-Hill.

Starratt, R. (1996). *Transforming educational administration: Meaning, community, and excellence*. New York: McGraw-Hill.

Swanson, C. B. (2004). *The truth about graduation rates: An evidence-based commentary*. Washington, DC: Urban Institute.

Tagiuri, R. (1968). The concept of organizational climate. In R. Tagiuri & G. H. Litwin (Eds.), *Organizational climate* (pp. 11–32). Boston: Harvard Graduate School of Business Administration.

Timperley, H. S. & Robinson, V. M. (1998). Collegiality in schools: Its nature and implications for problem solving. *Educational Administration Quarterly, 34*, 608–29.

Trimble, K. (1996). Building a learning community. *Equity and Excellence in Education, 29*(1), 37–40.

U.S. Department of Education. (2008). *A nation accountable: Twenty-five years after A Nation at Risk*. Washington, DC: Author.

Weiler, H. N. (1990). Comparative perspectives on educational decentralization: An exercise in contradiction? *Educational Evaluation and Policy Analysis, 12*(4), 433–48.

Zmuda, A., Kuklis, R., & Kline, R. (2004). *Transforming schools: Creating a culture of continuous improvement.* Alexandria, VA: Association for Supervision and Curriculum Development.

## CHAPTER 4

Bass, B. M. (1985). *Leadership and performance beyond expectations.* New York: Free Press.

Bassett, G. A. (1970). Leadership style and strategy. In L. Netzer, G. Eye, A. Graef, R. Drey, & J. Overman (Eds.), *Interdisciplinary foundations of supervision* (pp. 221–31). Boston: Allyn and Bacon.

Bennis, W. B. & Nanus, B. (1985). *Leaders: The strategies for taking charge.* New York: Harper & Row.

Burns, J. M. (1978). *Leadership.* New York: Harper & Row.

Fleishman, E. A. & Harris, E. F. (1962). Patterns of leadership behavior related to employee grievances and turnover. *Personnel Psychology, 15,* 43–56.

French, J. P. & Raven, B. (1960). The bases of social power. In D. Cartwright & A. Zander (Eds.), *Group dynamics* (pp. 607–23). New York: Harper and Row.

Getzels, J. W. & Guba, E. G. (1957). Social behavior and the administrative process. *School Review, 65,* 423–41.

Hallinger, P. & Heck, R. H. (1996). Reassessing the principal's role in school effectiveness: A review of empirical research, 1980–1995. *Educational Administration Quarterly, 32*(1), 5–44.

Halpin, A. W. (1966). *Theory and research in administration.* New York: Macmillan.

Hanson, E. M. (2003). *Educational administration and organizational behavior* (5th ed.). Boston: Allyn and Bacon.

Harris, M. M. & Willower, D. J. (1998). Principals' optimism and perceived school effectiveness. *Journal of Educational Administration, 36*(4), 353–61.

House, R. J. & Baetz, M. (1979). Leadership: Some empirical generalizations and new research directions. In B. M. Staw (Ed.), *Research in organizational behavior* (Vol. 1, pp. 341–423). Greenwich, CT: JAI Press.

Hoy, W. K. & Miskel, C. G. (2008). *Educational administration: Theory, research, and practice* (8th ed.). Boston: McGraw-Hill.

Immegart, G. L. (1988). Leadership and leader behavior. In N. J. Boyan (Ed.), *Handbook of research on educational administration* (pp. 259–77). New York: Longman.

Jackson, J. F. & Peterson, K. D. (2004). Executive behavior: An examination of selected studies for three decades of administrative work across organizational settings, industries, and contexts. *Journal of Leadership and Organizational Studies, 10*(3), 82–90.

Katz, R. L. (1974). Skills of an effective administrator. *Harvard Business Review, 52,* 80–108.

Kowalski, T. J. (2009). Evidence and decision making in professions. In T. J. Kowalski & T. J. Lasley (Eds.), *Handbook of data-based decision making in education* (pp. 3–19). New York: Routledge.

Kowalski, T. J., Lasley, T. J., & Mahoney, J. (2008). *Data-driven decisions and school leadership: Best practices for school improvement.* Boston: Allyn and Bacon.

Langer, S. & Boris-Schacter, S. (2003). Challenging the image of the American principalship. *Principal, 83*(1), 14–18.

Leithwood, K. & Duke, D. L. (1999). A century's quest for a knowledge base, 1976–1998. In J. Murphy & K. S. Louis (Eds.), *Handbook of research on educational policy* (pp. 45–72). San Francisco: Jossey Bass.

Leithwood, K. & Montgomery, D. J. (1982). The role of the elementary school principal in program improvement. *Review of Educational Research, 52*(3), 309–39.

Leithwood, K., Jantzi, D., & Steinbach, R. (1999). *Changing leadership for changing times.* Philadelphia: Open University Press.

Levin, H. M. (1999). Education as a public and private good. *Journal of Policy Analysis and Management, 6,* 628–41.

Lewin, K., Lippitt, R., & White, R. K. (1939). Patterns of aggressive behavior in experimentally created "social climates." *Journal of Social Psychology, 10,* 271–99.

Marks, H. M. & Printy, S. M. (2003). Principal leadership and school performance: An integration of transformational and instructional leadership. *Educational Administration Quarterly*, *39*(3), 370–97.

Marks, H. M. & Printy, S. M. (2006). Shared leadership for teacher and student learning. *Theory into Practice*, *45*(2), 125–32.

Marzano, R. J., Waters, T., & McNulty, B. A. (2005). *School leadership that works: From research to results*. Alexandria, VA: Association for Supervision and Curriculum Development.

Raven, B. H. (1992). A power/interaction model of interpersonal influence: French and Raven thirty years later. *Journal of Social Behavior and Personality*, 7(2), 217–44.

Reitzug, U. C. (1997). Images of principal instructional leadership: From super-vision to collaborative inquiry. *Journal of Curriculum and Supervision*, *12*, 324–43.

Reitzug, U. C., West, D. L., & Angel, R. (2008). Conceptualizing instructional leadership: The voices of principals. *Education and Urban Society*, *40*(6), 694–714.

Sarason, S. B. (1996). *Revisiting the culture of the school and the problem of change*. New York: Teachers College Press.

Schriesheim, C. S., House, R. J., & Kerr, S. (1976). Leader initiating structure: A reconciliation of discrepant research results and some empirical tests. *Organizational Behavior and Human Performance*, *15*, 297–321.

Sergiovanni, T. J. (2001). *The principalship: A reflective practice perspective* (4th ed.). Boston: Allyn and Bacon.

Sunderman, G. L., Kim, J. S., & Orfield, G. (2006). The principals denied by NCLB are central to visionary school reform. *Education Digest*, *72*(2), 19–24.

Yukl, G. A. (1989). *Leadership in organizations* (2nd ed.). Englewood Cliffs, NJ: Prentice Hall.

## CHAPTER 5

Agron, J. (1993). Stretching the school calendar. *American School & University*, *66*, 30–3.

Alexander, K. L., Entwisle, D. R., & Olson, L. S. (2001). Schools, achievement, and inequality: A seasonal perspective. *Educational Evaluation & Policy Analysis*, *23*(2), 171–91.

Alexander, W. & Kealy, R. (1969). From junior high school to middle school. *High School Journal*, *53*, 151–63.

Arnold, D. E. (2002). Block schedule and traditional schedule achievement: A comparison. *NASSP Bulletin*, *86*(630), 42–53.

Bidwell, C. (1965). The school as a formal organization. In J. March (Ed.), *Handbook of organizations* (pp. 972–1023). Chicago: Rand McNally.

Borba, J. A. (2000). Durability of multi-track year-round elementary school principals. *ERS Spectrum*, *18*(1), 41–6.

Bracey, G. W. (1999). Going loopy for looping. *Phi Delta Kappan*, *81*(2), 169–70.

Canady, R. L. (1990). Parallel block scheduling: A better way to organize a school. *Principal*, *69*(3), 34–6.

Canady, R. & Rettig, M. (1995). *Block scheduling: A catalyst for change in high schools*. Princeton, NJ: Eye on Education.

Chaika, G. (2007). *Is year-round schooling the answer?* Retrieved from http://www.educationworld.com/a_admin/admin/admin137.shtml

Covey, S., Merrill, A., & Merrill, R. (1996). *First things first: To live, to love, to learn, to leave a legacy*. New York: Fireside.

David, J. L. (2008). Small learning communities. *Educational Leadership*, *65*(8), 84–5.

Delany, M., Toburen, L., Hooton, B., & Dozier, A. (1998). Parallel block scheduling spells success. *Educational Leadership*, *55*(4), 61–3.

Denault, L. E. (1999). Restructuring? Keep it simple . . . consider looping! *Delta Kappa Gamma Bulletin*, *65*(4), 19–26.

DuFour, R. & Eaker, R. (1998). *Professional learning communities at work: Best practices for enhancing student achievement*. Alexandria, VA: Association for Supervision and Curriculum Development.

DuFour, R., DuFour, R., & Eaker, R. (2008). *Revisiting professional learning communities at work: New insights for improving schools*. Bloomington, IN: Solution Tree.

Duke, D. (2004). *The challenge of educational change*. Boston: Allyn and Bacon.

Elmore, R. F., Peterson, P. L., & McCarthey, S. J. (1996). *Restructuring in the classroom: Teaching, learning, and school organization*. San Francisco: Jossey-Bass.

Fennell, H. (1994). Organizational linkages: Expanding the existing metaphor. *Journal of Educational Administration*, *32*(1), 23–33.

Firestone, W. (1985). The study of loose coupling: Problems, progress and prospects. *Research in Sociology of Education and Socialization*, *5*, 3–30.

Fullan, M. G. (1990). Staff development, innovation, and institutional development. In B. Joyce (Ed.), *Changing school culture through staff development* (pp. 3–25). Alexandria, VA: Association for Supervision and Curriculum Development.

Fullan, M. G. (1991). *The new meaning of educational change* (2nd ed.). New York: Teachers College Press.

Fullan, M. (1999). *Change forces: The sequel*. Philadelphia: Falmer Press.

Fullan, M. (2001). *Leading in a culture of change*. San Francisco: Jossey-Bass.

Garvin, D. A. (1993). Building a learning organization. *Harvard Business Review*, *71*(4), 78–91.

Gaustad, J. (1992). *Nongraded primary education*. (ERIC Document Reproduction Service, No. ED347637).

Goodlad, J. I. & Anderson, R. H. (1987). *The nongraded elementary school*. New York: Teachers College Press.

Gruber, C. & Onwuegbuzie, A. J. (2001). Effects of block scheduling on academic achievement among high school students. *High School Journal*, *84*(4), 32–42.

Gullatt, D. E. (2006). Block scheduling: The effects on curriculum and student productivity. *NASSP Bulletin*, *90*(3), 250–66.

Hackman, D. G. (1995). Ten guidelines for implementing block scheduling. *Educational Leadership*, *53*(11), 24–7.

Hall, G. E. & Hord, S. M. (2001). *Implementing change: Patterns, principles, and potholes*. Boston: Allyn and Bacon.

Harp, L. (1995, November 15). Florida parents win retreat on year-round schools. *Education Week*, p. 10.

Hume, K. (2007). Academic looping: Problem or solution? *Education Canada*, *47*(2), 63.

Kneese, C. C. (1996). Review of research on student learning in year-round education. *Journal of Research and Development in Education*, *29*(2), 60–72.

Kowalski, T. J. (2002). *Planning and managing school facilities* (2nd ed.). Westport, CT: Bergin & Garvey.

Kowalski, T. J. (2003). *Contemporary school administration: An introduction* (2nd ed.). Boston: Allyn and Bacon.

Kowalski, T. J. (2005). Evolution of the school superintendent as communicator. *Communication Education*, *54*(2), 101–17.

Kowalski, T. J. (2006). *The school superintendent: Theory, practice, and cases* (2nd ed.). Thousand Oaks, CA: Sage.

Kowalski, T. J., Petersen, G. J., & Fusarelli, L. D. (2007). *Effective communication for school administrators: An imperative in an information age*. Lanham, MD: Rowman & Littlefield Education.

Kramer, S. L. & Keller, R. (2008). An existence proof: Successful joint implementation of the IMP curriculum and a 4 × 4 block schedule at a suburban U.S. high school. *Journal for Research in Mathematics Education*, *39*(1), 2–8.

Lashway, L. (1998). *Creating a learning organization*. (ERIC Document Reproduction Service No. ED420 897).

Lezotte, L., Edmonds, R., & Brookover, W. (n.d.). *Correlates of effective schools*. Retrieved from http://www.effectiveschools.com/

McMillen, B. J. (2001). A statewide evaluation of academic achievement in year-round schools. *Journal of Educational Research*, *95*(2), 67–74.

Meyer, H. (2002). From "loose coupling" to "tight management"? Making sense of the changing landscape in management and organization theory. *Journal of Educational Administration*, 40(6), 515–20.

Perrone, V. (1985). *Portraits of high schools*. Lawrenceville, NJ: Princeton University Press.

Queen, J. A. & Isenhour, K. G. (1998). *The 4 × 4 block schedule*. Princeton, NJ: Eye on Education.

Queen, J. A., Algozzine, R. F., & Eaddy, M. A. (1997). The road we traveled: Scheduling in the 4 × 4 block. *NASSP Bulletin*, 81, 88–99.

Roberts, A. & Cawelti, G. (1984). *Redefining general education in the American high school*. Alexandria, VA: Association for Supervision and Curriculum Development.

Sarason, S. B. (1996). *Revisiting the culture of the school and the problem of change*. New York: Teachers College Press.

Sargeant, J. C. (1967). *Organizational climate in high schools*. Danville, IL: Interstate Publishers.

Schön, D. (1987). *Educating the reflective practitioner*. San Francisco: Jossey-Bass.

Schroth, G. & Dixon, J. (1996). The effects of block scheduling on student performance. *International Journal of Education Reform*, 5, 472–6.

Schwahn, C. J. & Spady, W. G. (1998). *Total leaders: Applying the best future-focused change strategies in education*. Arlington, VA: American Association of School Administrators.

Senge, P. M. (1990). *The fifth discipline: The art and practice of the learning organization*. New York: Doubleday/Currency.

Sergiovanni, T. J. (2004). Collaborative cultures and communities of practice. *Principal Leadership*, 5(1), 48–52.

Shields, C. M. & LaRocque, L. J. (1996). *Literature review on year-round schooling*. Report prepared for the British Columbia Ministry of Education, British Columbia, Canada. (ERIC Document Reproduction Service No. ED399661).

Shields, C. M. & Oberg, S. L. (2000). *Year-round schooling: Promises and pitfalls*. Lanham, MD: Scarecrow Press.

Shortt, T. L. & Thayer, Y. (1995). What can we expect to see in the next generation of block scheduling? *NASSP Bulletin*, 79, 53–62.

Skrobarcek, S. A., Chang, H. M., & Thompson, C. (1997). Collaboration for instructional improvement: Analyzing the academic impact of a block scheduling plan. *NASSP Bulletin*, 81, 104–11.

Sørensen, A. B. (1989). Schools and the distribution of educational opportunities. In A. C. Kerckhoff (Ed.), *Research in sociology of education and socialization* (Vol. 8, pp. 3–26). Greenwich, CT: JAI Press.

Supovitz, J. A. (2002). Developing communities of instructional practice. *Teachers College Record*, 104(8), 1591–1626.

Thompson, K. F. & Homestead, E. R. (2004). Middle school organization through the 1970s, 1980s, and 1990s. *Middle School Journal*, 35(3), 56–60.

Weick, K. (1976). Educational organizations as loosely coupled systems. *Administrative Science Quarterly*, 21, 1–19.

Wilson, B. & Corbett, H. D. (1983). Organization and change: The effects of school linkage on the quality of implementation. *Educational Administration Quarterly*, 19(4), 85–104.

York, T. (1997). *A comparative analysis of student achievement in block and traditionally scheduled high schools*. Unpublished doctoral dissertation, University of Houston.

Zepeda, S. J. & Mayers, R. S. (2006). An analysis of research on block scheduling. *Review of Educational Research*, 76(1), 137–70.

## CHAPTER 6

Armistead, L. (2000). Public relations: Harness your school's power. *High School Magazine*, 7(6), 24–7.

Baker, B. (1997). Public relations in government. In C. L. Caywood (Ed.), *The handbook of strategic public relations and integrated communication* (pp. 453–80). New York: McGraw-Hill.

Barnett, K. & McCormick, J. (2004). Leadership and individual principal–teacher relationships in schools. *Educational Administration Quarterly, 40*(3), 406–34.

Batory, J. P. (1999). The sad state of education coverage. *School Administrator, 56*(8), 34–8.

Bauman, P. C. (1996). *Governing education: Public sector reform or privatization.* Boston: Allyn and Bacon.

Björk, L. G. & Gurley, D. K. (2005). Superintendent as educational statesman and political strategist. In L. G. Björk and T. J. Kowalski (Eds.), *The contemporary superintendent: Preparation, practice, and development* (pp. 163–85). Thousand Oaks, CA: Corwin Press.

Borja, R. R. (2004, October 24). Educators, journalists spar over media access. *Education Week*, pp. 1, 24–5.

Broom, G. M., Casey, S., & Ritchey, J. (2000). Concept and theory of organization: Public relationships. In J. Ledingham & S. Bruning (Eds.), *Public relations as relationship management* (pp. 3–22). Mahwah, NJ: Lawrence Erlbaum Associates.

Bruning, S. D. & Ledingham, J. A. (2000). Organization and key relationships: Testing the influence of relationship dimensions in a business to business context. In J. Ledingham & S. Bruning (Eds.), *Public relations as relationship management: A relational approach to the study and practice of public relations* (pp. 159–74). Mahwah, NJ: Lawrence Erlbaum Associates.

Brunner, J. & Lewis, D. (2006). Full court press: A principal's media management plan. *Principal Leadership, 7*(3), 65–6.

Bryk, A. S. & Schneider, B. (2002). *Trust in schools: A core resource for school improvement.* New York: Russell Sage Foundation.

Burgoon, J. K. & Hale, J. L. (1984). The fundamental topoi of relational communication. *Communication Monographs, 51*, 193–214.

Cambron-McCabe, N., Cunningham, L. L., Harvey, J., & Koff, R. H. (2005). *The superintendent's fieldbook.* Thousand Oaks, CA: Corwin.

Coleman, M. & Churchill, S. (1997). Challenges to family involvement. *Childhood Education, 73*(3), 144–8.

Conrad, C. (1994). *Strategic organizational communication: Toward the twenty-first century* (3rd ed.). Fort Worth, TX: Harcourt Brace College Publishers.

Cook-Sather, A. (2007). What would happen if we treated students as those with opinions that matter? The benefits to principals and teachers of supporting youth engagement in school. *NASSP Bulletin, 91*(4), 343–62.

Dahl, R. A. (1989). *Democracy and its critics.* New Haven, CT: Yale University Press.

Ferrari, J. (2005, November). *5 tips for professional marketing materials.* Retrieved from http://www. entrepreneur.com/

Frohlichstein, T. (1993). Dealing successfully with media inquiries. *NASSP Bulletin, 77*(555), 82–8.

Goldring, E. B. & Hausman, C. (2001). Civic capacity and school principals: The missing links for community development. In R. Crowson (Ed.), *Community development and school reform* (pp. 193–209). London: Elsevier.

Gonring, M. P. (1997). Global and local media relations. In C. L. Caywood (Ed.), *The handbook of strategic public relations and integrated communication* (pp. 63–76). New York: McGraw-Hill.

Grunig, J. E. (1989). Symmetric presuppositions as a framework for public relations theory. In C. H. Botan (Ed.), *Public relations theory* (pp. 17–44). Hillsdale, NJ: Lawrence Erlbaum Associates.

Grunig, J. E. & Huang, Y. H. (2000). Antecedents of relationships and outcomes. In J. Ledingham & S. Bruning (Eds.), *Public relations as relationship management* (pp. 23–54). Mahwah, NJ: Lawrence Erlbaum Associates.

Grunig, J. E. & Hunt, T. (1984). *Managing public relations.* New York: Holt, Rinehart and Winston.

Gutmann, A. (1987). *Democratic education.* Princeton, NJ: Princeton University Press.

Hallinger, P. & Heck, R. H. (1998). Exploring the principals' contributions to school effectiveness: 1980–1995. *School Effectiveness and School Improvement, 9*, 157–91.

Hanson, E. M. (2003). *Educational administration and organizational behavior* (5th ed.). Boston: Allyn and Bacon.

Hausman, C. & Goldring, E. B. (2001). Sustaining teacher commitment: The role of professional communities. *Peabody Journal of Education, 76*(2), 30–51.

Herman, H. T. (1998). Parent involvement: Must we choose sides? *High School Magazine*, *5*, 26–31.

Hord, S. M. (1997). *Professional learning communities: Communities of continuous inquiry and improvement*. Austin, TX: Southwest Educational Development Laboratory.

Horowitz, S. (1996). Media: Not your enemies—but not your friends. *Thrust for Educational Leadership*, *26*(2), 9.

Howard, C. M. & Mathews, W. K. (2000). *On deadline: Managing media relations* (3rd ed.). Prospect Heights, IL: Waveland Press.

Hoy, W. & Miskel, C. (2008). *Educational administration: Theory, research and practice* (8th ed.). New York: McGraw-Hill.

Hoy, W. K. & Sweetland, S. R. (2001). Designing better schools: The meaning and measure of enabling school structures. *Educational Administration Quarterly*, *37*(3), 296–321.

Hyde, J. (2004). The internet and beyond—mean business: 12 tips on writing better brochures. *Santa Cruz, CA: Persuasions Copywriting. Creative Search Media*. Retrieved from http://www.juliahyde.com/mw/issue-004

Johnson, G. S. & Venable, B. P. (1986). A study of teacher loyalty to the principal: Rule administration and hierarchical influence of the principal. *Educational Administration Quarterly*, *22*(4), 4–27.

Katz, M. (1971). *Class, bureaucracy and schools: The American illusion of educational change*. New York: Praeger.

Kidwai, S. (2008). Building relationships with reporters. *Techniques*, *83*(6), 44–5.

Kowalski, T. J. (2005). Evolution of the school superintendent as communicator. *Communication Education*, *54*(2), 101–17.

Kowalski, T. J. (2008). *School public relations* (4th ed.). Boston: Allyn and Bacon.

Kowalski, T. J., Petersen, G. J., & Fusarelli, L. D. (2007). *Effective communication for school administrators: An imperative in an information age*. Lanham, MD: Rowman & Littlefield.

Lan, Z. (1997). A conflict resolution approach to public administration. *Public Administration Review*, *57*(1), 27–36.

Leithwood, K. & Jantzi, D. (2000). The effects of transformational leadership on organizational conditions and student engagement with school. *Journal of Educational Administration*, *38*(2), 112–29.

Levin, H. M. (1999). The public–private nexus in education. *American Behavioral Scientist*, *43*(1), 124–37.

Littlejohn, S. W. (1992). *Theories of human communication* (4th ed.). Belmont, CA: Wadsworth.

Martin, R. P. (1978). Expert and referent power: A framework for understanding and maximizing consultation effectiveness. *Journal of School Psychology*, *16*, 49–55.

Martinson, D. L. (1999). School public relations: The public isn't always right. *NASSP Bulletin*, *83*(609), 103–9.

Marzano, R. J., Waters, T., & McNulty, B. A. (2005). *School leadership that works: From research to results*. Alexandria, VA: Association for Supervision and Curriculum Development.

Meier, K. J. (1993). Representative bureaucracy: A theoretical and empirical exposition. *Research in Public Administration*, *2*(1), 1–35.

Millar, F. E. & Rogers, L. E. (1976). A relational approach to interpersonal communication. In G. Miller (Ed.), *Explorations in interpersonal communication* (pp. 87–103). Newbury Park, CA: Sage.

Million, J. (2000). No comment, NO WAY! *Education Digest*, *65*(9), 59–60.

Ordovensky, P. & Marx, G. (1993). *Working with the news media*. Arlington, VA: American Association of School Administrators.

Parker, J. (1991). *Accessing the media.* (ERIC Document Reproduction Service No. ED339337).

Pateman, C. (1970). *Participation and democratic theory*. London: Cambridge University Press.

Pawlas, G. (2005). *Administrator's guide to school-community relations* (2nd ed.). Larchmont, NY: Eye on Education.

Pfeiffer, I. L. & Dunlap, J. B. (1988). Advertising practices to improve school–community relations. *NASSP Bulletin*, *72*(506), 14–17.

Pratchett, L. (1999). New fashions in public participation: Towards greater democracy? *Parliamentary Affairs*, *52*(4), 616–33.

Raisman, N. A. (2000). Building relationships with the media: A brief working guide for community college leaders. *New Directions for Community Colleges*, *28*(2), 21–7.

Rhoades, L. & Rhoades, G. (1991). Helping the media add depth to education news. *Clearing House*, *64*(5), 350–1.

Roberts, N. (2004). Public deliberation in an age of direct citizen participation. *American Review of Public Administration*, *34*(4), 315–53.

Shepard, R. G., Trimberger, A. K., McClintock, P. J., & Lecklider, D. (1999). Empowering family–school partnerships: An integrated hierarchical model. *Contemporary Education*, *70*(3), 33–7.

Sielke, J. (2000). So, you want positive press? An in-depth look at what the media really want when they come knocking. *School Business Affairs*, *66*(10), 26–9.

Smrekar, C. & Cohen-Vogel, L. (2001). The voices of parents: Rethinking the intersection of family and school. *Peabody Journal of Education*, *76*(2), 75–100.

Soholt, S. (1998). Public engagement: Lessons from the front. *Educational Leadership*, *56*(2), 22–3.

Solo, L. (1997). School success begins at home. *Principal*, *77*(2), 29–30.

Spicer, C. (1997). *Organizational public relations: A political perspective*. Mahwah, NJ: Erlbaum.

St. John, E. P. & Daun-Barnett, N. J. (2008). Public opinions and political contexts. In T. J. Kowalski (Ed.), *Public relations in schools* (4th ed., pp. 50–72). Upper Saddle River, NJ: Merrill, Prentice Hall.

Surra, C. A. & Ridley, C. A. (1991). Multiple perspectives on interaction: Participants, peers, and observers. In B. Montgomery & S. Duck (Eds.), *Studying interpersonal interaction* (pp. 35–55). New York: Guilford.

Tschannen-Moran, M. (2004). *Trust matters: Leadership for successful schools*. San Francisco: Jossey-Bass.

Wadsworth, D. (1997). Building a strategy for successful public engagement. *Phi Delta Kappan*, *78*(10), 749–52.

Wahlstrom, K. L. & Seashore Louis, K. (2008). How teachers experience principal leadership: The roles of professional community, trust, efficacy, and shared responsibility. *Educational Administration Quarterly*, *44*(4), 458–95.

Walker, J. E. (1987). Local opinion polling for educators. *Education Digest*, *53*(12), 26–9.

Waters, T., Marzano, R., & McNulty, B. (2004) Leadership that sparks learning. *Educational Leadership*, *61*(7), 48–52.

West, P. T. (1985). *Educational public relations*. Beverly Hills, CA: Sage.

Wherry, J. H. (2008). Working with parent diversity. *Principal*, *88*(2), 10.

White, J. (1998). Media misconceptions. *Thrust for Educational Leadership*, *27*(6), 8–10.

White, L. J. (1998). National PTA standards for family/parent involvement programs. *High School Magazine*, *5*, 8–12.

Zeichner, K. M. (1991). Contradictions and tensions in the professionalization of teaching and the democratization of schools. *Teachers College Record*, *92*(3), 363–79.

## CHAPTER 7

Addonizio, M. F. (2000). Private funds for public schools. *Clearing House*, *74*(2), 70–4.

Affleck, K. & Fuller, B. (1988). The integration of programming and educational specifications. *CEPF Journal*, *26*(6), 9–12.

Augenblick, J. & Silverstein, J. (2002). Financing facilities. *American School Board Journal*, *189*(10), 40–2, 44.

Brimley, V. & Garfield, R. R. (2008). *Financing education in a climate of change* (10th ed.). Boston: Allyn and Bacon.

Castaldi, B. (1994). *Educational facilities: Planning, modernization, and management* (4th ed.). Boston: Allyn and Bacon.

Chan, T. C. & Richardson, M. D. (2005). *Ins and outs of school facility management*. Lanham, MD: Scarecrow Education.

Drake, T. L. & Roe, W. H. (1994). *School business management: Supporting instructional effectiveness*. Boston: Allyn and Bacon.

Erwood, D. & Frum, R. D. (1996). Forming a united front. *American School & University*, *68*(8), 84–6.

General Accounting Office. (1996). *School facilities: America's schools report differing conditions*. Report to Congressional Requesters. (ERIC Document Reproduction Service No. ED 397 508).

Greenhalgh, J. (1978). *Practitioner's guide to school business management*. Boston: Allyn and Bacon.

Hartman, W. T. (1988). *School district budgeting*. Englewood Cliffs, NJ: Prentice Hall.

Hunter, M. (2004). Planning without politics. *American School & University*, *77*(3), 344–7.

Jordan, K., McKeown, M., Salmon, R., & Webb, L. (1985). *School business management*. Beverly Hills, CA: Sage.

Kedro, J. M. (2003). Controlling the purse strings. *Principal Leadership*, *3*(5), 19–23.

King, R. A., Swanson, A. D., & Sweetland, R. G. (2003). *School finance: Achieving high standards with equity and efficiency* (3rd ed.). Boston: Allyn and Bacon.

Kowalski, T. J. (1995). Chasing the wolves from the schoolhouse door. *Phi Delta Kappan*, *76*(6), 486–90.

Kowalski, T. J. (2002). *Planning and managing school facilities* (2nd ed.). Westport, CT: Bergin & Garvey.

Kowalski, T. J. (2006). *The school superintendent: Theory, practice, and cases* (2nd ed.). Thousand Oaks, CA: Sage.

Kowalski, T. J. & Schmielau, R. E. (2001). Potential for states to provide equality in funding school construction. *Equity and Excellence in Education*, *34*(2), 54–61.

Lewis, A. (1989). *Wolves at the schoolhouse door: An investigation of the condition of public school buildings*. Washington, DC: American Education Writers Association.

Lieberman, M. (1986). *Beyond public education*. New York: Praeger.

McKinley, S. K. & Phillis, W. L. (2008). Collaboration in search of a school funding remedy post DeRolph. *Journal of Education Finance*, *33*(3), 311–29.

Milshtein, A. (1998). Setting the cleaning standard. *School Planning and Management*, *37*(5), 29–31.

National School Foundation Association. (n.d.). *About NSFA*. Retrieved from http://www.schoolfoundations.org/en/about_nsfa/

Portland Schools Foundation. (n.d.). *The equity fund*. Retrieved from http://www.thinkschools.org/local-school-foundations/

Ray, J., Candoli, I., & Hack, W. (2005). *School business administration: A planning approach* (8th ed.). Boston: Allyn and Bacon.

Rondeau, E. (1989). The future of facility management. *CEFP Journal*, *27*(1), 9–14.

Sharp, W. L. (1994). Seven things a principal should know about school finance. *NASSP Bulletin*, *78*, 1–5.

Smith, S. J. (2003). The visionary master plan. *American School & University*, *75*(12), 142–5.

Tanner, C. K. & Lackney, J. A. (2006). *Educational facilities planning: Leadership, architecture, and management*. Boston: Allyn and Bacon.

Thompson, D. C., Wood, R. C., & Honeyman, D. S. (1994). *Fiscal leadership for schools: Concepts and practices*. New York: Longman.

Vann, A. S. (1995). Give us a say on school budgets. *Principal*, *74*, 41.

White, A. (1999). *Coke and Pepsi are going to school*. Retrieved from http://www.essentialaction.org/spotlight/CokeSchool.html

## CHAPTER 8

Attea, W. J. (1993). From conventional to strategic bargaining: One superintendent's experience. *School Administrator*, *50*(10), 16–19.

Clark, S. G. (1998). Interviewing job applicants: Asking the right questions. *West Education Law Reporter*, (128 Ed. Law Rep. 939).

Cole, P. (2004). *Professional development: A great way to avoid change*. Melbourne, Vic.: Centre for Strategic Education.

Daresh, J. C. & Playko, M. A. (1995). *Supervision as a proactive process: Concepts and cases* (2nd ed.). Long Grove, IL: Waveland Press.

Edwards, M. A. (1995). Growth is the name of the game. *Educational Leadership, 52*, 72–4.

Elmore, R. (2004). *School reform from the inside out*. Cambridge, MA: Harvard University Press.

Fullan, M. (2007). Change the terms for teacher learning. *Journal of Staff Development, 28*(3), 35–6.

Fullan, M. G., Bertani, A., & Quinn, J. (2005). *Leading in tough times: New lessons for district-wide reform*. Center for Development and Learning. Retrieved from http://www.cdl.org/resource-library/articles/leading_in_tough_times.php

Gorman, C. D., Clover, W., & Doherty, M. (1978). Can we learn anything about interviewing paper people from interviews of paper people? Two studies of the external validity of a paradigm. *Organizational Behavior and Human Performance, 22*, 165–92.

Gullattt, D. E. & Ballard, L. M. (1998). Choosing the right process for teacher evaluation. *American Secondary Education, 26*(3), 13–17.

Hanson, E. M. (2003). *Educational administration and organizational behavior* (5th ed.). Boston: Allyn and Bacon.

Harrington-Lueker, D. (1990). Some labor relations specialists urge caution. *American School Board Journal, 177*(7), 29.

Harvey, T. & Drolet, B. (1994). *Building teams, building people: Expanding the fifth resource*. Lancaster, PA: Technomic.

Hirsh, S. (2009). Before deciding what to do, determine what is necessary. *Journal of Staff Development, 30*(1), 71–2.

Jones, R. (1997). Showing bad teachers the door. *American School Board Journal, 184*(11), 20–4.

Kimball, S. M. & Milanowski, A. (2009). Examining teacher evaluation validity and leadership decision making within a standards-based evaluation system. *Educational Administration Quarterly, 45*(1), 34–70.

Kowalski, T. J. (2003). *Contemporary school administration: An introduction* (2nd ed.). Boston: Allyn and Bacon.

Kowalski, T. J. (2006). *The school superintendent: Theory, practice, and cases* (2nd ed.). Thousand Oaks, CA: Sage.

Kowalski, T. J., Petersen, G. J., & Fusarelli, L. D. (2007). *Effective communication for school administrators: An imperative in an information age*. Lanham, MD: Rowman & Littlefield.

Lieberman, A. & Miller, L. (1991). *Staff development in the '90s: New demands, new realities, new perspectives* (2nd ed.). New York: Teachers College, Columbia University.

Little, J. W. (1993). Teachers' professional development in a climate of educational reform. *Educational Evaluation & Policy Analysis, 15*(2), 129–51.

Loucks-Horsley, S. & Stiegelbauer, S. (1991). Using knowledge of change to guide staff development. In A. Lieberman & L. Milkler (Eds.), *Staff development for education in the '90s: New demands, new realities, new perspectives* (pp. 15–36). New York: Teachers College Press.

Manatt, R. (1988). Teacher performance evaluation: A total systems approach. In S. Stanley & J. Popham (Eds.), *Teacher evaluation: Six prescriptives for success* (pp. 79–109). Alexandria, VA: Association for Supervision and Curriculum Development.

Manatt, R. P. & Kemis, M. (1997). 360° feedback: A new approach to evaluation. *Principal, 77*(1), 24–7.

Medley, D. M., Coker, H., & Soar, R. S. (1984). *Measurement-based evaluation of teacher performance*. New York: Longman.

Misso, J. D. (1995). Consensus bargaining: A step toward rational thinking. *School Business Affairs, 61*(12), 26–8.

Norton, N. S. (2008). *Human resources administration for educational leaders*. Los Angeles, CA: Sage.

Peterson, K. (2004). Research on school teacher evaluation. *NASSP Bulletin, 88*(639), 60–79.

Peterson, K. D. (2000). *Teacher evaluation: A comprehensive guide to new directions and practices*. Thousand Oaks, CA: Corwin Press.

Place, A. W. & Kowalski, T. J. (1993). Principal ratings of criteria associated with teacher selection. *Journal of Personnel Evaluation in Education, 7*, 291–300.

Rahim, M. A. (2001). *Managing conflict in organizations*. Westport, CT: Quorum Books.

Sarason, S. B. (1996). *Revisiting the culture of the school and the problem of change*. New York: Teachers College Press.

Schwartz, R. A. (1997). Demystifying performance documentation. *School Administrator, 54*(3), 14–17.

Shedd, J. B. & Bacharach, S. B. (1991). *Tangled hierarchies: Teachers as professionals and the management of schools.* San Francisco: Jossey-Bass.

VanScriver, J. H. (1999). Developing rubrics to improve teacher evaluation. *High School Magazine, 7*(2), 32–4.

Wagner, R. F. (1949). The employment interview: A critical summary. *Personnel Psychology, 2*(1), 17–46.

Winter, P. A. (1995). Facts and fiction about teacher selection: Insights from current research findings. *High School Journal, 79*, 21–4.

Winter, P. A. (2006). Applicant evaluations of formal position advertisements: The influence of sex, job message content, and information order. *Journal of Personnel Evaluation in Education, 10*, 105–16.

Winter, P. A., Newton, R., & Kilpatrick, R. L. (1998). The influence of work values on teacher selection decisions: The effects of principal values, teacher values, and principal–teacher value interactions. *Teaching and Teacher Education, 14*(4), 385–400.

Woodruff, S. B. & Kowalski, T. J. (2009, April 16). *Problems encountered by novice high school principals: Implications for academic preparation and state licensing.* Paper presented at the annual meeting of the American Educational Research Association, San Diego, CA.

Young, I. P. (2008). *The human resource function in educational administration* (9th ed.). Boston: Allyn and Bacon.

Young, I. P. & Prince, A. L. (1999). Legal implications for teacher selection as defined by the ADA and the ADEA. *Journal of Law & Education, 28*(4), 517–30.

## CHAPTER 9

Anderson, K. M. & Durant, O. (1991). Training managers of classified personnel. *Journal of Staff Development, 12*(1), 56–9.

Barrios, L. C., Jones, S. E., & Gallagher, S. S. (2007). Legal liability: The consequences of school injury. *Journal of School Health, 77*(5), 273–9.

Black, S. (2002). The well-rounded student: Extracurricular activities and academic performance go hand in hand. *American School Board Journal, 189*(6), 33–5.

Boehrer, J. M. (1993). Managing to meet the bottom line. *School Business Affairs, 59*(11), 3–8.

Burnett, M. A. (2000). One strike and you're out: An analysis of no pass/no play policies. *High School Journal, 84*(2), 1–6.

Carroll, S. R. & Carroll, D. J. (2002). *Statistics made simple for school leaders: Data-driven decision making.* Lanham, MD: Scarecrow Press.

Clark, S. G. (2001). Confidentiality and disclosure: A lesson in sharing. *Principal Leadership, 1*(8), 40–3.

Coles, A. D. (2000, November 22). Federal breakfast program feeds record numbers. *Education Week*, p. 6.

Cook, G. (2003). Food safety questions continue in wake of ruling. *American School Board Journal, 190*(11), 10–12.

Daggett, L. M. & Huefner, D. S. (2001). Recognizing schools' legitimate educational interests: Rethinking FERPA's approach to the confidentiality of student discipline and classroom records. *American University Law Review, 51*, 2–48.

Dawson, J. & Sanders, D. (1997). A bus program that really works! *Principal, 76*(3), 38–9.

Dillon, J. E. (2001). Keeping peace on the school bus. *Principal, 81*(2), 39.

Essex, N. L. (2004). Confidentiality and student records: Ten ways to invite legal challenges. *Clearing House, 77*(3), 111–13.

Family Educational Rights and Privacy Act, 20 U.S.C. 123g, 34 C.F.R. Part 99 (2000).

Feldman, A. F. & Matjasko, J. L. (2005). The role of school-based extracurricular activities in adolescent development: A comprehensive review and future directions. *Review of Educational Research, 75*(2), 159–210.

Fitzgerald, P. L. (2002). Serving up safety. *Principal, 82*(1), 56–8.

Fredricks, J. A. & Eccles, J. S. (2006). Is extracurricular participation associated with beneficial outcomes? Concurrent and longitudinal relations. *Developmental Psychology, 42*(4), 698–713.

George, K. L. (1995). Fuss on the bus. *American School Board Journal, 182*(11), 33–7.

Hoff, D. L. & Mitchell, S. N. (2007). Should our students pay to play extracurricular activities? *Education Digest, 72*(6), 27–34.

Holloway, J. H. (2002). Extracurricular activities and student motivation. *Educational Leadership, 60*(1), 80–1.

Jones, R. (1996). Salad daze. *American School Board Journal, 183*(2), 20–2.

Kaldahl, M. A. & Blair, E. H. (2005). Student injury rates in public schools. *Journal of School Health, 75*(1), 38–40.

Kennedy, R. (2008). The need for high school extracurricular activities. *Coach and Athletic Director, 78*(4), 38–9.

Knorr, J. (1996). The need to rethink coaching certification. *Coach and Athletic Director, 65*(1), 4–7.

Kowalski, T. J. (2002). *Planning and managing school facilities* (2nd ed.). Westport, CT: Bergin & Garvey.

Kowalski, T. J., Lasley, T. J., & Mahoney, J. (2008). *Data-driven decisions and school leadership: Best practices for school improvement.* Boston: Allyn and Bacon.

McNeal, R. B., Jr. (1995). Extracurricular activities and high school dropouts. *Sociology of Education, 68*, 62–81.

O'Neill, S. (2000). Playing it safe. *American School & University, 73*(1), 36–9.

Petrides, L. A. & Guiney, S. Z. (2002). Knowledge management for school leaders: An ecological framework for thinking schools. *Teachers College Record, 104*(8), 1702–17.

Potter, R. L. & Stefkovich, J. A. (2009). Legal dimensions of using employee and student data to make decisions. In T. J. Kowalski & T. J. Lasley (Eds.), *Handbook of data-based decision making in education* (pp. 38–53). New York: Routledge.

Sarmiento, J. W. (2006). *Technology tools of the analysis of achievement data: An introductory guide for educational leaders.* Retrieved from http://www.nwrel.org/scpd/sslc/federal_grantees/cohort2/data_institutes/binder/resources/C2DataTechToolsforAnalysis.pdf#search='Sarmiento%20and%20Technology%20Tools'

Shoop, R. J. (2008). Student records. *Principal Leadership, 8*(6), 65–7.

Stuart, S. P. (2005). A local distinction: State education privacy laws for public school children. *West Virginia Law Review, 108,* 361.

Torres, M. S. & Stefkovich, J. A. (2005). The No Child Left Behind act. In K. E. Lane, M. J. Connelly, J. F. Mead, M. Gooden, & S. Eckes (Eds.), *The principal's legal handbook* (3rd ed., pp. 365–81). Dayton, OH: Education Law Association.

Woodruff, S. & Kowalski, T. J. (2008, November). *Problems identified by novice principals.* Paper presented at the annual meeting of the University Council for Educational Administration, Orlando, FL.

Young, S. J. (2004). Is school recess a recreational activity? *Journal of Physical Education, Recreation and Dance, 75*(5), 7–9.

Zirkel, P. A. (2007). Liability for off-campus school bus activity. *Principal, 86*(4), 12–14.

## CHAPTER 10

Amberger, K. & Shoop, R. (2006). A principal's guide to manifestation determination. *Principal Leadership, 6*(9), 16–21.

American Psychological Association Zero Tolerance Task Force (2008). Are zero tolerance policies effective in schools? *American Psychologist, 63*(9), 852–62.

Baker, D. E. (2005). Lockdown! *Principal Leadership, 6*(2), 8–9.

Bear, G. G. & Duquette, J. F. (2008). Fostering self-discipline. *Principal Leadership, 9*(2), 10–14.

Brickman, H. K., Jones, S. E., & Groom, S. E. (2004). Evolving school-crisis management since 9/11. *Education Digest, 69*(9), 29–35.

Campbell, J. (1999). *Student discipline and classroom management: Preventing and managing discipline problems in the classroom.* Springfield, IL: C. C. Thomas Publisher.

Clarksean, L. & Pelton, M. H. (2002). Safe schools: A reality check. *Leadership*, *32*(1), 32–5.

Clemmer, E. F. (1991). *The school policy handbook*. Boston: Allyn and Bacon.

Duke, D. L. (2002). *Creating safe schools for all children*. Boston: Allyn and Bacon.

Dunklee, D. R. & Shoop, R. J. (2006). *The principal's quick-reference guide to school law: Reducing liability, litigation, and other potential legal tangles*. Thousand Oaks, CA: Corwin Press.

Essex, N. L. (2000). Zero tolerance approach to school violence: Is it going too far? *American Secondary Education*, *29*(2), 37–40.

Fink, S. (1986). *Crisis management*. New York: American Management Association.

Fiore, D. J. (2002). *School community relations*. Larchmont, NY: Eye on Education.

Gillens, H. (2005). Assessing safety. *American School & University*, 77(11), 30–3.

Hanson, E. M. (2003). *Educational administration and organizational behavior* (5th ed.). Boston: Allyn and Bacon.

Heath, M. A. & Sheen, D. (2005). *School-based crisis intervention: Preparing all personnel to assist*. New York: Guilford Press.

Henley, M. (1997). Why punishment doesn't work. *Principal*, 77(2), 45–6.

Horner, R. H., Horner, H. F., & Sugai, G. M. (2005). A schoolwide approach to student discipline. *School Administrator*, 57(2), 20–3.

Jones, F. (1987). *Positive classroom discipline*. New York: McGraw-Hill.

Jones, M. & Paterson, L. (1992). *Preventing chaos in times of crisis: A guide for school administrators*. Los Alamitos, CA: Southwest Regional Lab.

Kowalski, T. J. (2002). Working with the media during a crisis situation. *Journal of School Public Relations*, *23*(3), 178–86.

Kowalski, T. J. (2005). Revisiting communication during a crisis: Insights from Kenneth Trump. *Journal of School Public Relations*, *26*(1), 47–55.

Kowalski, T. J. (2006). *The school superintendent: Theory, practice, and cases* (2nd ed.). Thousand Oaks, CA: Sage.

Kowalski, T. J. (2008). *School public relations* (4th ed.). Boston: Allyn and Bacon.

Kowalski, T. J., Petersen, G. J., & Fusarelli, L. D. (2007). *Effective communication for school administrators: An imperative in an information age*. Lanham, MD: Rowman & Littlefield Education.

Marzano, R. (2003). *What works in schools: Translating research into action*. Alexandria, VA: Association for Supervision and Curriculum Development.

*Merriam-Webster's collegiate dictionary*. (1993). Springfield, MA: Merriam-Webster.

Peterson, R. L. (2005). Ten alternatives to suspension. *Impact: Feature Issue on Fostering Success in School and Beyond for Students with Emotional/Behavioral Disorders*, *18*(20), 10–11.

Quinn, T. (2002). The inevitable school crisis: Are you ready? *Principal*, *81*(5), 6–8.

Raffaele-Mendez, L. M. (2003). Predictors of suspension and negative school outcomes: A longitudinal investigation. In J. Wald & D. J. Losen (Eds.), *New directions for youth development: Vol. 99. Deconstructing the school-to-prison pipeline* (pp. 17–34). San Francisco: Jossey-Bass.

Rettig, M. A. (1999). Seven steps to schoolwide safety. *Principal*, *71*(9), 10–13.

Rollo, J. M. and Zdziarski, E. L. (2007). The impact of crisis. In E. L. Zdziarski, N. W. Dunkel, & J. M. Rollo (Eds.), *Campus crisis management. A comprehensive guide to planning, prevention, response, and recovery* (pp. 3–34). San Francisco: Jossey-Bass.

Ruder, R. (2006). Four steps to address student discipline. *Education Digest*, *71*(7), 32–5.

Seyfarth, J. T. (1999). *The principal: New leadership for new challenges*. Upper Saddle River, NJ: Merrill, Prentice Hall.

Skiba, R. & Sprague, J. (2008). Safety without suspensions. *Educational Leadership*, *66*(1), 38–43.

Smiar, N. P. (1992). Cool heads: Crisis management for administrators. *Child Welfare*, *71*(2), 147–56.

Spitalli, S. J. (2005). The don'ts of student discipline. *Education Digest*, *70*(5), 28–31.

Thompson, J. C. & Walter, J. K. (1998). School discipline: Becoming proactive, productive, participatory, and predictable. *Educational Horizons*, *76*(4), 195–8.

Thompson, R. (2004). *Crisis intervention and crisis management: Strategies that work in schools and communities*. New York: Brunner-Routledge.

Tobin, T., Sugai, G., & Colvin, G. (1996). Patterns in middle school discipline records. *Journal of Emotional and Behavioral Disorders, 4*(2), 82–94.

Trump, K. S. (1998). *Practical school security: Basic guidelines for safe and secure schools*. Thousand Oaks, CA: Corwin Press.

U.S. Department of Education (2003). *Practical information on crisis planning: A guide for schools and communities*. Washington, DC: U.S. Department of Education, Office of Safe and Drug Free Schools.

Walker, H., Colvin, G., & Ramsey, E. (1995). *Antisocial behavior in school: Strategies and best practices*. Pacific Grove, CA: Brooks/Cole.

Warner, C. (1994). *Promoting your school: Going beyond PR*. Thousand Oaks, CA: Corwin Press.

Yell, M. L. & Rozalski, M. E. (2008). The impact of legislation and litigation on discipline and student behavior in the classroom. *Preventing School Failure, 52*(3), 7–16.

## CHAPTER 11

Biesta, G. (2007). Why "what works" won't work: Evidence-based practice and the democratic deficit in educational research. *Educational Theory, 57*(1), 1–22.

Bridges, D. (2008) Evidence-based reform in education: A response to Robert Slavin. *European Educational Research Journal*, 7(1), 119–33.

Clark, S. N., Clark, D. C., & Irvin, J. L (1997). Collaborative decision making. *Middle School Journal, 28*(5), 54–6.

Cohen, M. D., March, J. G., & Olsen, J. P. (1972). A garbage can model of organizational choice. *Administrative Science Quarterly*, 7(1), 1–25.

Cooper, B. S., Fusarelli, L. D., & Randall, E. V. (2004). *Better policies, better schools: Theories and applications*. Boston: Allyn and Bacon.

Cray, D., Haines, G. H., & Mallory, G. R. (1994). Programmed strategic decision making: The view from Mintzberg's window. *British Journal of Management*, 5, 191–204.

Doyle, D. P. (2002). Knowledge-based decision making. *School Administrator, 59*(11), 30–4.

Doyle, D. P. (2003). Data-driven decision-making. *T.H.E. Journal, 30*(10), S19–21.

Eraut, M. (2004). Practice-based evidence. In G. Thomas & R. Pring (Eds.), *Evidence-based practice in education* (pp. 91–102). Maidenhead, UK: Open University Press.

Estler, S. (1988). Decision-making. In N. J. Boyan (Ed.), *Handbook of research in educational administration* (pp. 305–19). White Plains, NY: Longman.

Giesecke, J. (1993). Recognizing multiple decision-making models: A guide for managers. *College & Research Libraries, 54*(2), 103–14.

Hanson, E. M. (2003). *Educational administration and organizational behavior* (5th ed.). Boston: Allyn and Bacon.

Hellreigel, D. & Slocum, J. W. (1996). *Management* (7th ed.) Cincinnati, OH: South-Western College Publishing.

Howard, M. O., McMillen, C. J., & Pollio, D. E. (2003). Teaching evidence-based practice: Toward a new paradigm for social work education. *Research on Social Work Practice, 13*(2), 234–59.

Hoy, W. K. & Tartar, C. J. (1995). *Administrators solving the problems of practice: Decision making concepts, cases, and consequences*. Boston: Allyn and Bacon.

Janis, I. L. (1982). *Groupthink* (2nd ed.). Boston: Houghton Mifflin.

Kowalski, T. J. (2003). *Contemporary school administration: An introduction* (2nd ed.). Boston: Allyn and Bacon.

Kowalski, T. J. (2008). *Case studies on educational administration* (5th ed.). Boston: Allyn and Bacon.

Kowalski, T. J. (2009a). Evidence and decision making in professions. In T. J. Kowalski & T. J. Lasley (Eds.), *Handbook of data-based decision making in education* (pp. 3–19). New York: Routledge.

Kowalski, T. J. (2009b). Need to address evidence-based practice in educational administration. *Educational Administration Quarterly, 45*, 375–423.

Kowalski, T. J., Lasley, T. J., & Mahoney, J. (2008). *Data-driven decisions and school leadership: Best practices for school improvement.* Boston: Allyn and Bacon.

Kowalski, T. J., Petersen, G. J., & Fusarelli, L. (2009). Novice superintendents and the efficacy of professional preparation. *AASA Journal of Scholarship and Practice, 5*(4), 16–26.

Levin, H. M. (1999). The public–private nexus in education. *American Behavioral Scientist, 43*(1), 124–37.

Lindblom, C. E. (1993). *The science of muddling through.* New York: Irvington.

Luthans, F. (1985). *Organizational behavior* (4th ed.). New York: McGraw-Hill.

Malen, B. & Ogawa, R. T. (1992). Site-based management: Disconcerting policy issues, critical policy choices. In J. J. Lane & E. G. Epps (Eds.), *Restructuring the schools: Problems and prospects* (pp. 185–206). Berkeley, CA: McCutchan Publishing.

March, J. G. & Simon, H. (1958). *Organizations.* New York: John Wiley.

Mayer, R. E. (1983). *Thinking, problem solving, cognition.* New York: W. H. Freeman and Company.

McBeath, J. (2001, December 14). Too many heads improve the broth. *Times Educational Supplement,* p. 26.

No Child Left Behind Act of 2001, Pub. L. No. 107–110, 115 Stat. 1425 (2002).

Ogawa, R. T., Crowson, R. L., & Goldring, E. B. (1999). Enduring dilemmas of school organization. In J. Murphy & K. S. Louis (Eds.), *Handbook of research on educational administration* (2nd ed., pp. 277–95). San Francisco: Jossey-Bass.

Parsley, D., Dean, C., & Miller, K. (2006). Selecting the right data. *Principal Leadership, 7*(2), 38–42.

Picciano, A. G. (2006). *Data-driven decision making for effective school leaders.* Upper Saddle River, NJ: Pearson/Merrill, Prentice Hall.

Popham, W. J. (2006). *Assessment for educational leaders.* Boston: Allyn and Bacon.

Pring, R. (2004). Conclusion: Evidence-based policy and practice. In G. Thomas & R. Pring (Eds.), *Evidence-based practice in education* (pp. 201–11). Maidenhead, UK: Open University Press.

Razik, T. A. & Swanson, A. D. (2002). *Fundamental concepts of educational leadership* (2nd ed.). Boston: Allyn and Bacon.

Reitman, W. R. (1965). *Cognition and thought: An information processing approach.* New York: Wiley.

Reitz, H. J. (1987). *Behavior in organizations* (3rd ed.). Homewood, IL: Irwin.

Reys, R., Lindquist, M., Lambdin, D., Smith, N., & Suydam, M. (2003). *Helping children learn mathematics* (6th ed.). New York: John Wiley and Sons.

Schein, E. H. (1996). Culture: The missing concept in organization studies. *Administrative Science Quarterly, 41*(2), 229–40.

Schön, D. A. (1987). *Educating the reflective practitioner: Toward a new design for teaching and learning in the profession.* San Francisco: Jossey-Bass.

Simon, H. A. (1960). *The new science of management decisions.* New York: Harper & Row.

Wayman, J. C. (2005). Involving teachers in data-driven decision making: Using computer data systems to support teacher inquiry and reflection. *Journal of Education for Students Placed at Risk, 10*(3), 295–308.

Welch, D. A. (2002). *Decisions, decisions: The art of effective decision making.* Amherst, NY: Prometheus Books.

Whitehurst, G. J. (n.d.). *Evidence-based education.* Retrieved from http://www.ed.gov/nclb/methods/whatworks/eb/evidencebased.pdf

Wirt, F. & Kirst, M. (2001). *The political dynamics of American education* (2nd ed.). Berkeley, CA: McCutchan.

# CHAPTER 12

Bauman, P. C. (1996). *Governing education: Public sector reform or privatization.* Boston: Allyn and Bacon.

Belasen, A. T. (2000). *Leading the learning organization: Communication and competencies for managing change.* Albany: SUNY.

Björk, L. G. & Gurley, D. K. (2005). Superintendent as educational statesman and political strategist. In L. G. Björk & T. J. Kowalski (Eds.), *The contemporary superintendent: Preparation, practice, and development* (pp. 163–85). Thousand Oaks, CA: Corwin Press.

Blase, J. R. & Blase, J. (1999). Shared governance principals: The inner experience. *NASSP Bulletin*, *83*(606), 81–90.

*Brown v. Board of Education of Topeka*, 347 U.S. 483 (1954).

Chin, R. & Benne, K. D. (1985). General strategies for effecting changes in human systems. In W. G. Bennis, K. D. Benne, & R. Chin (Eds.), *The planning of change* (4th ed., pp. 22–43). New York: Holt, Rinehart, and Winston.

Cooper, T. L., Bryer, T. A., & Meek, J. W. (2006). Citizen-centered collaborative public management. *Public Administration Review*, *66*, 76–88.

Datnow, A. (2005). The sustainability of comprehensive school reform models in changing district and state contexts. *Educational Administration Quarterly*, *41*(1), 121–53.

Edelman, M. (1985). *The symbolic uses of politics* (2nd ed.). Urbana: University of Illinois Press.

Education for All Handicapped Children Act. P.L. 94-142, 20 USC 1401 et seq.

Eliasoph, N. (1998). *Avoiding politics: How Americans produce apathy in everyday life*. Cambridge, UK: Cambridge University Press.

Feuerstein, A. (2002). Elections, voting, and democracy in local school district governance. *Educational Policy*, *16*(1), 15–36.

Finn, C. E. (1991). *We must take charge*. New York: The Free Press.

Flinspach, S. L. & Ryan, S. P. (1994). Diversity of outcomes: Local schools under school reform. *Education and Urban Society*, *26*(3), 292–305.

Frohlichstein, T. (1993). Dealing successfully with media inquiries. *NASSP Bulletin*, 77(555), 82–8.

Fullan, M. (2001). *Leading in a culture of change*. San Francisco: Jossey-Bass.

Fusarelli, L. D. (1999). Education is more than numbers: Communitarian leadership of schools for the new millennium. In L. T. Fenwick (Ed.), *School leadership: Expanding horizons of the mind and spirit* (pp. 97–107). Lancaster, PA: Technomic.

Hall, G. E. & Hord, S. M. (2001). *Implementing change: Patterns, principles, and potholes*. Boston: Allyn and Bacon.

Hanson, E. M. (2003). *Educational administration and organizational behavior* (5th ed.). Boston: Allyn and Bacon.

Hawley, W. D. (1988). Missing pieces of the educational reform agenda: Or, why the first and second waves may miss the boat. *Educational Administration Quarterly*, *24*(4), 416–37.

Hodgkinson, H. L. (2002). *A demographic look at tomorrow*. Washington, DC: Institute for Educational Leadership.

Howard, C. M. & Mathews, W. K. (2000). *On deadline: Managing media relations* (3rd ed.). Prospect Heights, IL: Waveland Press.

Hoyle, J. (1994). Can a principal run the show and be a democratic leader? *NASSP Bulletin*, *78*, 33–9.

Kirst, M. W. (1988). Recent state education reform in the United States: Looking backward and forward. *Educational Administration Quarterly*, *24*(3), 319–28.

Kowalski, T. J. (2005). Evolution of the school superintendent as communicator. *Communication Education*, *54*(2), 101–17.

Kowalski, T. J. (2006). *The school superintendent: Theory, practice, and cases* (2nd ed.). Thousand Oaks, CA: Sage.

Kowalski, T. J. (2008). *School public relations* (4th ed.). Upper Saddle, NJ: Merrill, Prentice Hall.

Kowalski, T. J., Petersen, G. J., & Fusarelli, L. D. (2007). *Effective communication for school administrators: An imperative in an information age*. Lanham, MD: Rowman & Littlefield Education.

Lan, Z. (1997). A conflict resolution approach to public administration. *Public Administration Review*, *57*(1), 27–36.

Leithwood, K., Jantzi, D., & Steinbach, R. (1999). Do school councils matter? *Educational Policy*, *13*(4), 467–93.

Levin, H. M. (1999). The public–private nexus in education. *American Behavioral Scientist*, *43*(1), 124–37.

Lutz, F. W. & Iannoconne, L. (1978). *Public participation in local school districts: The dissatisfaction theory of democracy*. Lexington, MA: Lexington Books.

Marks, H. M. & Printy, S. M. (2003). Principal leadership and school performance: An integration of transformational and instructional leadership. *Educational Administration Quarterly*, *39*(3), 370–97.

McQuaid, E. P. (1989). The rising tide of mediocre education coverage. *Education Digest*, *54*(8), 7–10.

Medearis, J. (2005). Social movements and deliberative democratic theory. *British Journal of Political Science*, *35*(1), 53–75.

Metz, M. H. (1990). Hidden assumptions preventing real reform: Some missing elements in the educational reform movement. In S. Bacharach (Ed.), *Education reform: Making sense of it all* (pp. 141–54). Boston: Allyn and Bacon.

Million, J. (2000). No comment, NO WAY! *Education Digest*, *65*(9), 59–60.

Murphy, J. (1994). The changing role of the superintendency in restructuring districts in Kentucky. *School Effectiveness and School Improvement*, *5*(4), 349–75.

Passow, A. H. (1988). Whither (or wither?) school reform? *Educational Administration Quarterly*, *24*(3), 246–56.

Posner, M. A. (1994). Read all about it. *Case Currents*, *20*(1), 8–13.

Putnam, R. D. (2000). *Bowling alone: The collapse and revival of American community*. New York: Touchstone.

Raisman, N. A. (2000). Building relationships with the media: A brief working guide for community college leaders. *New Directions for Community Colleges*, *28*(2), 21–7.

Rubin, L. (1984). Formulating education policy in the aftermath of the reports. *Educational Leadership*, *42*(2), 7–10.

Sarason, S. B. (1996). *Revisiting the culture of the school and the problem of change*. New York: Teachers College Press.

Schlechty, P. C. (1990). *Schools for the twenty-first century: Leadership imperatives for educational reform*. San Francisco: Jossey-Bass.

Senge, P. M. (1990). *The fifth discipline: The art and practice of the learning organization*. New York: Doubleday/Currency.

Silins, H. C., Mulford, W. R., & Zarins, S. (2002). Organizational learning and school change. *Educational Administration Quarterly*, *38*(5), 613–42.

Spring, J. (1990). *The American school: 1642–1990* (2nd ed.). New York: Longman.

St. John, E. P. & Daun-Barnett, N. J. (2008). Public opinions and political contexts. In T. J. Kowalski (Ed.), *Public relations in schools* (4th ed., pp. 50–72). Upper Saddle River, NJ: Merrill, Prentice Hall.

Stone, C., Orr, M., & Worgs, D. (2006). The flight of the bumblebee: Why reform is difficult but not impossible. *Perspectives on Politics*, *4*(3), 529–46.

Tracy, K. & Durfy, M. (2007). Speaking out in public: Citizen participation in contentious school board meetings. *Discourse & Communication*, *1*(2), 223–49.

Weiler, H. N. (1990). Comparative perspectives on educational decentralization: An exercise in contradiction? *Educational Evaluation and Policy Analysis*, *12*(4), 433–48.

White, J. (1998). Media misconceptions. *Thrust for Educational Leadership*, *27*(6), 8–10.

# CHAPTER 13

Arthur, M. B., Hall, D. T., & Lawrence, B. S. (1989). Generating new directions in career theory: The case for a transdisciplinary approach. In M. Arthur, D. Hall, & B. Lawrence (Eds.), *Handbook of career theory* (pp. 7–25). Cambridge, UK: Cambridge University Press.

Begley, P. T. (2006). Self-knowledge, capacity and sensitivity: Prerequisites to authentic leadership by school principals. *Journal of Educational Administration*, *44*(6), 570–89.

Blanchard, K. & Peale, N. V. (1988). *The power of ethical management*. New York: William Morrow and Company.

Brown, G. & Irby, B. J. (1995). The portfolio: Should it also be used by administrators? *NASSP Bulletin*, *79*(570), 82–5.

Burns, J. M. (1978). *Leadership*. New York: Harper & Row.

Buskirk, R. H. (1976). *Your career: How to plan it, manage it, change it*. Boston: Cahners Books.

Day, C. (2007). What being a successful principal really means: An international perspective. *Educational Leadership and Administration*, *19*, 13–24.

DiPaola, M. F. & Tschannen-Moran, M. (2003). The principalship at a crossroads: A study of the conditions and concerns of principals. *NASSP Bulletin*, *87*(634), 43–65.

Doud, J. L. & Keller, E. P. (1998). The K–8 principal in 1998. *Principal*, *78*(1), 5–12.

Fullan, M., Bertani, A., & Quinn, J. (2004). New lessons for districtwide reform. *Educational Leadership*, *61*(7), 42–6.

Fuller, E. (n.d.). *Principal turnover, teacher turnover and quality, and student achievement*. Retrieved from www.npbea.org/meetings/NPBEA_12.9.07.ppt

Giles, C. & Hargreaves, A. (2006). The sustainability of innovative schools as learning organizations and professional learning communities during standardized reform. *Educational Administration Quarterly*, *42*(1), 124–56.

Graen, G. B. (1989). *Unwritten rules for your career*. New York: John Wiley & Sons.

Graham, J.W. (1991). Servant-leadership in organizations: Inspirational and moral. *Leadership Quarterly*, *2*(2), 105–19.

Greenfield, T. B. (1991). Foreword. In C. Hodgkinson (Ed.), *Educational leadership: The moral art* (pp. 3–9). Albany: SUNY Press.

Greenfield, W. D., Jr. (1995). Toward a theory of school administration: The centrality of leadership. *Educational Administration Quarterly*, *31*(1), 61–85.

Greenleaf, R. K. (1977). *Servant leadership: A journey into the nature of legitimate power and greatness*. Mahwah, NJ: Paulist Press.

Hodgkinson, C. (1991). *Educational leadership: The moral art*. Albany: SUNY Press.

Howlett, P. (1991). How you can stay on the straight and narrow. *Executive Educator*, *13*(2), 19–21, 35.

Johnson, L. (2005). Why principals quit. *Principal*, *84*(3), 21–3.

Kimbrough, R. B. & Nunnery, M. Y. (1988). *Educational administration: An introduction*. New York: Macmillan.

Kowalski, T. J. (2003a). Superintendent shortage: The wrong problem and wrong solutions. *Journal of School Leadership*, *13*, 288–303.

Kowalski, T. J. (2003b). *Contemporary school administration: An introduction* (2nd ed.). Boston: Allyn and Bacon.

Kowalski, T. J., Lasley, T. J., & Mahoney, J. (2008). *Data-driven decisions and school leadership: Best practices for school improvement*. Boston: Allyn and Bacon.

Kwan, P. (2009). Vice-principals' dilemma: Career advancement or harmonious working relationship. *International Journal of Educational Management*, *23*(3), 203–16.

Lashway, L. (1999). *Holding schools accountable for achievement*. (ERIC Document Reproduction Service No. ED 434 381).

Leithwood, K. & Jantzi, D. (1997). Explaining variation in teachers' perceptions of principals' leadership: A replication. *Journal of Educational Administration*, *35*, 312–31.

Leithwood, K. & Jantzi, D. (2000). The effects of transformational leadership on organizational conditions and student engagement with school. *Journal of Educational Administration*, *38*, 112–29.

Lyon, D. W. & Kirby, E. G. (2000). The career planning essay. *Journal of Management Education*, *24*(2), 276–87.

McDaniels, C. & Gysbers, N. C. (1992). *Counseling for career development: Theories, resources, and practices*. San Francisco: Jossey-Bass.

Norton, M. S. (2003). Let's keep our quality school principals on the job. *High School Journal*, *86*(2), 50–6.

Pond, B. N., Burdick, S. E., & Yamamoto, J. K. (1998). Portfolios: Transitioning to the future. *Business Education Forum*, *52*(4), 50–4.

Quick, P. M. & Normore, A. H. (2004). Moral leadership in the 21st century: Everyone is watching—especially the students. *Educational Forum*, *68*(4), 336–47.

Rait, E. (1995). Against the current: Organizational learning in schools. In S. B. Bacharach & B. Mundell (Eds.), *Images of schools: Structures and roles in organizational behavior* (pp. 71–107). Thousand Oaks, CA: Sage.

Sergiovanni, T. J. (1992). *Moral leadership: Getting to the heart of school improvement.* San Francisco: Jossey-Bass.

Silins, H. (1994). The relationship between transformational leadership and school improvement outcomes. *School Effectiveness and School Improvement, 5,* 272–98.

Starratt, R. J. (1991). Building an ethical school: A theory for practice in educational leadership. *Educational Administration Quarterly, 27*(2), 185–202.

Starratt, R. J. (1995). *Leaders with vision: The quest for school renewal.* Thousand Oaks, CA: Corwin Press.

Steele, J. E. & Morgan, M. S. (1991). *Career planning and development for college students and recent graduates.* Lincolnwood, IL: VGM Career Horizons.

Washington, R. R., Sutton, C. D., & Field, H. S. (2006). Individual differences in servant leadership: The roles of values and personality. *Leadership & Organization Development Journal, 27*(8), 700–16.

Wirt, F. & Kirst, M. (2005). *The political dynamics of American education* (3rd ed.). Richmond, CA: McCutchan.

Woodruff, S. & Kowalski, T. J. (2009, April). *Frequency and severity of problems identified by novice Ohio principals.* Paper presented at the annual meeting of the American Education Research Association, San Diego, CA.

Zunker, V. G. (1990). *Career counseling: Applied concepts of life planning* (3rd ed.). Pacific Grove, CA: Brooks/Cole.

# Index

programs 141–2; playgrounds 139–40; pupil transportation 140–1; relevance in student activities 137; risk avoidance in food services 142; routes for pupil transportation, design of 140; school records, management of 135–6; student activities programs 132, 136–9; student information, maintenance of 132–6; student privacy rights 133–5; supervision of activity programs 138; supervision of food services 142; supervision of pupil transportation 140; supervision outside classrooms 132, 139–41; time and energy needed for 132

pupil transportation 140–1
purchasing 105
Purkey, S.C. and Smith, M.S. 16, 28
purpose and mission 37
Putnam, R.D. 191

**Q**

Queen, J.A., Algozzine, R.F., and Eaddy, M.A. 70
Queen, J.A. and Isenhour, K.G. 70
questions *see* knowledge-based questions
Quick, P.M. and Normore, A.H. 199
Quinn, T. 154, 155

**R**

Radin, B.A. and Hawley, W.D. 7
Raffaele-Mendez, L.M. 151
Rahim, M.A. 125
Raisman, N.A. 91, 194
Rait, E. 201
rational decision-making models 177
Raven, B.H. 209n5
Ray, J., Candoli, L. and Hack, W. 104, 105
Razik, T.A. and Swanson, A.D. 12, 180
Rebell, M.A. 9
record correction, media relationships and 92
recruitment 117–18
reflections: collaborative school improvement 195; commitment to school administration 206; complex nature of schools 18; decision making 181–2; effective schools for all 45; human resources, management of 129; instructional programs, organization and evaluation of 78; material resources, management of 112–13; principal behavior and instructional leadership 62; principal roles and responsibilities 31; problem solving 181–2; pupil services, management of 143;

relationships, building and maintenance of 96; school environment, safety in 161
regulations 12; directory regulations 13; discretionary regulations 13; mandatory regulations 13; proscriptive regulations 13; rules and regulations 12
Rehabilitation Act (1973) 134, 152
Reitman, W.R. 168–9
Reitz, H.J. 180
Reitzug, U.C. 59
Reitzug, U.C., West, D.L., and Angel, R. 59
relational communication 29–30, 77, 86–8
relationships, building and maintenance of: communicating with stakeholders 93–5; communicative behavior 86–8; constructive exchanges 88; credibility 89; deadlines with media 91; democratic localism 83; educational reasons for positive relationships 82, 83; focus groups 94–5; focused relationships 88–93; goodwill building 84; internal relations 88–90; interpersonal communications 87; journalism, relationships with 91; media relations 91–3; media relations, dangers in 92; multi-directional communications 87, 88; mutual influence 87; negative news, dealing with 92; objective communications 87; opinion polls 94–5; parental relations 90; philosophical reasons for positive relationships 82–3; planning media relations 91; political reasons for positive relationships 82, 84; positive media relations 91–2; power, dominance and 88; principal leadership, relationships and 81; principal–teacher relationships 90; print material, communicating with 94; public forums 95; record correction, media relationships and 92; relational communication 86–8; relationship building 88; reporters, meeting with 91; representative democracy 83; school–community relations 84; school public relations 84–6; school public relations, breadth of 86; school public relations, normative definition of 85–6; school Web pages 93–4; shared leadership 89; stakeholder involvement, relationships and 82–4; student-centered leadership 89; symmetrical communications 87, 88; trust building 83, 89
representative democracy 9–10, 14, 83
resource rooms 67
results orientation 77
Rettig, M.A .156